George E. Gee

The Silversmith's Handbook

Containing full instructions for the alloying and working of Silver

George E. Gee

The Silversmith's Handbook
Containing full instructions for the alloying and working of Silver

ISBN/EAN: 9783742833556

Manufactured in Europe, USA, Canada, Australia, Japa

Cover: Foto ©Lupo / pixelio.de

Manufactured and distributed by brebook publishing software (www.brebook.com)

George E. Gee

The Silversmith's Handbook

THE

SILVERSMITH'S HANDBOOK

CONTAINING

FULL INSTRUCTIONS

FOR THE

ALLOYING AND WORKING OF SILVER

INCLUDING THE DIFFERENT MODES OF REFINING AND MELTING
THE METAL; ITS SOLDERS; THE PREPARATION OF IMITATION
ALLOYS; METHODS OF MANIPULATION; PREVENTION OF
WASTE; INSTRUCTIONS FOR IMPROVING AND
FINISHING THE SURFACE OF THE WORK;
TOGETHER WITH OTHER USEFUL
INFORMATION AND MEMORANDA

By GEORGE E. GEE

JEWELLER

AUTHOR OF THE "PRACTICAL GOLD-WORKER"

LONDON
CROSBY LOCKWOOD & CO.
7, STATIONERS' HALL COURT, LUDGATE HILL
1877

I

PREFACE.

The object of this Treatise is to supply a want long felt in the Silver Trade, namely, a work of reference from which workmen, apprentices, and manufacturers, employing the material upon which it treats, may find information which will be of assistance to them in the performance of their daily duties, and by which their operations may be rendered more successful. The Author was led to undertake the present work from having had many opportunities, during his lengthened experience in the art of silver-working, of observing the difficulties and stumbling-blocks that are constantly to be met with in the manifold branches of this important trade, by those *practically* engaged in it, and also by those persons who are desirous of acquiring a *thorough* knowledge of the mechanical and manipulative details belonging to it. To assist his object, numerous illustrations have been prepared for this Treatise, with the view of rendering the various processes of the art more readily comprehensible, and to save a lengthened or detailed description of them.

The different modes of alloying and melting silver; its solders; the preparation of imitation alloys; methods of working; the prevention of waste; instructions for improving and finishing the surface of the work, together with other useful information and memoranda—all these have been carefully collected and placed in order in the body of the work.

The Author has endeavoured, throughout, to present the contents (which he has with some little difficulty and labour brought together) in as practical and readable a form as is compatible with accuracy and efficiency.

G. E. GEE.

189 HERBERT ROAD, SMALL HEATH, BIRMINGHAM.
S. N. 1877.

CONTENTS.

INTRODUCTORY CHAPTER.

	Page
Silver a Precious Metal	1
Economy of Treatment	1
Working Silversmiths	2
English and Foreign Workmen	2
Technical Education	2
Pure Silver	3
Plate and Ornamental Wares	4

CHAPTER I.

Silver.

Silver, Characteristics of	5
Silver for Filigree Work	5
Indian Filigree Workers	5
Malleability of Silver	6
Ductility of Silver	6

CONTENTS.

	Page
Test for Pure Silver	6
Silver known to the Ancients	6
Silver Currency	6
Polished Silver	7
Tarnishing of Silver	7
Density of Silver	7
Fusibility of Silver	7
Heating Power of Silver	7
Action of Silver under Great Heat	8
Hardness of Silver	8
Nitrate of Silver	8
Silver resists Aqua-regia	8
Chief Places of Filigree Manufacture	8
Chief Uses of Silver	9
Price of Silver, Commercial	9
Ores of Silver	9
Dissolution of Silver	9
Caustic Alkalies	10
Nitre	10
Vegetable Acids	10

CHAPTER II.

Sources of Silver.

Silver-mining	11
Great Britain	11
British Isles' Yield of Silver	11

	Page
Spain	11
America	11
Native Silver	11
European Supplies of Silver . . .	12
American Supply of Silver . . .	12
The Richest Mine	12
State of the Jewellery Trade . . .	12
Yield of Silver	13
Foreign Silver Currency . . .	13
Chief Sources of British Silver . .	13
State in which it is found . . .	14

CHAPTER III.

The Assay of Silver Ores.

Silver and Mercury	15
Assaying of Silver Ores	16
Crucible Assay	16
Fluxes for Crucible Assay . . .	16
Assay of Genuine Silver Ores . .	16
Carbonate of Soda	16
Dimensions of Crucible	16
Litharge	17
Preparation and Charge for Assay .	17
Treatment in the Furnace . . .	18
Casting-mould	18
Scorification Process	18

CONTENTS.

	Page
Fusing Cup or Scorifier	19
Special Form of Scorifier	19
Scorification Assay the Reverse of Crucible Assay	19
Charge for Scorification Assay	20
Advantages of the Process	20
Anthracite and its Object	21
Separation of the Silver from the Slag	21
Borax, use of, in Assaying	22
Continental Method of Assaying	22
Flux and Charge for Crucible	23
Details of the Process	23, 24
Skittle-pot	25
Cupellation	26
Cupel, its Mode of Manufacture	26
Cupel-mould	27
Assayer's Muffle	28
Cupel-tongs	28
Brightening	29
Sprouting	29
Weighing of Silver Assay	30
Chief Alloy of Silver	30

CHAPTER IV.

The Cupellation of Silver Ores.

	Page
Test-ring	31
Preparation of Bone-ash	32
Defects in Bone-ash Cupel	33
Currents of Air to the Furnace	33
Withdrawal of the Silver from the Cupel	34
Removal of the Litharge, Manner of	35
Quantity of Alloy per Cupel	35
Purity of Silver after Cupellation	37
Ancient Method of Assaying	37
Dr. Lamborn on Assaying	38
Scriptural Testimony	37, 38
English System of Assay	39

CHAPTER V.

The Alloys of Silver.

Silversmith's Alloys	40
Filigree Work	40
Alloy	41
Amalgam	41
Metals employed in the Industrial Arts	41

CONTENTS.

	Page
Metals, their various Characteristics	41
Principal Alloys of Silver	42
Copper	42
Characteristics of Copper	43
Protoxide of Copper	44
Action of Acids on Copper	44
Bean-shot Copper for Alloying	44
Chemical name for Copper	44
Nickel	45
Cronstedt	45
Density of Nickel	45
Ductility of Nickel	45
Malleability of Nickel	45
Fusibility of Nickel	45
Nickel Coinage	45
Nickel Alloys	46
Electro-plate	46
Zinc	46
Spelter	46
Zinc in Silver Solder	46
Annealing of Zinc	47
Specific Gravity of Zinc	47
Spelter used by Jewellers	47
Tarnishing of Zinc	47
Malleability of Zinc	48
Ductility of Zinc	48
Tenacity of Zinc	48
Tin	48

	Page
Ancient Workers in Tin	48
Density of Tin	48
Christianity and Tin	48
Fusibility of Tin	48
Dissolving of Tin	48
Tin alloyed with Gold	49
Tin alloyed with Silver	49
Tin in Silversmith's Solders	49
Vapours of Tin injurious to Gold	49
Malleability of Tin	49
Ductility of Tin	49
Tenacity of Tin	49
Scientific Name for Tin	50
Table of Metallic Elements	50
Melting-points of the Principal Metals	51
Physical Properties of the Principal Metals	51

CHAPTER VI.

Various Qualities of Silver.

Mechanical Uses of Silver	52
Filigree Work	52
Birmingham	52
London	52
Indian	53
Chief Places of Filigree Manufacture	53

CONTENTS.

	Page
Continental Cheap Labour	54
Hand-made Articles	54
Process of Workmanship	55
Maltese Filigree	55
Chinese and Japanese Filigree	56
Filigree of Norway and Sweden	56
Filigree working, Necessity for Pure Metal	56
Old Method of making Filigree	57
Twisting of the Wire	58
Lathe, Use of	58
Flattening of Twisted Wire for Filigree	59
New Method of preparing Filigree Wire	59
English Standards for Silver	60
English Coinage	61
Standard Silver Alloy	61
Alloy for Hall-marking	62
Standard Alloy of the Highest Quality	62
Standard Alloy for Hall-marking	62
Alloy commonly used in England	63
Qualities used by English Silversmiths	63
Drawbacks to Hall-marking	63
Method of calculating the Qualities of Silver	63
Silver Alloy No. 1, cost 4s. 7d. per oz.	64
,, No. 1, differently calculated	64
,, No. 2, cost 4s. 1d. per oz.	64
,, No. 2, differently calculated	64
,, No. 3, cost 3s. 10d. per oz.	65
,, No. 3, differently calculated	65

CONTENTS.   xv

Silver Alloy No. 4, cost 3s. 7d. per oz.	. .	65
,, No. 4, differently calculated	.	65
,, No. 5, cost 3s. 6d. per oz.	. .	66
,, No. 5, differently calculated	.	66
,, No. 6, cost 3s. 3d. per oz.	. .	66
,, No. 6, differently calculated	.	66
,, No. 7, cost 3s. 2d. per oz.	. .	67
,, No. 7, differently calculated	.	67
,, No. 8, cost 3s. per oz.	. .	67
,, No. 8, differently calculated	.	67
Instructions in the Preparation of Alloys	.	68
Copper for Alloying	.	68
French Standards	.	69
Silver Ware	.	69
Coinage	.	69
French Alloy for Coinage . . .	.	70
French Alloy for Plate	.	70
French Alloy for Silver Ware . .	.	70
Instructions in the Preparation of these Alloys	.	70
German Standards	.	71
Silver Ware	.	71
Coinage	.	71
Silver Alloy for the German Coinage	.	72
Alloy for Plate	.	72
Alloys for Silver Wares . . .	.	72, 73
Law on the Manufacture of Silver Wares	.	73
Remedy allowed in Fineness . .	.	73
Government Exports . . .	.	73
Guarantee Marks	.	73

CHAPTER VII.

Silver Solders: their Uses and Applications.

	Page
The Act of Soldering	74
Cause of Inferior Manufactures	74
Tin in Solders	75
Filed Solders	76
Zinc in Silver Solder	76
Solders made with Copper and Silver	76
Hard Silver Solders	77
Medium Solders	77
Easy Solders	77
Connections for Soldering	77
Flux for Soldering	77
Fusibility of Silver Solders	78
Hardest Silver Solder, cost 4s. 1d. per oz.	78
Ditto, differently calculated	79
Medium Silver Solder, cost 3s. 10d. per oz.	79
Ditto, differently calculated	79
Easy Silver Solder, cost 3s. 5d. per oz.	79
Ditto, differently calculated	80
Remarks on Silver Solders	80
Composition for Solder	81
Best Hard Solder, cost 4s. 1d. per oz	81
Ditto, differently calculated	81
Medium Solder, cost 3s. 10d. per oz.	82
Ditto, differently calculated	82

	Page
Easy Solder, cost 3s. 7d. per oz.	82
Ditto, differently calculated	82
Common Solder, cost 3s. 3d. per oz.	83
Ditto, differently calculated	83
Directions on the Melting of Solders	83
Solder for Enamelling, cost 4s. 1d. per oz.	84
,, ,, cost 3s. 6d. per oz.	84
Easy Solder for Filigree Work	84
Quick Running Solder, cost 3s. 3d. per oz.	85
Silver Solder for Chains, cost 3s. 3d. per oz.	85
Easy Solder for Chains, cost 3s. 3d. per oz.	85
Common Silver Solder, cost 3s. per oz.	85
Common Easy Solder, cost 3s. per oz.	86
Arsenic Solder, cost 4s. 1d. per oz.	86
Silver Solder with Arsenic, 3s. 10d. per oz.	86
Easy Silver Solder, cost 3s. 6d. per oz.	86
Common Easy Solder, cost 3s. per oz.	87
Another Common Solder	87
Very Common Solder	87
Directions in the Preparation of Solders	87
Drossy Solders	88
Mode of Soldering Gold and Silver	88
Pallion Solder	88
Blowpipes	89
Solder-dish and Charger	89
Soft Solder	90
Art in Soldering	90
Solder for Filigree	91

xviii   CONTENTS.

	Page
Lemaille Solder . .	91
English Filigree Workers	91
Sprinkle Borax . .	92
Special Soldering Flux .	92
Boiling-out Pickle . .	93

CHAPTER VIII.

On the Melting of Silver.

Directions on Melting . . .	94
Weighing Metal for the Crucible .	94
Crucibles	95
Best Crucibles to employ . .	95
Fluxes: their Action on Crucibles . .	96
Fluxes employed in Melting . .	96
Testing the Soundness of a Crucible .	97
Mixing various Metals for melting .	97
Zinc a fusible Metal . . .	98
Charcoal	99
Bad working Material . . .	99
Plumbago Crucible for Melting .	99
Tongs for Melting . . .	100
Ingot-mould	100
Flux and the Pouring of Molten Metal .	101
Protoxide of Zinc . . .	102
Scrap Silver	102

CONTENTS.   ix

	Page
Carbonate of Soda	102
Dissolving Impurities	103
Lead and Tin in Silver	103
Salammoniac	103
Lemel	103
Mixture prepared for Crucible	104
Burning of Lemel	104
Skittle-pot for Lemel	104
Melting of Lemel	105
Another Mode of melting Lemel	106
Crucible for Lemel	106
Pouring of Lemel from Crucible	107

CHAPTER IX.

On the Working of Silver.

Rolling Silver	108
Annealing Silver	109
Irregularities in Rolling-mills	110
Messrs Kemp's Mill	110, 111
Table of the Cost of Silver-rolling	112
Slitting Rollers	112
Breaking-down Rollers	112
Wire-rolling	113
Wire-drawing	113

Draw-plate	114
Draw-bench	110, 115
Draw-tongs	115
Drum used by Wire-drawers	115
Fine Wire-drawing	115, 116
Wire-drawer's Punch and Hammer	117
Wrought Work	118
Sparrow-hawk	119
Raised Work	120
Cement for Chasers	121
Snarling-tools for Raising	122
Art in the Silver Trade	123
Burnished Silver Work	124
Silver Filigree Work	125
Stamped or Struck-up Work	126
Press	127
Plain Solid Work	127
Chain Bracelets	128
Present State of Silver Trade	128
Silver, Liability to become tarnished	129
Enamelling	129
Galvanic Ring	129
Mode of preparing Ring	129, 130
Hollow Silver Work	131
Stamping-press	132
Spinning	134, 135
Polishing	135
Water-of-Ayr Stone	136

	Page
Polishing-lathe	137
Washing-out Mixture	138

CHAPTER X.

Enriching the Surfaces of Silver.

Production of the best and richest Surface	139
Oldest Method for Whitening	140
East Indian Silversmiths	141
Indian Mode of Whitening Silver	142
Another Mode of Whitening	142
Boiling-out Pan	143
Boiling-out Mixture	143, 144
Our Mode of Whitening	145
Surface Refining of Silver	146
Brown Colour on Silver Goods	146
Common Articles of Silver	147
Whitening Powder or Mixtures	147
Nitrate of Silver Mixture	148
Improving the Colour of Electro-plate	149
Electro-plating	149
Discoverer of Electro-plating	149, 150
Constant Battery	150
Best Battery for Plating	151
Strength of Battery Solution	151
Bunsen's Battery	152
Exciting Mixture for Battery	152

	Page
Zinc Amalgamation	153
Conducting Wires	154
Preparation of Plating Solution	155
Cyanide Solution	156
Black Cyanide	157
Strength of Plating Solution	157, 158
Inferior Plating Solution	159
Recovery of Silver from Plating Solutions	160
Scratch-brushing	161
Scratch-brush Lathe	161
Burnishing Silver Work	161, 162
Oxidizing Silver Work	163
Solution No 1.	163
Solution No 2.	164
Solution No 3.	164
Producing various Shades	165

CHAPTER XI.

Imitation Silver Alloys.

	Page
Melting Imitation Alloys	166
Common Silver Alloy	167
Another	167
Another	168
Another	168
Another	168

	Page
Common Silver Alloy	168
Another	169
Another	169
Another	169
Another	169
Another	170
Another	170
Chinese Silver	170
Imitation Silver	170
Another	171
Another	171
Another	171
Another	171
White Alloy	172
Clark's Patent Alloy	172
White Alloy	172
Alloy with Platinum	172
Alloy with Palladium	173
Uses for Imitation Alloys	173
Characteristics of Imitation Alloys	174

CHAPTER XII.

Economical Process.

Working Loss	175
Lowest Estimate Real Loss	175
Total Working Loss	176

xxiv   CONTENTS.

	Page
Shop Floors	177
Waste-saving Precautions	177, 178
Treatment of Waste	178
Burning of Polishings	179
Treatment of Waste Liquids	180
Processes for the Recovery of Silver from Waste Waters	180, 182
Chloride of Silver	183
Aqua-regia	183
Precipitating Silver in Waste Waters	183
Solution for Precipitation	184
Sediment in Collecting-vessels	185

CHAPTER XIII.

Licences and Duties.

Acts of the Legislature	186
43 George III., c. 69	186
6 George I., c. 11	187
31 George II., c. 32	188
32 George II., c. 14	188
24 George III., c. 53	188
37 George III., c. 90	188
44 George III., c. 98	189
55 George III., c. 185	189
Table of Various Duties	189

	Page
Manufactured Plate	190
Remarks on the Licence Question	161, 196
Act of Parliament in Licences	193
Clause of Act	193, 194
Tax or Licence unjustly Assessed	195, 196

CHAPTER XIV.

Useful Information for the Trade.

	Page
Silversmith's Alloys	197
Silver Wares	197
Cleaning Plate	198
Imitation Silver	198
Another	198
Removing Gold from Silver Articles	198
Oxidizing Silver	198
Dipping Mixture	199
Silver Powder for Copper	199
Powder for Silver	200
To protect the Polish of Metals	200
Silver-stripping Mixture	200
Stripping Silver	201
Soft Solder	201
Soldering Fluid	201
Dissolving Silver	202
Dissolving Silver Alloy	202

CONTENTS.

	Page
Dissolving Copper	202
Dissolving Soft Solder	202
Dissolving Silver Solder	202
Dissolving Sealing-wax	202
Resist Varnish	202
Plate Powder	202
Electro-plating Soft Solder	202
Another Recipe	203
Testing Silver Wares	203
Another Test	204
Perchloride of Iron	205
Aluminium Alloy	205
New Alloy	205
Removing Gold from Silver Wares	205
Silver Plating Fluid	206
Plate-cleaning Powder	206
Solder for Aluminium	206

CHAPTER XV.

Foreign Silver Standards	207
French Work, Duty on	208
Continental Silversmiths	209
French Style of Work	209
German Style of Work	210
Indian Style of Work	210
Austrian Style of Work	211
English Style of Work	211
Index	212

THE SILVERSMITH'S HANDBOOK.

INTRODUCTORY CHAPTER.

IN reviewing the rise and progress of the silversmith's beautiful and interesting art, in its relation to the manufacture of articles of personal ornament and luxury at home and abroad, we may observe at the outset, that the material of which they are composed differs widely in character from that employed by the ordinary "metalsmiths" and the manufacturer of "electro-plated wares." Silver, the material of which we are now treating, being a precious metal and of considerable value, it is essentially necessary that the most careful means be exercised in dealing with it from the commencement—that is, from the pure or fine state— and also that the utmost economy be observed in reference to the kind of mechanical treatment to which it is subjected in the production of the silversmith's work, in order to prevent too great a quantity of waste or loss of material. For it should be borne in mind that silver, like gold, begins to lose, in one way or another, every time it is touched; therefore, carefulness and economy will be the characteristics of our teaching, so far as regards the present subject.

The vast majority of working silversmiths know very little of the physical and chemical properties of the metal they employ, and still less of the comparison it bears with other metals in the field of science; and this want of scientific knowledge is nowhere more apparent than in our own country, where the English workman, in art education, is much behind the foreigner; and yet we have some of the finest and best workmen, in their *special* branches, in the whole world. The English workman believes that if the work is worth doing at all, it is worth doing well; and we have no hesitation in saying, that, if a good technical education were afforded, concerning the precious metal trades, he would scarcely have an equal, and certainly no superior, abroad, in art workmanship, both in respect to the display of good taste and judgment, combined with a knowledge of design, so far as the exercise of these qualities is compatible with the manufacture of articles specially designed for use and ornament.

INTRODUCTORY CHAPTER.

The object of the information we are about to supply is to enable the practical silversmith to become a perfect master of his art or profession; and such a condition, when once achieved, will be found of considerable assistance to him in the various kinds of manufacture that present themselves; so that he will know how to begin a piece of work and when to leave it off; be able to remedy a defect in the metal when required, as well as be in a position to form an opinion as to the relative treatment of its different alloys; all of which invariably require different treatment.

We shall commence by describing the characteristics of *fine silver*, carefully narrating the distinctive features of its alloys; then give an account of the processes employed, mechanical and chemical, in the silversmith's workshop; and conclude by pointing out the difference between English and foreign work in regard both to style and workmanship.

It may be thought by the reader, if uninitiated in the art, that the costly plate and other articles made from the precious metal are manufactured from entirely *pure* silver, and therefore that they possess absolute freedom from alloy; but this is not the case. Pure silver being far too soft to stand the necessary wear and tear of (metallic) life, it is mixed with some other metal, to give it increased hardness. In the manufacture of plate and ornamental wares the metal employed is always copper, in various proportions, thus forming different commercial qualities; and of these we shall speak hereafter. Our first object is to treat of the chemical and physical properties of the pure metal.

CHAPTER I.

Silver.

PURE silver is, next to gold, the finest metal, but of a smoother and more polished nature. It may be said to be almost infinitely malleable, but it will not so easily yield or extend under the hammer as fine gold. As a malleable metal, however, it stands next to it in this respect. It is characterized by its perfectly white colour, being the whitest of all the metals. It is harder than gold, yet in a pure state it is so soft that it can easily be cut with a knife. On account of its extreme softness, when in a pure state, it is employed for filigree work, being utterly devoid of that elastic power which is found in the metal when alloyed. It is for this reason that the Indian filigree workers, who are the finest in the world, are so very particular about the absolute purity of the metal before commencing the manufacture of their artistic work; all of which is exceedingly beautiful.

It is reported that fine silver is capable of being beaten into leaves of less than one-hundred-thousandth part of an inch in thickness. For the accuracy of this statement we cannot vouch, never having had occasion to try the experiment; its employment in that form being unknown in the ordinary industrial pursuits. Fine silver is extremely ductile, and may be drawn into the very finest wire without breaking, and almost without annealing. Its purity can be partly ascertained by the latter process; for perfectly fine silver never changes colour by heat, whereas when it contains alloy it blackens if heated in contact with a current of air, and soon hardens in wire-drawing.

Silver was a metallic element known to the ancients, and it is repeatedly mentioned in the Holy Scriptures. In the time of the patriarchs we read of it as having been constantly employed in the transactions of nations, and that it was in use as a standard of value; thus forming a circulating medium for the purpose of exchange. This function it has always continued to fulfil down to the present day, except that since the year 1816 it has not been so employed in the English currency. However, as token money, it is everywhere recognised as a circulating medium of trade. The Egyptian symbol for silver was represented by

Fig. 1, relating to the moon; in modern chemistry it is understood by *ag.* from the Latin name *argentum*, denoting silver.

Fine silver is capable of receiving a polish scarcely inferior in lustre to that of highly polished steel, and in this state it reflects more light and heat than any other metal, without any perceptible change of colour for some considerable time. It is chiefly on this account, as well as its resistance to oxidation in air and water, that it is used for such a variety of purposes, not only of ornament and luxury, but also in a domestic way. Silver, unlike gold, cannot resist the influence of sulphuretted hydrogen, from the action of which it very soon becomes much tarnished if left exposed in damp rooms, &c.

Luna. Fig. 1. Egyptian mark for Silver.

Silver ranks next to gold in point of ductility and malleability. Its density, or specific gravity, lies between 10.47 and 10.50, taking water as 1, according to the degree of compression it has received by rolling and hammering. It is fusible at a full red heat, or about 1873° Fahr. It is a metal having a very low radiating power for heat; hence silver wire of given dimensions retains and conducts heat better than a similar piece of another metal; for the same reason, a liquid contained in a silver vessel retains its heat much longer than if placed in one made of some other substance. Silver volatilises when subjected to a very great temperature in the fire, emitting rather greenish fumes. It loses between $\frac{1}{10}$th and $\frac{2}{10}$nds of its absolute weight in air when weighed in water. In point of tenacity it occupies the fifth position among the useful metals. In hardness it lies between copper and gold; and a small addition of the former substance considerably increases this quality, in which state it is largely employed in the arts. Nitric acid is the proper solvent for silver, as it dissolves it with the greatest ease and rapidity, forming *nitrate* of silver, which is much used for medical purposes, and in art. Sulphuric and hydrochloric acids act upon it but slowly in the cold. Silver resists partially the best aqua-regia, probably on account of the dense chloride which forms on the surface of the metal, from the action of the hydrochloric acid in the mixture of aqua-regia.

Fine silver is largely used in the industrial and commercial arts, in the manufacture of silver lace and fine filigree work; the latter branch being more commonly practised in India, Sweden, Norway, and some parts of Germany, where labour is cheap, than in England. This class of silversmith's work takes a long time to produce, and as labour forms the chief item of its cost, this, not unnaturally, acts as a great drawback in the extension of the art of very fine filigree working, in all its intricate variety, in countries where labour is dear. To this subject we shall subsequently refer again in detail. Fine silver, with a small proportion of alloy, is largely used by all nations for purposes of coinage. It amalgamates with nearly all the metals, but is principally used in alloys suitable to the watchmaker's and silversmith's art. The purchasable price of fine silver for manufacturing purposes is about five shillings and twopence per ounce, troy weight, varying however in value according to the total amounts purchased; for which see refiners' and assayers' charge lists, to be procured at the offices of any bullion dealer. The silver ores of commerce have generally an intermixture of a small quantity of gold, and sometimes instances have occurred in which it has been employed in manufactures without a proper chemical investigation; and in such cases the loss resulting from the omission would have amply paid the expenses of the process.

Exposed to the action of hot and concentrated sulphuric acid, silver dissolves, setting free sulphurous acid. By the application of this process—which is one of the most advantageous methods—silver may readily be separated from gold, sulphuric acid having no action upon the latter metal. With the exception of gold, silver perhaps more perfectly resists the action of the *caustic alkalies* and the powerful effects of *nitre* (saltpetre) than any other metal, if we omit platinum from the list of elements at present known to metallurgical chemistry. For reasons such as these its superiority for the manufacture of utensils for culinary and other domestic purposes is at once apparent, and because it is a metal upon which *vegetable acids* produce no effect.

CHAPTER II.

Sources of Silver.

STRICTLY speaking, silver mining does not exist as a distinct operation in Great Britain, for it can hardly be said that this country possesses any great quantity of silver ore. Yet we must not disguise or leave unnoticed, in dealing with this subject, the positive fact that silver is found to some extent in our copper and lead mines, principally in the latter; but in no case, as far as we know, have mines been worked for the sake of the silver alone. It is almost always found in conjunction with lead, and it is from that source that we have a good supply of British silver. The average annual yield in the British Isles for some years has been equal to 800,000 ounces—a position in regard to the quantity produced ranking second only to Spain amongst the nations of the world, America, of course, being excepted. Silver is found in a native state, the commonest ore being a sulphuret.

The chief European supplies are derived from Spain, in which country genuine silver ore exists; from Saxony and Prussia, where the ores are principally associated with lead, as in England; and from Austria, where it is for the greater part found mixed with copper. Silver is nearly always to be found in copper and lead mines, but generally in such small quantities that it is rarely worth the trouble and expense of separation.

Considerably more than three-fourths of the whole total supply of silver comes from America; and in fact nearly the whole territory of America is said to be more or less argentiferous. Until lately Mexico carried off the palm, as containing and yielding the largest percentage of silver; but through the discovery of another mine in the United States, at Nevada, of considerable richness, which has yielded enormous supplies, we shall not be far wrong in pronouncing the silver mines in the State of Nevada to be the richest in the whole world. The extensive production of these mines, combined with other causes, has led to a considerable depreciation in the value of silver, and probably this may yet lead to its more extensive employment in the arts and manufactures; and, in the midst of the very general depression of the jewellery trade, any change extending in that direction would be joyfully accepted by the thousands of workmen in the precious metal trades now standing idle. We are told that, since the year 1860, the production of silver has increased from an average yield of eight or nine to fourteen millions per annum, or about 60 per cent.; while, on the other hand, the foreign demand for the metal formerly largely employed for the currency) has greatly diminished. This decrease in the demand has been caused by the adoption in the following countries of a gold currency, viz., Holland, Germany, and the Scandinavian Governments in Northern Europe, &c.; and also by a diminution in the amount of silver coined by the undermentioned powers: France, Belgium, Switzerland, Italy, and Greece.

The chief sources of supply in the British Isles, according to Professor George Gladstone, are as given below; and as all the silver found in this country is produced from lead ores, the average yield here given must be understood to exist in about that proportion to every ton of lead ore assayed:—Isle of Man, 50 or 60 oz.; Cornwall, about 30 oz.; Devonshire, about 30 oz.; Cardiganshire, 15 to 20 oz.; Montgomeryshire, 15 to 20 oz. Thus, it will be seen the lead ores of the Isle of Man yield the greatest proportion of silver in the British dominions. Silver is also found in the undermentioned counties, in all of which it is produced from lead ore :—Cumberland, Durham, and Northumberland, Denbighshire, Flintshire, and Derbyshire; but the percentage is much smaller than in the preceding cases. Ireland also yields a fair percentage of silver.

CHAPTER III.

The Assay of Silver Ores.

A LARGE proportion of the silver of commerce is extracted from ores (which are too poor to allow of their being smelted or fused) by a process called amalgamation. Founded on the ready solubility of silver, &c., in metallic mercury, the ore is first crushed to powder, then mixed with common salt, and afterwards roasted. By the adoption of this plan the silver is reduced to a state of chloride. The roasting is done in a reverberatory furnace, in which the heat is very gradually raised, the ore being constantly stirred; the heat is then increased sufficiently to raise the ore to a good red heat. It is then put into wooden barrels, revolving on iron axles attached to the ends, and scraps of iron are then added to it; both are then agitated together by rotary motion, the effect of which is to reduce the chloride of silver to a metallic state. When this is effected, it is again agitated with mercury, and a fluid amalgam is formed with the metal, together with any other metallic ingredient that may happen to be present in the roasted ore. Subsequently, to recover the silver, the mercury is driven off by heat, and the silver is thus left behind in an impure state.

There are three ways of assaying silver ores; they are in the *test* assay as follows:—

1. Melting in a crucible.
2. Scorification.
3. Cupellation.

In the crucible assay the ore is commonly run down with a suitable flux, those most frequently employed being litharge, carbonate of soda, borax, and charcoal. These four substances are all that are required by the practical assayer in the treatment of the regular ores of silver.

The assaying of the genuine ores is performed in the following manner; that is, if they contain but little earthy matter. They may then be conveniently treated by fusing with carbonate of soda, on account of its cheapness, and borax, in a fire-clay crucible (Fig. 2). The dimensions of the crucible should be as follows: $4\frac{1}{2}$ inches in height, and $2\frac{1}{2}$ inches

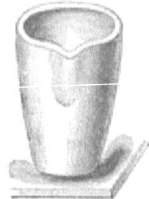
Fig. 2. Fire-clay Crucible.

in its greatest diameter, which should be at the top. A quantity of litharge (a semi-vitrious substance, oxide of lead), more than is actually necessary to take up the whole of the silver in the ore, should be added, so as to promote fusion, and collect the ingredients into one mass at the bottom of the crucible. In preparing the ore for the crucible, it must be well pounded, and intimately mixed with the undermentioned chemicals:—

Pounded silver ore	240 grains.
Litharge	800 ,,
Carbonate of soda	700 ,,
Borax	300 ,,
Charcoal	50 ,,

Place two crucibles to warm during the time occupied in the preparation of the mixture, then put it into the warm crucible; take 100 grains more of litharge, and powder it over the contents in the vessel. Prepare in this manner a second mixture for the other crucible, place them both in the furnace, and put plenty of coke round them. The mixtures may be melted in an ordinary wind or melting furnace, such as is used by jewellers in the preparation of their material for art working. The fusion should take place very gradually at first, as silver in combination with lead is sensibly volatile at a high temperature: it may then be continued at a low heat for twenty-five minutes, and finally the operation may be completed with a full red heat for five minutes longer.

During the process of fusing the contents of the crucible may be watched by removing one of the bricks from the top of the furnace, and when the whole mass has become quite liquid the crucible must be seized with a pair of suitable tongs, tapped once or twice very lightly against the side of the furnace to procure the settlement of the contents, and immediately poured into an iron mould, previously warmed and greased to prevent adhesion and spitting. Allow the mould to remain for some time, in order to partially cool, and then plunge it into a vessel of cold water. On cooling, the metallic elements will be found incorporated into a button, the slag can then easily be removed by tapping with a hammer on the edge, and the plunging into cold water greatly facilitates this separation. The whole mass has then to be cupelled, in order to separate the silver from the lead and other metals.

Silver ores, containing a large proportion of the sulphides (chemical combinations of sulphur with metallic substances) of other metals, may be easily assayed by the scorification process, which is, without exception, applicable to the assay of all kinds of argentiferous ores; and is one of the best, most simple, and most exact methods that can possibly be employed in the extraction of silver from its ores. This process, like that of fusion with litharge, already described, has the effect of producing an alloy, and subsequently requires cupellation. The ore is first well pounded, and then put into a small shallow vessel made of close-grained refractory fire-clay (Fig. 3), with an excess of finely granulated lead and some borax. The fusing cup or scorifier employed in this process should be about 1½ in.

Fig. 3. Fire-clay Fusing Cup.

high and 2¼ ins. in its greatest diameter; some assayers, however, use them deeper in proportion to their width, and representing in form the end of an egg. The object of this shape is to preserve the bath of molten metal at the bottom, and that it may always be well covered and protected by the slag on the top during the process of fusing. In the scorification method the principles are exactly the reverse of those of the crucible assay; for in the latter the object is to reduce the oxide of lead to a metallic state, whereas in the former the metallic lead added to the pounded ore in the scorifier is oxidized by being fused in contact with the air. The charge for this assay may be as follows:—

Well pounded ore	60 grains.
Finely granulated lead	600 ,,
Borax anhydrous	100 ,,
Powdered anthracite	5 ,,

The cups or scorifiers should be charged in the following manner: well mix the silver ore with 300 grains of granulated lead; place this mixture in a scorifier, and add 300 grs. more of granulated lead, and over the top of the whole put the burnt borax. The vessel may then be placed in an ordinary assay furnace or muffle, as many being introduced at one time as there is room for in the furnace, and submitted to the strongest heat for about thirty minutes; during the greater portion of this time the door should be kept closed, especially for the first fifteen minutes. On opening the muffle-door a current of air passes through the furnace, converting a portion of the lead into litharge; this enters into combination with the earthy portions of the ore, the other metallic sulphides, and also the borax, producing a fusible slag on the surface of the metallic bath, extending over the whole surface of the scorifier. The excess of lead is thus protected by this film or flux from the oxidizing effects of the currents of air admitted into the furnace, and remains united with whatever silver there may be in the ore, in a metallic state.

The fusing should be continued longer than the

thirty minutes—in fact until the slag or flux is reduced into a perfectly liquid state; stirring it well with a slender iron rod will facilitate the operation, as it will tend to mix with the mass any hard portions remaining undissolved and attached to the sides or other parts of the vessels. This condition of the flux is absolutely indispensable; when the slags are quite liquid, which with a strong fire will take place in from thirty to forty minutes, wrap up in a piece of paper the powdered anthracite, and drop it into the scorifier while still in the furnace or muffle. The object of adding the anthracite at the last moment is to reduce any minute portions of the metal that may exist in the slags, and remain separated from the bulk. When the anthracite has burnt off, which process usually takes about five minutes, this point is considered to have been attained, and the operation is then complete. The scorifier may be immediately withdrawn from the fire, and the contents poured into a suitable casting-mould, of the form represented in Fig. 4, a button of silver lead being the result. When cold, the metallic mass is readily separated from the slag or flux by slightly tapping with a hammer; the former may then be passed on to the next operation, viz. to be purified of its lead by the process of cupellation, which will be presently described.

When there is not enough borax present, the assayer will observe an infusible skin floating upon the surface; should this be the case more borax must at once be employed, in order to dissolve such impurity. When a chloride of silver ore is to be assayed, carbonate of soda must be added to the mixture to prevent sublimation.

The following method of assaying is adopted in several large Continental establishments, where the ores have, beside the usual earthy matter and the sulphides of lead, an admixture of zinc, iron, and copper. The process is precisely similar to the crucible assay, in the case of genuine silver ores, as already described—with this exception, that no more lead is added than the ores then contain— that is, if we are treating *galena* or *silver lead;* other ores require different treatment according to their known composition. In this process wrought-iron crucibles are employed having the form and shape as shown in Fig. 5. They are made of thick iron plate, and are rendered secure by welding the edges firmly together. Their dimensions are as follows: a depth of $4\tfrac{1}{2}$ ins., with a thickness of iron at the bottom of $1\tfrac{1}{2}$ in., and a $\tfrac{1}{4}$ of an inch in the sides; the diameter at the top of the crucible should be about $2\tfrac{1}{2}$ ins., and at the bottom between 2 and $2\tfrac{1}{4}$ ins. A mechanical mixture or flux is prepared to use with the ores to which we have referred, consisting of the following chemicals, all of which should be finely powdered and well mixed with the ore to be assayed :—

Carbonate of soda	6 parts.
Tartar	3 ,,
Saltpetre	2 ,,
Borax	1 part.

The furnace used for this assay is the ordinary one, having rather a high chimney, to insure a perfect draught. In effecting the reduction of the silver, the crucible is first placed as before on the fire, and allowed to become hot; when this is accomplished, take

Well powdered ore	480 grains.
Prepared flux	500 ,,

These ingredients should be thoroughly mixed together, and put into the red hot crucible. Fuse at a low heat for about twenty minutes, when the whole will be in a perfect state of fusion; then give about five minutes strong heat, and at the end of that time the crucible may be withdrawn, and its contents poured into an iron mould, as represented in Fig. 4, having one or two conical holes for the reception of the fused mass. The silver and lead collect at the bottom of the mould by reason of its high specific gravity. It may be removed by reversing the position of the latter, when a gentle tap or two will deprive it of that slag or flux which is usually attached to it. A

Fig. 5. Iron Casting-moulds.

large quantity of silver can be readily collected from its ores by an alternate use of crucibles, in which case it is possible to make a regular number of fusions per hour. Wrought-iron crucibles, when strongly prepared and carefully made, will stand about thirty of these fusions, giving way in the end on account of the action of the sulphur contained in the ores.

Another kind of crucible, in addition to those already mentioned, is used by the trade, and is recommended by many assayers as superior to all others. Fig. 6 represents the form of it. It is about 4½ ins. high, and 2 ins. in its greatest interior diameter, being in the form of a skittle. The charge consists of the following in this assay:

Finely powdered ore	60 grains.
Small pieces of iron	12 ,,
Black flux	180 ,,
Common salt	50 ,,

Put the powdered ore into the crucible, and

place upon it the iron, which should not be in the form of filings or dust, but in small pieces; upon

 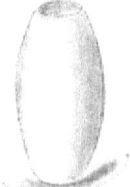

Fig. 5. Iron Crucible for Assay.   Fig. 6. Fireclay Crucible for Assay.

the ore and iron should be put the black flux, and lastly the common salt must be placed above all these substances as a protection against the air. The crucibles, as many as convenient, may now be introduced into the furnace, and slowly raised to a strong red heat, at which temperature they should be kept for about half an hour; at the end of that period they should be removed from the fire, slightly tapped to settle the contents, and then placed aside to cool. When this has taken place, a few blows with a hammer near the base of the crucibles, each in turn, will soon expose the button of silver attached to the undecomposed iron; the latter substance may, however, be easily detached by a few well-directed blows with the hammer.

In order to ascertain the exact amount of the

precious metal—that is, the silver—contained in the buttons of lead obtained as the results of the foregoing operations, they are subjected to a purifying process by the metallurgist, called cupellation. By this means the lead and other impurities are driven off by heat in contact with a current of air, and the silver is left behind in a pure state. To perform this operation it is necessary to expose the buttons on some absorbing medium or porous support, and this support is commonly known as a *cupel*. No doubt many porous substances could be made available for the formation of cupels, but bone-ash is the best for all practical purposes, such as are required by the assayer. The bone-ash, in the condition of a very fine powder, is mixed with a little water in which has been dissolved a small quantity of potash, and moulded into the desired shape. The cupels are tightly consolidated by pressure in an iron mould of the form shown in Fig. 7, which is the best in use, being well adapted for the manufacture of cupels. It consists of a slightly conical steel ring, 2 ins. in depth, and about 1½ in. in diameter at the top internally; a steel die with a wooden handle (Fig. 8) is made to fit the mould. To make a cupel the space in the ring is nearly filled with the moistened bone-ash, and pressed down by the hand, and afterwards by

THE CUPEL.

the die, the latter being driven into the ring by the application of a wooden mallet (Fig. 9) to the handle

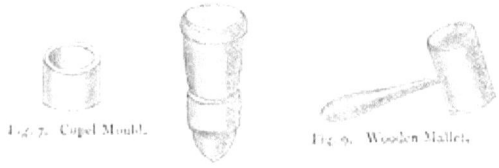

Fig. 7. Cupel Mould.   Fig. 9. Wooden Mallet.

Fig. 8. Die for Cupel.

of the die. It will be seen from the illustration that the die forms a cavity in the cupel capable of receiving the charge of metal for assay. When the bone-ash has been sufficiently compressed, the die is withdrawn, and the cupel removed from the ring. This is a delicate operation, as sometimes the edges of the cupel are liable to be injured; to prevent which and facilitate the removal a loose plate of iron, exactly fitting the bottom of the mould, should be introduced previous to putting in the bone-ash. The iron plate of course being removed with the cupel, it must be replaced before another can be made. By introducing a cylindrical piece of wood to the lower aperture of the steel ring, the cupel can be removed without difficulty.

The size of the cupel should always be regulated according to the quantity of foreign matter to be absorbed, it being generally understood that the material of which it is formed takes up double its weight of lead. The process of cupelling is conducted in the furnace of the assayer, an apparatus of peculiar construction, the most important part of which, however, is the muffle (Fig. 10), consisting of a small arched oven of fire-clay closed at one end, and furnished with perpendicular slits in the sides, in order to allow of a free access of air to the cupels inside.

Fig. 10. Assayer's Muffle for Cupels.

The position of the muffle in the furnace is so arranged that it can be readily heated on every side; and when it has become red hot, six or eight cupels, previously well dried, are taken and placed on the floor of it, which should be covered with a thin layer of bone-ash. The form of tongs required for this purpose is shown in Fig. 11. When the

Fig. 11. Cupel Tongs.

cupels have been raised to the temperature of the muffle itself, the assays are put in by a very slender pair of tongs, the door of the furnace is then closed for a few minutes, when the metal will have become fused, and the litharge will begin to be taken up by the bone-ash of which the cupel is composed. The

Fig. 12. Cupels, section and perspective views.

temperature of the furnace is now lowered as much as possible, although not to such an extent that it will retard the progress of oxidation and absorption. When nearly the whole of the lead has been thus absorbed, the bead remaining will have become very rich in silver, and, as the oxidation proceeds, will appear much agitated, assuming a rapid circular movement, and revolving with great rapidity. The silver gradually concentrates itself in the centre of the cupel, taking the form of a globule, and at this stage the fire should be made sharper, the operation being carefully watched. When the last particle of lead leaves the silver, the agitation will suddenly cease, and a beautiful phenomenon be witnessed, called by assayers the *brightening*. The button of silver then becomes brilliant and immovable, and the operation, when this takes place, is complete. The cupel must be cooled with very great care, in order to prevent the silver from *sprouting*; which if allowed to take place would result in considerable loss, besides destroying the accuracy of the assay. To prevent this sprouting it is a good plan immediately to cover the cupel by another, which has been heated for that purpose; the two are withdrawn together, and allowed to remain at the mouth of the muffle until the silver has become solid; the metal is then in a state of almost chemical purity, and may be detached and weighed. Previous to the latter, however, it should be carefully cleansed from all foreign matter, and flattened on a smooth-faced anvil, this process greatly assisting in the removal of any oxide of lead, which not unfrequently attaches itself to the globule of silver. The weighing is conducted with a pair of scales having an extremely delicate balance; and where any commercial transaction depends upon the accuracy of the assay, it is always imperative to make several tests of the same sample, to avoid the consequences of any accident or mistake.

The chief element in combination with silver on the large scale is lead. Formerly the plan adopted in the separation of this metal was cupellation alone. This process on the large scale is somewhat different from that just described; and as it may appear to the reader interesting and instructive, a brief explanation of it may not be considered out of place.

CHAPTER IV.

The Cupellation of Silver Ores.

This interesting process is performed in a reverberatory furnace of a very peculiar construction, the cupel employed on the large scale differing somewhat from the ordinary one, being considerably larger and varying also in form. It consists of a strong oval wrought-iron ring, with a part of the full shape omitted, as shown in accompanying sketch, in order to allow of the overflow of lead during the process, in the form of litharge. This iron ring, known as the *test ring*, contains the cupel, and in order to prepare the latter, the frame, which measures about 60 ins. in its longest diameter, 40 ins. in breadth, and 6 ins. in depth, is strengthened by having a number of broad strips of iron seamed across the bottom by riveting to the sides of it. The cupel itself is prepared for use by taking finely ground bone-ash, together with a little carbonate of potash, and working them up with just sufficient water to make the mass cohere properly; the carbonate of potash may be advantageously dissolved in the water; the latter is then applied in small quantities at a time to the bone-ash until the proper coherency has been obtained; of the total quantity of bone-ash employed in the operation, 2 per cent. of potash will be *quantum sufficit* to mix with it. The iron frame, or test, is then filled with the mixture, and it is pressed down into a solid compact mass, the centre part being hollowed out with a small trowel, the sides sloping towards the concavity in the middle; the hollow should not however be extended more than within 1 to 1½ in. of the bottom of the frame, and above the iron bars. The cupel forms the hearth of the furnace we have spoken of, and of which Fig. 13 is a sectional view; it is removable, and not a fixture in the furnace. It must be left for several days to dry, after having been constructed as described, when it is ready for use, and only requires firmly

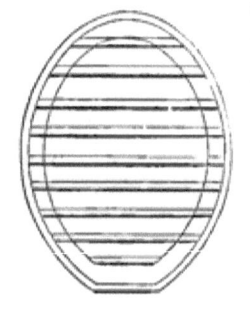

Fig. 13. Cupels, section and perspective views.

wedging in its place beneath the arch of the furnace.

The fire should be only very moderate at the commencement of the operation, and the furnace slowly raised in temperature, lest the cupel should crack by being too quickly heated. As the temperature increases, if without any apparent defects in the bone-ash cupel, or hearth, which it may now be termed, the wind or blast, generally driven by a fan, is thrown in through a nozzle, or an aperture in the furnace, which, for facilitating the immediate removal of the bone-ash hearth, is placed upon an iron car, and runs beneath the vault of the furnace on rails, so that it may thus be very readily withdrawn when found necessary. The admission of a current of air into the furnace oxidizes the excess of lead, in combination with the silver, producing litharge on the surface of the molten mass; the formation of the litharge takes place rapidly, and it is continually blown forward by the strength of the blast as fast as it is produced, running through a gap or channel specially made for the purpose in the mouth of the cupel into a movable iron pot which is placed for its reception. The continual oxidization and flow-off of the lead alters the respective proportions of the metals in the cupel. For this reason it is always kept full of lead ore, which is effected by taking it in its fused state from a kettle in which it is ready melted by means of a long-handled ladle; and thus about 500 or 600 lbs. of metal are constantly kept in this bone-ash cupel or hearth.

As the silver necessarily increases in the hearth, it will require to be occasionally withdrawn, in order to make room for a further supply of lead ore. This process is adopted when it reaches about from 8 to 10 per cent. of silver to the ton (between 2,000 and 3,000 ozs.), and may be effectually performed by drilling a hole underneath the cupel, and letting the silver flow through it into a receptacle placed to receive it. Of course the operations of the furnace are arrested while these manipulations are being carried on. After the withdrawal of the silver, the hole is closed up again with a plug of moistened bone-ash prepared as before; when the process may be continued a second time by giving 500 or 600 lbs. of fresh lead ore to the cupel. Thus a single cupel will often last 48 hours, and 6 or 7 tons of lead may be oxidized upon it.

We have already observed that the prolongation of the cupelling process increases the richness of the remaining alloy, and this very rich silver-lead alloy is again subjected to a second operation in cupelling. This process of assaying or refining is similar in every respect to the former, and is often performed in the same furnace, the cupel being first of all brought to almost a bright red heat, when about 600 lbs. of the silver-lead alloy are added, and a strong current of air given in order to oxidize the remaining lead in combination with the silver. In this operation the material under treatment, previous to its introduction to the cupel, should be melted in a kettle easy of access, and added in its fused state. The current of air in connection with the heat of the furnace immediately begins to purify the silver by oxidizing the lead, and forms litharge, which passes off through the channel provided in the mouth of the cupel; as this proceeds, fresh silver-lead alloy is added, to keep the level of the metal always at the same height. This is continued until some three tons of the alloy from the first cupellation have been put in, and when about 600 or 700 lbs. of silver are collected in the cupel.

When the cupel has received the above proportion of metal, the addition of the alloy ceases, and the silver is allowed to purify. The litharge which passes off towards the close of this process will be richer in silver than in the former one; consequently it is found best in practical metallurgical operations to treat in a special manner the last part of silver cupelling on the large scale, for it needs very careful management indeed to secure all the silver, especially to do so in a fine state. Towards the completion of the process the fire should be increased considerably, in order to keep the silver thoroughly melted, and also to oxidize and completely remove every trace of lead that is possible. As it begins to purify itself from the remaining lead a characteristic brightness will be perceived. When this takes place the fire must be lowered, the wind or blast stopped, and the metal left to cool gradually. This latter proceeding is of some importance, as a too sudden cooling of the surface causes the interior of the metal to expand and shoot, by which means little globules of silver may be lost; therefore it should be allowed to cool very slowly.

The iron ring encircling the cupel with its contents may now be drawn from beneath the arch of the furnace, and the cake of silver taken from its bed in the bone-ash which formed the vessel, and cleaned of any impurity; when it may be remelted in a plumbago crucible, and cast into ingot moulds. These moulds should be made of iron, and should always, when used for this purpose, be warmed and greased a little, previous to the introduction of the melted material, to prevent the metal from spitting and adhering to it. If skilfully treated during the process of cupellation, the desilvered lead seldom contains more than ·002 to ·003 per cent. of silver to the test assay of 200 grs., or between six and ten pennyweights to the ton, beyond which point it is unprofitable to carry on the operation.

The litharge which is formed and passes off during the process gradually grows richer in silver towards the end of the cupellation. It probably contains after concentration about thirty to forty ounces of silver to the ton of litharge. This is again subjected to the several operations of the same kind for the recovery of the silver.

It is somewhat remarkable that the present method of recovering and purifying this metal bears a strong resemblance to that employed in ancient times, and which is spoken of in the Holy Scriptures by the prophet Ezekiel [xxii. 18 and 20]: " Son of man, the house of Israel is to me become dross : all they are brass, and tin, and iron, and lead, in the midst of the furnace; they are even the dross of silver." And also, " As they gather silver, and brass, and iron, and lead, and tin, into the midst of the furnace, to blow the fire upon it, to melt it ; so will I gather you in mine anger and in my fury, and I will leave you there, and melt you." The celebrated metallurgist Dr. Lamborn says, "Only those who have seen, beneath the glowing arch at the smelting works, flames surging wave after wave across the surface of the liquid metal, carrying all the substances, here called dross, from the pure silver; and only those who have heard the roar of the fiery blast, that ceases neither day nor night, until its task of purification is accomplished,—can appreciate the terrible force of the figure made use of by the prophet." According to the above scriptural passage it is evident that the ancients were in possession of the first rudiments of assaying, and understood to some extent the purification of metals; but scriptural testimony does not point out with what amount of skill and success these operations were performed. Judging from the appliances which have been handed down from generation to generation, we are inclined to think they must have been practised somewhat rudely; for it has been left to the present school of scientific and practical metallurgists to found and develop the art in the direction of that commercial success to which it has at the present day attained.

This plan of cupellation which we have just described is still adopted in many continental works in the assaying of silver-lead ores. In

England the system has been almost entirely superseded by one invented by the late Mr. Pattinson of Newcastle, and which is confidently stated to be far more convenient in practice. For a full and comprehensive description of this and other processes relating to the metallurgy of silver, we refer the reader to an admirable little work on the subject, by Dr. Robert H. Lamborn, issued by the publishers of the present volume.

CHAPTER V.

The Alloys of Silver.

FINE silver enters freely into combination with nearly all the useful metals, but its most important alloys are those prepared from copper, the latter substance being more suitable for the production of silversmith's work than any other; whilst it produces a more pleasing effect, if not over-alloyed, in regard to finish. Silver articles, especially of the *filigree* kinds, if the designs are good, possess a very tasteful appearance. In treating of the alloys of silver, it is our intention, first, to give a cursory glance at the chemical and physical properties of the metals which form these alloys. Such a description, although brief, will, we believe, prove of essential service, not only to working silversmiths and metalsmiths, but also to goldsmiths and jewellers, who are constantly manipulating with these inferior metals in precisely the same way as the silversmith. Besides, such information cannot, we apprehend, fail to be useful, whether to the student, the theorist, or the practical worker.

An alloy is the union of two or more metals by fusion, so as to form a metallic compound. It may consist of any number of the metallic elements, and in any proportion, provided they will chemically combine, always excepting mercury as one of the ingredients. In this latter case the mixture is called an *amalgam*. Chemistry has made us acquainted with about forty-nine metals; of that number, however, not more than fourteen are employed to any considerable extent for industrial art purposes. They are as follow: Gold, silver, copper, zinc, platinum, aluminum, nickel, iron, mercury, lead, tin, arsenic, antimony, and bismuth. Some of these are occasionally employed for *special* purposes in the arts in their pure state; but where hardness is to be a distinguishing characteristic, combined with certain variations in shades of colour, a union is effected of two or more of these metals in different proportions, by fusion and stirring, so as to form the requisite alloy. Metals used in the pure state, that is, without any mixture of alloy, have very few applications in regard to industrial pursuits and the arts. The precious metals—gold, silver, &c.—would be much too soft, while, on the other hand, arsenic, bismuth, and antimony would be far too brittle to be employed alone for manufacturing purposes. It is quite possible to effect some thousands of alloys, but there do not appear to have been more than about three hundred practised successfully for commercial purposes.

The principal alloy of silver, as we have already remarked, is copper; but, occasionally, nickel, and even zinc are employed in the case of the commoner qualities of silver. Tin is also used in the preparation of solder for these qualities, in order to render it the more easy of fusion when used for soldering the work. Of the distinctive features of these elements of silver-alloy we shall now speak with some amount of detail.

Silver will unite with copper in various proportions by melting the two ingredients together, and stirring them whilst in a fused state. A product will thus be formed differing physically in character from fine silver, caused by the loss of some little of the latter's ductility and malleability; but, on the other hand, a compound will be produced harder and more elastic, which is in every sense better adapted to the manufacture and also to the durability of the articles made by the silversmith.

Copper, like the precious metals, appears to have

been known from a very early age, being one of the six metals spoken of in the Old Testament; and described by the historian as being also one of the seven made use of by the ancient philosopher. It is of a reddish colour, malleable, ductile, and tenacious. It is largely employed in alloying both gold and silver for the manufacture of jewellery and other articles. With regard to malleability, it stands next to gold and silver in the list of useful metals; in ductility it occupies the fifth position; and in tenacity one only is superior, viz. iron. It is not very fixed in the fire, for if subjected to a long-continued heat it loses a part of its substance; for this reason the alloys of silver and copper should be carefully watched in the crucible to prevent this loss when under the action of the fire.

When struck copper gives only a feeble sound, and is easily abraded by the file. It fuses at a good white heat, or about 1994° Fahr., although some authors have given it as 1996° Fahr. Its specific gravity varies between 8·88 for cast copper, and 8·96 when rolled and hammered. It loses between one-eighth and one-ninth of its weight in water. When exposed to a damp atmosphere a greenish oxide, called verdigris, is produced on its surface, and this is one of the reasons why silver articles containing a percentage of copper become so readily discoloured if left exposed to atmospheric influences; copper also, if heated in contact with the air, quickly becomes oxidized, and, on being touched, scales fall off: these form the *protoxide of copper*. If this process is frequently repeated under a great heat, each time the metal is operated upon it loses a part of its malleability and ductility, which are both eminent characteristics of the pure metal. Most of the ordinary acids act on copper but slowly in the cold, but nitric acid very readily dissolves it, even if largely diluted. Copper amalgamates with most of the metals, and its subsidiary alloys are very largely employed in the arts and manufactures of every kind.

The bean-shot copper of commerce, costing about a shilling per pound avoirdupois weight, is quite good enough for all the practical purposes of the silversmith.

The name given to this metal by the alchemists was *Venus* (Fig. 14), which is one of the principal planets, whose orbit is situated between the Earth and Mercury. The scientific name of *cuprum* for copper is derived from the Isle of Cyprus, where, it is said by Pliny, the Greeks discovered the method of mining and working it. Copper is found distributed all over

Fig. 14. Venus. Egyptian Mark for Copper.

the world; a considerable portion, however, is found in the United Kingdom.

Nickel.—This metal is found chiefly in the Hartz Mountains. It was formerly called by the Germans "Kupfer nickel," or false copper, "nickel" being a term of detraction. It was first discovered about a century and a half ago by Cronstedt. It has a greyish-white colour, and is slightly magnetic, *i.e.* it is attracted by the magnet in the same way as iron and steel, but it loses this property if heated to about 600° Fahr. Its specific gravity varies between 8·30 and 8·50, according to the amount of compression it has received, and it is rather brittle; it may, however, be drawn into wire, and rolled flat, or into sheets. It is considerably harder and less ductile than any of the other metals employed in jeweller's and silversmith's work. In hardness it nearly approaches iron, and on this account, when polished, a characteristic brightness is produced. The malleability of nickel is less than that of iron, standing tenth in the list of useful metals; and in ductility it also occupies the tenth position. Nickel is very infusible, and does not so easily oxidize or tarnish at ordinary temperatures as copper does. Several countries have tried to employ it in the manufacture of small coin for the currency, but its use has now been almost abandoned.

Nickel alloys are much used in the arts for manufacturing purposes, under the name of "German silver," there being large demand for this metal, as it forms the hard white alloy much used in making "electro-plate," and on which silver is afterwards deposited. It also is used in common silver alloys, in order to keep up the whiteness of the latter element, the addition of too large a proportion of copper maintaining the tint of the latter metal, in too strong a degree to be altogether employed by the silverworker. Nickel is sometimes *specially* employed, in combination with other metals, to replace or imitate silver in the manufacture of commercial wares, while with copper, zinc, tin, &c., it forms very useful alloys, producing great hardness.

Zinc.—This metal in its pure state is sometimes called *spelter*. At the present day it is not much used for alloying silver; but, as it is commonly employed in the preparation of silver-solder, it is necessary that the amateur and the student should know, as well as the practical mechanic, the distinctive characteristics of it, together with the qualities it imparts to others when in combination with them. As a metallic substance it was unknown until a long time subsequent to the discovery of the principal metals; and only since the commencement of the present century has its uses been thoroughly known and appreciated in the industrial world. In its pure state, zinc is a bluish-white metal, hard and highly crystalline; but, when raised to a heat of between 250° and 300° Fahr., it is malleable, and may safely be rolled and hammered: it is in this way that the zinc of commerce is produced.

Zinc may be annealed by placing it for a time in boiling water. Its specific gravity varies between 6.8 and 7.2 Fahr., according to the previous kind of mechanical treatment it has received. At 773° it melts, and is quickly oxidized by exposure to a current of air, emitting white vapours, which rise into the air, and are not unlike cotton-flakes; oxide of zinc is thus formed by the burning away of the zinc. Spelter or zinc is employed by jewellers in the manufacture of bright gold alloys, as it gives liveliness of colour to their wares not to be equalled by any other metal. (For the proportions and treatment of this composition see the "Practical Goldworker.") It may be alloyed with most of the metals we have named; its uses in roofing, gutters, spouting, and chimney-pots being all well known. All the acids very readily attack it in the cold, and even when largely diluted; it speedily tarnishes, and becomes covered with a white oxide which protects the metal from atmospheric influences. In point of malleability zinc stands eighth among the metals, seventh in ductility, and as regards tenacity about seventh also. In chemistry it is represented by the symbol Zn. Its value when in a state of purity, commercially speaking, is about 4*d.* per. lb.

Tin.—This appears to have been one of the oldest known metals, and was employed in the Egyptian arts by the ancients, in combination with copper. Its colour is white, with a shining lustre almost as brilliant as that of silver, but it tarnishes much more quickly than alloys of the latter metal. With the exception of aluminum and zinc, it is the lightest of all the metals, its density being between 7·0 and 7·3, whether cast, hammered, or rolled. It is found in abundance in Cornwall, where it was also obtained at a very early period by the Phœnicians; and it is reported in Soame's "Latin Church," p. 30, that it was through the medium of the trade in tin that Christianity was first introduced into this country. Tin is not of a fixed nature like gold or silver, but melts in a moderate fire long before it becomes red hot, or about 442° Fahr. It is rapidly oxidized when kept for a long time in a fire having a free access to the air; and it is dissolved by hydrochloric, sulphuric, and nitric acids, the latter acting on it most powerfully. Tin should not be alloyed with gold or silver, as with either of these it easily enters into combination by fusion, rendering them extremely brittle, especially in the case of silver, which becomes by the least mixture of it so brittle that it is totally unfit for the work of the silversmith. However, for solder, for filing into dust, it may be advantageously employed to promote a quicker fusion; but even for this it should be avoided where it is possible to do so. The vapours of tin are also permanently injurious in the melting of gold, silver, and their alloys, as they render them very unworkable, and the operator being often at a loss to understand the cause of his misfortune; therefore, in melting silver alloys, it is advisable to avoid as much as possible the introduction of little bits of scrap tin into the furnace. If such a thing should happen, however, make the fire once or twice stronger in order that the tin may all be destroyed before the crucible containing the silver alloy is put in.

Tin is very malleable, moderately ductile, and tenacious, being fifth on the list for malleability, eighth for ductility, and eighth for tenacity. The Egyptian mark or symbol for tin (sign of "Jupiter") was the same as is represented in Fig. 15, and related to the planet of that name, one remarkable for its brightness. *In mythology* it is understood as representing the supreme deity of the Greeks and Romans. The modern scientific name for tin is Sn.

Fig. 11. *Jupiter.* Egyptian mark for Copper.

Tin loses one-seventh of its weight in water from its absolute weight in air. In the next chapter we shall treat of the mixing of silver alloys, &c., and in order to make our information regarding the various metals so employed as complete as possible, we shall conclude this one with the following tables, each of which will no doubt be found useful:—

Table of Metallic Elements.

Names of Elements.	Symbols.	Specific Gravities.
Platinum	Pt	21·40 to 21·50
Gold	Au	19·25 ,, 19·30
Mercury	Hg	13·56 ,, 13·59
Lead	Pb	11·40 ,, 11·45
Silver	Ag	10·47 ,, 10·50
Bismuth	Bi	9·82 ,, 9·90
Copper	Cu	8·89 ,, 8·96
Nickel	Ni	8·50 ,, 8·40
Iron	Fe	7·77 ,, 7·80
Tin	Sn	7·25 ,, 7·30
Zinc	Zn	6·80 ,, 7·20
Antimony	Sb	6·75 ,, 6·80
Arsenic	As	5·70 ,, 5·90
Aluminum	Al	2·56 ,, 2·60

Melting-points of the Principal Metals.

Names of Elements	Fahrenheit	Centigrade
Platinum	Infusible, except by the oxyhydrogen blow-pipe.	
Cast Iron	2786	1530
Nickel	2700	1482
Gold	2016	1102
Copper	1994	1090
Silver	1873	1023
Aluminum	1300	705
Zinc	773	412
Lead	612	322
Bismuth	497	258
Tin	442	228
Antimony	Fuses a little below red-heat.	
Arsenic	Volatilises before it fuses.	

Physical Properties of the Principal Metals.

Malleability.	Ductility.	Tenacity.	
Gold	Gold	Iron	549
Silver	Silver	Copper	302
Copper	Platinum	Aluminum	300
Aluminum	Iron	Platinum	274
Tin	Copper	Silver	187
Platinum	Aluminum	Gold	$150\frac{1}{2}$
Lead	Zinc	Zinc	$109\frac{1}{2}$
Zinc	Tin	Tin	$34\frac{1}{2}$
Iron	Lead	Lead	$27\frac{1}{2}$
Nickel	Nickel		

* The above weights were lbs. sustained by 0.787 of a line in diameter, in wires of the various metals.

CHAPTER VI.

Various Qualities of Silver.

THE chemical and physical properties of fine silver having been dealt with in a preceding chapter, we shall not refer to them again in detail; but, as we have already observed that it is sometimes employed in *its pure* state for special purposes, it is desirable that we should point out the uses to which it has been applied, especially those of a mechanical nature. With reference to the latter part of the subject we will now proceed to describe the commercial utility of the metal with some amount of detail.

One of the greatest demands for pure silver—if not the greatest of all—is in the manufacture of fine filigree work, a branch of industry extensively practised on the Continent. This kind of silversmith's work was attempted to be revived in this country some twelve or fifteen years ago, Birmingham and London being the principal places where the manufacture was carried on; but the success of the undertaking as a staple industry must, at the most, have been only a partial one, for it soon declined, and the trade was thus virtually left, as before, in the hands of our Eastern competitors; most of whom produce splendid specimens of the art of filigree and fine wire-working. In India this work is wonderfully performed, and it is truly marvellous to witness the beautiful handiwork of the natives who practise this craft. Their productions are quite the work of the true artist, almost every article representing Nature in some of her various forms, such as flowers, animals, serpents, &c., and these are so skilfully imitated that no one could possibly dispute either the faithfulness of the representation or the ability of the workman. This is all the more surprising, because in India the natives have not the modern mechanical appliances which we possess in this country. The jeweller there represents to some extent our travelling tinker, only with this difference, that the travelling tinker in this country is generally an inexperienced and unskilful workman, whereas the Indian, if we are to judge him by his work, must be just the reverse.

Filigree wire-work is manufactured in Italy, Germany, Norway, and Sweden, and the secret of these countries maintaining the monopoly in this branch of the silversmith's trade is that labour there is cheap; and not in any sense because English workmen cannot make the articles in question. It is owing to this cheapness of labour and the inexpensiveness of living that our Continental competitors can beat us by underselling us in the market; and to no other cause can the production of the foreign cheap article be assigned.

In India the art of working in silver and gold has long been practised, and so particular are the workmen there about the absolute purity of the metals they use, that they refine them by melting five times, under a very strong blast heat, before commencing the work of manufacture. The principal places where these art-manufactures are carried on are in Southern India and at Trichinopoly; and in these districts the delicacy and intricacy of the workmanship are brought to the greatest possible perfection. The articles produced there are all "hand-made," and wrought entirely with a few simple tools, such as a hammer and an anvil (both of which are highly polished and burnished), a few fine pliers, blow-pipes, burnishers, scrapers, a pair of fine dividers, and some delicate scales and weights; these, with a few perforated steel-plates for drawing the wire through, comprise the chief appliances of the travelling native jewellers. The process of the work is very simple. It is commenced by hammering out the metal upon the anvil, and when it has assumed a certain degree of thinness the dividers are next brought into requisition to mark it into certain widths, which are subsequently cut into strips and drawn into very fine wire through perforated steel-plates, a pair of strong pliers being used for the purpose. The holes in the steel-plates consist of graduated sizes, and by this means the strips of metal are soon considerably reduced; and when the proper thinness has been attained the wire is ready for the exercise of the practical skill and dexterity of the artisan, who produces from it the best filigree work in the world. Most of the native jewellers have books containing a variety of designs, but they more commonly work from memory, without any reference to patterns.

The principal localities where this description of work is produced in the highest perfection are Delhi, Cuttack, and Trichinopoly, in India; and Genoa, Paris, Florence, Malta, Norway, and Sweden. The Indian filigree work is the finest and cheapest in the world. The Maltese manufacture a very good kind, and their crosses are much admired;

so also do the Chinese and Japanese, but the manufactures of these latter countries are not so tasteful as those of India, consequently they have not been so highly appreciated. Norway and Sweden produce filigree work of a very light weight; but still their productions in this art will not compare in regard to effect with the finest specimens from India.

We have said that the silver employed by the filigree worker should be in every case absolutely pure; because, when it is quite fine, it is extremely soft and pliable, so that it will remain in almost any form the artist may choose to work it, without that springiness which is found in all alloyed metals. However small might be the amount of alloy contained in the metal, the least admixture of it would produce an elasticity in the wire when pressed into form which would make it unworkable for fine filigree purposes; and in this state it would be the utter bane of the workman, as his progress would be altogether impeded in the production of his work. It is of the greatest importance that the spirals, and all the various forms required in filigree working, should remain steadily in their places when pressed into shape, without that rebounding which happens in the case of metals of an elastic nature, and in consequence of which no really first-class work can be performed in connection with this art. For such reasons as these it will be at once palpable even to the ordinary reader that fine silver should always be used in preference to alloyed in the manufacture of filigree work.

The various ornaments of the filigree kind are commonly enclosed in a rim of plain and somewhat stronger wire, which gives additional strength to each part; and, when put together, tends to compose an article of considerably greater durability. In England these outside rims consist exclusively of sterling or standard silver, whilst all the inner work is of the finer material.

There are several methods of preparing the wire called "filigree." The oldest and the one almost invariably practised in India consists in the first place in drawing down the wire in a circular form until the very lowest possible thinness has been attained, and frequently annealing it during the process, which is done by heating it to a red heat in a muffle placed upon an iron or copper pan. When this process has been effectually performed the wire is taken (if of the proper degree of thinness) and doubled together; these two fine wires are then twisted into one cord, which should be of the fineness desired. The wire requires annealing more than once during the process of twisting, and when it is completed it has a corded appearance; it is then ready for the manufacture of the various articles comprised in this kind of work.

The old plan of twisting was accomplished in the following manner. One end of the doubled wire being firmly secured in a vice or some other suitable instrument, so as to prevent it from turning round and so prevent the progress of the work, the other end of it was also firmly secured in a small hand machine or vice, which was made to revolve by turning a small handle with the right hand, the machine being held and regulated with the left, in order to keep the wire out at its full length so as to avoid knotting in the various parts of it; it was in this manner that fine filigree wire was in the first instance made.

The second plan was somewhat different, and in regard to the last part of the process it was certainly a great advantage, especially in the saving of labour, as a greater quantity could be prepared in a much less time than by the old method, that being slow in its progress. Here the lathe was made to supply the place of the small hand machine, the speed of which soon brought about the object in view.

The flattening of this twisted wire has now commonly come into use, and is effected by passing it through small steel rollers, hardened and polished. The object of this is soon manifest, as the labour-saving process is brought prominently into play; the wire in the first place need not be so finely drawn, and secondly the same filigree surface can be made to appear upon the articles as before, by securing the edges of the wires which show the filigree uppermost; and this is always the case in manipulating with this kind of wire. This method is generally in vogue with most filigree workers.

A third plan of preparing the material for the manufacture of filigree work is, we believe, due to the ingenuity of a celebrated Birmingham firm, who extensively practised this kind of work some years ago. The secret is not now generally known to the trade, therefore a few observations bearing upon it will not be unacceptable to those for whose benefit we are writing. The process is commenced in the same manner as before, in the preparation of the round wire, though this need not be drawn so fine, because by this method we have no twisting. When the round wire has arrived at the proper size it is flattened in the manner already explained; and when this is done it should be annealed, but experience will dictate best when this particular process should be carried out.

After this latter operation the wire is submitted to the action of very small rollers, and bearing the pattern required in small grooves of various sizes. The pattern takes effect upon the edges of the wires only, and resembles the milled or serrated edges of our coinage, only of course the latter bears no comparison with regard to fineness. Lastly, the wire is again passed through the flattening rollers, and then it is ready to be worked up into the object desired.

Having gone through the general details of filigree working we shall next direct our attention to the component parts and commercial uses of the English standards, together with those of some other countries. In England there are two silver standards, called respectively the old and the new standards. They are as follows:—

Fine silver per lb. troy.

Old Standard, 11 oz. 2 dwts. = 925 millims.
New Standard, 11 oz. 10 dwts. = 959 millims.

The older of these appears to have been always the legally recognised standard for the coinage, and also for the manufacture of plate. By a law passed, however, in the reign of William III. (1697) it was raised to 11 oz. 10 dwts. of fine silver in the pound troy weight. The manufacture of silver articles from this standard was soon found to be not so durable as those made under the older one; consequently the silversmiths were permitted by a law passed in the reign of George III. (1819) to manufacture from the former standard of 11 oz. 2 dwts., the use of the new one being likewise permitted for the benefit of those who chose to avail themselves of it; and to this day it remains an English standard, though hardly ever employed.

The English coinage contains 37-40ths of fine silver and 3-40ths of alloy, which is always copper; or millesimal fineness 925 parts of fine silver and 75 parts of copper per 1,000 parts; the remedy allowed by law being millesimal fineness 0·004 parts. The copper which composes the alloy in the silver coinage is added for the purpose of hardening the material employed, and it has been found to wear much better with the above proportion of alloy.

In order to make the matter as simple as possible, we purpose giving a few practical alloys, as follows:—

Old standard silver alloy, cost 4s. 9d. per oz.

	oz.	dwts.	grs.
Fine Silver	0	18	12
Shot Copper	0	1	12
	1	0	0

If it is intended that the above alloy should be for Hall marking, it will be advisable to add a little extra silver to the prepared composition, because fine silver purchased from the refiner or bullion dealer is never absolutely pure, consequently the work will not pass the Hall; or better still alloy as follows:—

Old standard silver for Hall marking.

	oz.	dwts.	grs.
Fine Silver	0	18	14
Shot Copper	0	1	10
	1	0	0

The new standard silver is composed of $38\frac{1}{2}$-40ths of fine silver and $1\frac{1}{2}$-40ths of copper alloy; or millesimal fineness 959 parts of fine silver and 41 parts of copper per 1,000 parts; the remedy being as before 0·004 parts.

New standard silver alloy, cost 4s. 11d. per oz.

	oz.	dwts.	grs.
Fine Silver	0	19	4
Shot Copper	0	0	20
	1	0	0

New standard silver for Hall marking.

	oz.	dwts.	grs.
Fine Silver	0	19	6
Shot Copper	0	0	18
	1	0	0

Quality commonly used in England.

	oz.	dwts.	grs.
Fine Silver	0	18	0
Shot Copper	0	2	0
	1	0	0

The qualities of the silver employed by the English silversmiths are invariably below the standard, the duties, assay charges, and loss of time in sending the work to the Hall to be marked acting as a great drawback to the trade in the midst of the keen competition of the present day. Silver chains, brooches, buckles, collarets, &c. are for the most part manufactured from inferior metal. In fact, some manufacturers positively refuse to make Hall-marked goods, on account of the great drawbacks attending the marking.

The alloys of silver are not calculated on the carat system, like gold, but by certain numbers, or other distinctive features, well understood by the particular firms which trade in silver wares. For our present purpose it will be sufficient to distinguish them by using the numerals, 1, 2, 3, 4, &c.; the alloy nearest approaching sterling or standard we shall call No. 1, and so on downwards until the lowest quality has been reached. We may state that silver does not lose its whiteness if not alloyed below equal quantities of the two metals; however, the alloys used in manufactures seldom reach so low a limit.

Silver alloy No. 1, cost 4s. 7d. per oz.

	oz.	dwts.	grs.
Fine Silver	0	18	0
Shot Copper	0	2	0
	1	0	0

Silver alloy No. 1, same as above.

	oz.	dwts.	grs.
Fine Silver	1	0	0
Shot Copper	0	2	6
	1	2	6

Silver alloy No. 2, cost 4s. 1d. per oz.

	oz.	dwts.	grs.
Fine Silver	0	16	0
Shot Copper	0	4	0
	1	0	0

Silver alloy No. 2, same as above.

	oz.	dwts.	grs.
Fine Silver	1	0	0
Shot Copper	0	5	0
	1	5	0

TABLE OF ALLOYS.

Silver alloy No. 3, cost 3s. 10d. per oz.

	oz.	dwts.	grs.
Fine silver	0	15	0
Shot copper	0	5	0
	1	0	0

Silver alloy No. 3, same as above.

	oz.	dwts.	grs.
Fine silver	1	0	0
Shot copper	0	6	16
	1	6	16

Silver alloy No. 4, cost 3s. 7d. per oz.

	oz.	dwts.	grs.
Fine silver	0	14	0
Shot copper	0	6	0
	1	0	0

Silver alloy No. 4, same as above.

	oz.	dwts.	grs.
Fine silver	1	0	0
Shot copper	0	8	12
	1	8	12

F

VARIOUS QUALITIES OF SILVER.

Silver alloy No. 5, cost 3s. 6d. per oz.

	oz.	dwts.	grs.
Fine silver	0	13	12
Shot copper	0	6	12
	1	0	0

Silver alloy No. 5, same as above.

	oz.	dwts.	grs.
Fine silver	1	0	0
Shot copper	0	9	18
	1	9	18

Silver alloy No. 6, cost 3s. 3d. per oz.

	oz.	dwts.	grs.
Fine silver	0	13	0
Shot copper	0	7	0
	1	0	0

Silver alloy No. 6, same as above.

	oz.	dwts.	grs.
Fine silver	1	0	0
Shot copper	0	11	0
	1	11	0

SILVER ALLOYS.

Silver alloy No. 7, cost 3s. 2d. per oz.

	oz.	dwts.	grs.
Fine silver	0	12	12
Shot copper	0	7	12
	1	0	0

Silver alloy No. 7, same as above.

	oz.	dwts.	grs.
Fine silver	1	0	0
Shot copper	0	12	0
	1	12	0

Silver alloy No. 8, cost 3s. per oz.

	oz.	dwts.	grs.
Fine silver	0	12	0
Shot copper	0	8	0
	1	0	0

Silver alloy No. 8, same as before.

	oz.	dwts.	grs.
Fine silver	1	0	0
Shot copper	0	13	12
	1	13	12

The qualities of the silver alloys have been reduced in this list to various values, and the latter ones are as common as it is possible to make them, without a great and perceptible change of colour taking place in the prepared material. But if it be desired to work a still more inferior metal, then another ingredient must enter into its composition, in order to keep up the whiteness of the silver; and this other metal employed is nickel, the alloys with which we shall have occasion to refer to hereafter. Suffice it to say, however, that these inferior alloys of silver, prepared with nickel, are not now much employed by silversmiths in their art-manufactures. It will be observed that we have recommended the employment of *shot* copper in the manufacture of silver alloys: we do so for two reasons—first, because it can be purchased at a considerably cheaper rate than can the ordinary forms of copper, costing only one shilling per lb., whilst the ordinary prepared copper for alloying will cost double that amount; and, secondly, if proper attention has been given to the melting and casting process, the workable qualities of the metal will be found everything that could be desired. Therefore an excellent material in all respects can be produced by the means suggested at half the cost of alloy. A considerable saving to a large firm might thus be easily effected by its employment.

In France there are three silver standards—two to be employed by silversmiths, and one for the coinage, as follows:—

Fine silver per lb. troy.

Silver ware,	11 oz. 8 dwts.	=	950 millims.
Coinage,	10 oz. 16 dwts.	=	900 millims.
Silver ware,	9 oz. 12 dwts.	=	800 millims.

It will be seen from the above table that the coinage in France does not represent the highest standard, and also that the principal one in that country is inferior to our highest standard. The French coinage contains 36-40ths of fine silver and 4-40ths of copper alloy, or millesimal fineness 900 parts of fine silver and 100 parts of copper per 1,000 parts of metal; the highest standard for silver wares contains 38-40ths of fine silver and 2-40ths of copper alloy, or millesimal fineness 950 parts of fine silver and 50 parts of copper per 1,000 parts of metal; the lowest French standard for silver wares contains 32-40ths of fine silver and 8-40ths of copper alloy, or millesimal fineness 800 parts of fine silver and 200 parts of copper per 1,000 parts of metal. The remedy is millesimal fineness 0·005.

French alloy for coinage, 4s. 7d. per oz.

	oz.	dwts.	grs.
Fine silver	0	18	0
Copper	0	2	0
	1	0	0

French alloy for plate, 4s. 10d. per oz.

	oz.	dwts.	grs.
Fine silver	0	19	0
Copper	0	1	0
	1	0	0

French alloy, lowest standard, 4s. 1d. per oz.

	oz.	dwts.	grs.
Fine silver	0	16	0
Copper	0	4	0
	1	0	0

In the preparation of these alloys with French silver it is undesirable to make any addition of fine silver, in order to enable goods manufactured from them to pass the Hall in safety, because the former is assayed before it leaves the bullion dealers, and the bars of metal are marked with their various standards. Such is not the case in England, and refiners' fine metal is sometimes two or three grains under what it is supposed to be; hence the necessity for the further addition of some fine metal as we have already pointed out, when the object in view is to have goods Hall marked; without which addition it cannot be effected.

In Germany there are four silver standards—one for the coinage, and three to be employed in the manufacture of silversmiths' wares; and in that country the various standards are severally applied in the production of fine filigree and other artistic work. The fineness of the standards is as follows:—

Fine silver per lb. troy.

    Silver ware, 11 oz. 8 dwts. = 950 millims.
    Coinage,   10 oz. 16 dwts. = 900 millims.
    Silver ware, 9 oz. 12 dwts. = 800 millims.
    Silver ware, 9 oz. 0 dwts. = 750 millims.

As regards the alloy to be employed in the manufacture of these various qualities, copper only must be used, all other metals being forbidden. These standards represent all home manufactured articles of silver having reference to the standards of that country, as lately appointed by law.

The German coinage is the same as the French and contains 36-40ths of fine silver and 4-40ths of copper, or millesimal fineness 900 parts of fine silver and 100 parts of copper per 1,000 parts of metal. The highest standard of all is used for silver wares, and contains 38-40ths of fine silver and 2-40ths of copper, or millesimal fineness 950 parts of fine silver and 50 parts of copper per 1,000 parts of metal. The next German standard for silver wares contains 32-40ths of fine silver and 8-40ths of copper, or millesimal fineness 800 parts of fine silver and 200 parts of copper per 1,000 parts of metal. The commonest German standard employed by the silversmiths of that country contains 30-40ths of fine silver and 10-40ths of copper, or millesimal fineness 750 parts of fine silver and 250 parts of copper per 1,000 parts of metal indicated. Remedy 0·003.

Silver alloy for the German coinage.

	oz.	dwts.	grs.
Fine silver	0	18	0
Copper	0	2	0
	1	0	0

Alloy for silver wares of the first standard.

	oz.	dwts.	grs.
Fine silver	0	19	0
Copper	0	1	0
	1	0	0

Alloy for silver wares of the second standard.

	oz.	dwts.	grs.
Fine silver	0	16	0
Copper	0	4	0
	1	0	0

Alloy for silver wares of the third standard.

	oz.	dwts.	grs.
Fine silver	0	15	0
Copper	0	5	0
	1	0	0

Silver goods manufactured according to these standards in Germany, which have recently become law, may be alloyed only with copper, and any foreign substance is not allowed to enter into their composition. The remedy permitted in the actual fineness of the silver must not be under three thousandths of the standard specified. The goods to be stamped with the number of thousandths and the name of the manufacturer of them, and the correctness to be certified by the firm named. Experts are appointed by the Government to test this correctness, and if the provisions of the law have been justly observed a government guarantee mark is applied to them.

CHAPTER VII.

Silver Solders: their Uses and Applications.

SOLDERING as applied to silversmith's work is an art which requires great care and practice to perform it neatly and properly. It consists in uniting the various pieces of an article together at their junctions, edges, or surfaces, by fusing an alloy specially prepared for the purpose, and which is more fusible than the metal to be soldered. The solder should in every way be well suited to the particular metal to which it is to be applied, and should possess a powerful chemical affinity to it; if this be not the case, strong, clean, and invisible connections cannot be effected, whilst the progress of the work would be considerably retarded. This is partly the cause of inferior manufactures, and not, as might be frequently supposed, from the want of skill on the part of the workman who makes them.

The best connections are made when the metal

and solder agree as nearly as possible in uniformity, that is, as regards fusibility, hardness, and malleability. Experience has proved, more especially in the case of plain and strong work (or work that has to bear a strain in the course of manufacture), that the soldering is more perfect and more tenacious as the point of fusion of the two metals approaches each other; the solder having a greater tendency to form a more perfect alloy with the metal to which it is applied than under any other conditions. The silver or other metal to be operated upon by soldering being partly of a porous nature, the greater the heat required in the fusion of the solder the more closely are the atoms of the two metals brought into direct relationship; thus greater solidity is given to the parts united, and which are then capable of forming the maximum of resistance. It is thus obvious that tin should not be employed in forming solders possessing the characteristics we have just described, for being a very fusible metal it greatly increases the fusibility of its alloys; but when very *easy* solder is required, and this is sometimes the case, especially when zinc has been employed in the preparation of the silver alloy, its addition is a great advantage when it comes to be applied to the work in hand. Solders made with tin are not so malleable and tenacious as those prepared without it, as it imparts a brittleness not usually to be found in those regularly employed by silversmiths; for this reason it is advisable to file it into *dust*, and apply it in that state to the articles in course of manufacture.

The best solders we have found to be those mixed with a little zinc. These may be laminated, rolled or filed into dust; if the latter, it should be finely done, and this is better for every purpose. Too much zinc, however, should not be added under any conditions, as it has a tendency to eat itself away during wear, thus rendering the articles partly useless either for ornamental or domestic purposes earlier than might be anticipated. Solders thus prepared also act with some disadvantage to the workman using them, for they possess the property of evaporating or eating away during the process of soldering, leaving behind scarcely anything to indicate their presence; consequently the workman has to keep on repeating the process until the connection is made perfect, which is always done at the expense of a quantity of solder as well as loss to the workman as regards time.

Solders made from copper and silver only are, generally speaking, too infusible to be applied to all classes of silversmith's work.

FUSIBILITY OF SOLDERS.

Solders are manufactured of all degrees of hardness; the hardest of all being a preparation of silver and copper in various proportions; the next being a composition of silver, copper, and zinc; and the easiest or most fusible being prepared from silver, copper, and tin, or silver, brass, and tin. Arsenic sometimes enters into the composition of silver solders, for promoting a greater degree of fusion; and we have heard of workmen actually refusing to work with any other solder. The employment of arsenic has, however, a tendency to slightly endanger the health of those persons using it in large quantities; and of late its employment has not been persevered in.

In applying solder of whatever composition it is of the utmost importance that the edges or parts to be united should be chemically clean; and for the purpose of protecting these parts from the action of the air, and oxidation during the soldering process, they are covered by a suitable flux, which not only prevents oxidation, but has also a tendency to remove any portion of it left on the parts of the metal to be united. The flux employed is always borax, and it not only effects the objects just pointed out, but greatly facilitates the flow of the solder into the required places. Silver solder should be silver of a little inferior quality to that about to be worked up. The various degrees of fusibility of the several solders are occasioned by the different proportions of the component parts of the elements which enter into their existence. For instance, a solder in which tin forms a component part will flow or fuse much sooner than one in which copper and silver alone enter into composition, or of one wholly composed of copper, silver, and zinc, or of silver and brass; therefore it must be understood that tin is the best metal for increasing the fusibility of silver solders, and for keeping up their whiteness. Nevertheless it should always be used sparingly, and even then drawbacks will present themselves such as we have already alluded to.

It is our intention to give a list of the various solders which have been usually employed with more or less success, so that the silversmith and the art workman will be enabled to select the one most suitable to the particular branch of his trade; and we contend, from experience in the craft, that success of workmanship mainly depends upon this point.

Hardest silver solder, cost 4s. 1d. per oz.

	oz.	dwts.	grs.
Fine silver	0	16	0
Shot copper	0	4	0
	1	0	0

Hardest silver solder, same as above.

	oz.	dwts.	grs.
Fine silver	1	0	0
Shot copper	0	5	0
	1	5	0

Hard silver solder, cost 3s. 10d. per oz.

	oz.	dwts.	grs.
Fine silver	0	15	0
Brass	0	5	0
	1	0	0

Hard silver solder, same as above.

	oz.	dwts.	grs.
Fine silver	1	0	0
Brass	0	6	16
	1	6	16

Easy silver solder, cost 3s. 5d. per oz.

	oz.	dwts.	grs.
Fine silver	0	13	8
Brass	0	6	16
	1	0	0

Easy silver solder, same as above.

	oz.	dwts.	grs.
Fine silver	1	0	0
Brass	0	10	0
	1	10	0

The silver solders here given are not such as we can confidently recommend to the general silversmith, having proved them to be very unsatisfactory in certain classes of work. For example, the first solder, except in the case of plain strong work, would be far too infusible to be generally used by the silversmith; the second, although much more fusible, cannot safely be applied to very fine and delicate wire-work, because the brass in its composition is so uncertain; unless specially prepared by the silversmith, it probably, if purchased from the metal warehouses, contains lead; the latter is injurious, and in process of soldering it burns and eats away, much resembling the application of burnt sawdust to the work. No really effective work can be produced when the above symptoms present themselves. The same remarks apply to No. 3, which is the most fusible, and when free from lead or other base metal it may be classed as a tolerably fair common solder. In the preparation of the solders to which we are alluding, it is preferable to employ, instead of the brass, a composition consisting of a mixture of copper and zinc, in the proportion of two parts of copper to one part of zinc; the operator then knows of what the solder is composed, and if it should turn out bad he will partly know the cause, and be able to supply a remedy.

The solders that we have found to answer our purpose best are composed of the following elements. The first is described again as *hard* solder, but it is not nearly so hard as the one previously described.

Best hard silver solder, 4s. 1d. per oz.

	oz.	dwts.	grs.
Fine silver	0	16	0
Shot copper	0	3	12
Spelter	0	0	12
	1	0	0

Best hard silver solder, same as above.

	oz.	dwts.	grs.
Fine silver	1	0	0
Shot copper	0	4	9
Spelter	0	0	15
	1	5	0

SILVER SOLDERS.

Medium silver solder, 3s. 10d. per oz.

	oz.	dwts.	grs.
Fine silver	0	15	0
Shot copper	0	4	0
Spelter	0	1	0
	1	0	0

Medium silver solder, same as above.

	oz.	dwts.	grs.
Fine silver	1	0	0
Shot copper	0	5	8
Spelter	0	1	8
	1	6	16

Easy silver solder, 3s. 7d. per oz.

	oz.	dwts.	grs.
Fine silver	0	14	0
Shot copper	0	4	12
Spelter	0	1	12
	1	0	0

Easy silver solder, same as above.

	oz.	dwts.	grs.
Fine silver	1	0	0
Shot copper	0	6	12
Spelter	0	2	4
	1	8	16

TABLES OF QUALITIES.

Common silver solder, 3s. 3d. per oz.

	oz.	dwts.	grs.
Fine silver	0	12	12
Shot copper	0	6	0
Spelter	0	1	12
	1	0	0

Common silver solder, same as above.

	oz.	dwts.	grs.
Fine silver	1	0	0
Shot copper	0	9	15
Spelter	0	2	9
	1	12	0

The whole of the above-named solders will bleach or whiten properly if applied to silver of the suitable quality for such purposes. We have used copper and spelter in our silver solders, because we have found from experience that the fewer number of times a solder is melted the better it is for all purposes. This result of our experience is in direct opposition to those authors who have professed to treat upon this subject, and who can have had but a small amount of real practical knowledge, for it is argued by them that the oftener a solder is melted the more properly does it become mixed, and, consequently, the more fit is it for the workman's use. To such arguments we are prepared to give a blank denial, and our reasons for so doing we will state further on in this treatise.

There are various other silver solders used by silversmiths; some few of which it will be as well perhaps, while we are on the point, to enumerate:—

Silver solder for enamelling, cost 4s. 1d. per oz.

	oz.	dwts.	grs.
Fine silver	1	0	0
Shot copper	0	5	0
	1	5	0

Silver solder for enamelling, cost 3s. 6d. per oz.

	oz.	dwts.	grs.
Fine silver	1	0	0
Shot copper	0	10	0
	1	10	0

Easy silver solder for filigree work, cost 4s. 1d. per oz.

	oz.	dwts.	grs.
Fine silver	0	16	0
Shot copper	0	0	12
Composition	0	3	12
	1	0	0

TABLES OF QUALITIES. 85

Quick running silver solder, cost 3s. 3d. per oz.

	oz.	dwts.	grs.
Fine silver	1	0	0
Composition	0	10	0
Pure tin	0	2	0
	1	12	0

Silver solder for chains, cost 3s. 3d. per oz.

	oz.	dwts.	grs.
Fine silver	1	0	0
Shot copper	0	10	0
Pure spelter	0	2	0
	1	12	0

Easy solder for chains, cost 3s. 3d. per oz.

	oz.	dwts.	grs.
Fine silver	1	0	0
Composition	0	10	0
Pure spelter	0	2	0
	1	12	0

Common silver solder, cost 3s. per oz.

	oz.	dwts.	grs.
Fine silver	1	0	0
Shot copper	0	12	0
Pure spelter	0	3	0
	1	15	0

SILVER SOLDERS.

Common easy solder, cost 3s. per oz.

	oz.	dwts.	grs.
Fine silver	1	0	0
Composition	0	12	0
Pure spelter	0	3	0
	1	15	0

Silver solder with arsenic, cost 4s. 1d. per oz.

	oz.	dwts.	grs.
Fine silver	1	0	0
Shot copper	0	3	0
Yellow arsenic	0	2	0
	1	5	0

Silver solder with arsenic, cost 3s. 10d. per oz.

	oz.	dwts.	grs.
Fine silver	1	0	0
Composition	0	6	0
Yellow arsenic	0	1	0
	1	7	0

Easy silver solder, cost 3s. 6d. per oz.

	oz.	dwts.	grs.
Fine silver	1	0	0
Composition	0	5	0
Tinsel	0	5	0
	1	10	0

TABLES OF QUALITIES.

Common easy solder, cost 3s. per oz.

	oz.	dwts.	grs.
Fine silver	1	0	0
Tinsel	0	10	0
Arsenic	0	5	0
	1	15	0

Another common silver solder.

	oz.	dwts.	grs.
Fine silver	1	0	0
Composition	0	15	0
Arsenic	0	1	6
	1	16	6

A very common solder.

	oz.	dwts.	grs.
Fine silver	1	0	0
Composition	1	0	0
White arsenic	1	0	0
	3	0	0

The solders here given will be found amply sufficient to select from, for every operation of the silversmith, and will answer the several purposes for which they have been described. When tin and arsenic are employed in the composition of solder, either together or separately, they should be withheld until the more infusible metals with which they are to be united have become melted; the tin or tinsel should then be added, and when this is well melted with the mass, fling on the top the arsenic, let it melt, stir it well together, and pour it out quickly into an ingot mould already prepared for its reception.

When silver and brass, or silver and composition, alone form the component parts of the solder, these metals may be put into the melting-pot together, well fused, stirred, and poured out as before.

Solders into which volatile metals enter, upon repeated meltings, become hard, brittle, and drossy, and are therefore not so good as when the metal has received only one melting; it is for this reason that we have always preferred to manufacture our solders from metals which have not been melted before, or from those which have gone through the process as few a number of times as possible.

The mode of soldering gold and silver is as follows: Take the solder and roll it out thin between the flattening rollers, or file it into dust, according to the kind of work in hand. If filed into dust, it is all the better if done very fine; and if reduced to a flat state, which should be tolerably thin, cut it into little bits, or pallions, which may easily be performed with a pair of hand-shears,

PROCESS OF SOLDERING.

length-ways and afterwards cross-ways. When this is done, take the work which is to be soldered, join it together by means of fine binding-wire (very thin iron wire), or lay it upon the pumice so that the joinings can come close together, and will not be liable to move during the process; wet the joinings with a solution of borax and water, mixed into a thick paste, applying it with a small camel-hair pencil; then lay the bits or pallions of solder upon the parts to be united, and having placed the article upon some suitable object, take your blowing instrument (Fig. 16) and blow with it, through

Fig. 16. Blowpipe.

a gas jet, a keen flame upon the solder in order to melt it; this will render the unification of the parts complete and compact.

When filed solder is used, the process of charging the article is rather different from the above. In the latter case the filings are commonly put into a small cup-shaped vessel (Fig. 17), in most cases the bottom of a tea-cup, or some other similar vessel, being

Fig. 17. Solder-dish.

used for the purpose; a lump of borax is then taken

and rubbed upon a piece of slate, to which a little water is occasionally added during the rubbing; when this solution attains the consistency of cream, it is put into the solder-dish and well mixed with the solder. This is then applied to the article to be soldered, by means of a charger, consisting of a piece of round metal wire, flattened at one end, and shaped for the purpose it has to serve. The joinings, when this kind is employed, require no boraxing with the pencil, as described under pallion solder; the borax being intermixed with the solder flushes with it through the joinings to be united, thus rendering any further application unnecessary. The process to which we are alluding is called "hard soldering," and cannot be applied to metals of a fusible nature; neither must it be attempted in the case of goods bearing the name of plated, which are put together with soft or pewter solder, similar to that used by tinsmiths and gasfitters. If there should be any soft solder about the article, to be soldered by the means we are describing, it would be almost certain to destroy it, the soft solder having such an affinity for entering into combination with metals more infusible than itself when overheated.

There is an art in soldering greater than some people would believe. The heat required is of various degrees, some articles requiring a broad rough flame, others a smooth one, and others again a fine pointed one. All these circumstances connected with the process, together with others which we could detail, proving that it is an art only to be acquired by practice, must be considered enough; and we proceed to observe that the skilful jeweller in soldering a large piece of work will direct the flame of the gas jet to all parts of it, until it is tolerably hot, and then return to the spot to be soldered, and by a very dexterous movement of the flame, produced by the blowpipe, increase the heat at that spot until the solder has flushed and the parts are rendered thoroughly secure. So far as some of the work of the silversmith is concerned, the process of soldering is a very delicate operation, and ought not to be undertaken by an unpractised hand.

The method of preparing solder for filigree work is worthy of a passing notice. It is called by the Germans Lemaille solder. In the first place it is reduced to very fine filings, mixed with burnt borax powdered fine, and in this state it is sprinkled from a spouted grater over the work to be soldered. The English filigree workers commonly use clean filed solder, and by means of the camel-hair pencil apply a solution of borax to the work, and then sprinkle the dry solder upon it from the grater.

In Vienna a kind of powdered borax is employed, called *Streu borax*, or sprinkle borax. It is composed of the following ingredients, which should be gently annealed to expel their water of crystallization, the whole well pounded and mixed together, and sprinkled over the parts to be joined from the spouted grater as before:—

	oz.	dwts.	grs.
Calcined borax	0	17	12
Carbonate of soda	0	1	12
Common salt	0	1	0
	1	0	0

The object of this mixture is to prevent the rising of the solder, and to facilitate its flushing. Too much of it should not, however, be put with solder in the grater at one time, as it is as objectionable as too much borax applied in the ordinary way, but every workman will learn from experience concerning these matters. We have tried this mixture, prepared with filed solder in the ordinary way, and found it advantageous at first; but its greatest drawback is the turning of the solder yellow if not quickly used upon the work after mixing, thus rendering the solder permanently injured. For this reason we have had to abandon its employment in the wet state. But, in its dry state, to the silversmith for filigree purposes it is likely to be of advantage. It may be remarked that this preparation encumbers the work with a great deal more flux than borax does, and consequently it requires to be more often boiled out during the period of soldering together the component parts. This is effected by boiling in a weak pickle of sulphuric acid and water, composed of the following proportions: one part of acid to thirty parts of water.

CHAPTER VIII.

On the Melting of Silver.

The processes of melting and properly mixing silver with its alloys in a crucible are among the first operations of the silversmith, and are, moreover, of great importance in the production of intimate and homogeneous alloys. In order to effect these, however simple they may appear, various precautions are necessary, and certain principles require carrying out to arrive at the best possible results, otherwise a great loss or waste of material may take place. To direct attention to those principles, which from very careful attention to the subject we have found to answer best, will first be our aim, and if we succeed in rendering some little service to our fellow-workers in the craft to which our toil and leisure have been devoted we shall feel highly gratified.

The weighing of the component metals, the selection of the crucible, the charging of it, and the attention it requires whilst in the furnace are considerations to which we cannot too strongly call attention. The regulations with regard to weighing should be strictly and accurately carried out. The best and safest plan is, after the various metals have been separately weighed, to re-weigh them, this time collectively, in order to ascertain whether the total weight corresponds with the previous calculation; if it does, the mixture has been properly prepared. We have known both time and trouble saved by the adoption of this precaution, after mistakes had occurred which could not have been detected until the weighing of the bar of metal had taken place after melting. There are various kinds of crucibles manufactured for the use of the precious metal workers. Crucibles were so-called from originally being impressed by the alchemists with the sign of the cross. They are calculated to bear very high temperatures, and consist of English, Hessian, Cornish, Black-lead, and Plumbago. The last two are by far the best; the plumbago, however, being the hardest, and capable of standing the highest temperature, is to be preferred before all others. It will also stand more frequent meltings than any of the rest. Such crucibles have been known to withstand the heat of the furnace for upwards of fifty times without giving way. The wear of them is very strong and resisting, as they only *gradually* become reduced in thickness, so that it is easy to distinguish their unfitness for use. Fluxes act on earthern crucibles, particularly English at a high temperature, whilst nitre and carbonate of soda soon destroy them.

Fluxes are necessary in most cases of metallic reductions: they protect the metal from the air, and dissolve impurities. They are of several kinds, as follows:—

> Vegetable charcoal.
> Carbonate of potash.
> Carbonate of soda.
> Common salt.
> Salammoniac.
> Sal-enixum.
> Saltpetre.
> Borax.
> Sandiver.
> Yellow soap.
> Black flux.
> White flux.
> Crude tartar.
> Brown potash.
> Sub-carbonate of potash.

All these fluxes have occasional duties to perform, and are therefore of great service to the metallurgist.

To prevent the cracking or flying of the crucible, when newly employed, it should, before being charged with the precious metal, be well annealed; that is, heated to redness upon a very slow fire—one that is gradually going down, and in which there is no blaze is to be preferred, because the flame has a tendency, on the introduction of a new crucible, to make it fly to pieces. When it has become red-hot, if a cold bar of iron be introduced it will soon show whether there are any cracks, and if so the crucible should be rejected; on the contrary, if it withstands this test it may be placed aside until required for use, when it may be employed with perfect safety in the melting of silver and its alloys.

When copper and silver only form the alloys of the silversmith, they should both be added to the crucible at the commencement of the operation; and it is the best plan to put the copper at the bottom, because it is the most infusible metal. By doing so, it will receive the greatest degree of heat, which in jewellers' furnaces always comes upwards and the higher specific gravity of the silver has a tendency to force that metal downwards; consequently, when the two metals have become fused, upon well stirring—which should be done with an iron stirrer tapered at the point, and previously heated to redness—a perfectly homogeneous mass will be the result. When the more fusible metals of which we have spoken are to form the component parts of the mixture, different treatment with regard to them will be required. They should not be added at the commencement of the operation, but should be dealt with afterwards, in the following manner:—

Zinc is one of the more fusible metals, and is sometimes employed by the silversmith in his alloys, for the purpose of imparting a greater degree of whiteness to them, as well as rendering inferior silver more easily bleached or whitened; thus assisting to bring back the natural colour of fine silver to manufactured articles, which have partially lost it by the addition of alloy of some other colour. Zinc, when employed in silver alloys, should be cautiously used, and care should be taken not to add too much to a given quantity of material. The solder used with silver-zinc alloys should be far more fusible than that employed with the other alloys. If too much zinc be added in the preparation of these alloys, in the course of the work, particularly in the process of soldering, they have a tendency to *sweat*, and sometimes to *eat* the metals into holes around the parts to be united; such alloys, therefore, render this process very difficult to perform, besides entailing more labour in the production of a clean and smooth finish.

In melting an alloy of silver, copper, and zinc,

the silver and copper should first be melted in a plumbago crucible of the form shown in Fig 18, and well stirred together in order that they may become properly mixed. The zinc is sold in flat cakes under the name of spelter, and, when required, is usually cut up with a chisel into pieces of various weights suitable for the object in view. When the copper and silver have become well incorporated, the mixture should be protected from the air by a

Fig. 18. Plumbago Crucible for melting.

suitable flux, charcoal being the best for this purpose. The most suitable time to add it to the crucible in the furnace is when the metals are just beginning to fuse. This flux covers the whole of the surface of the molten mass, and so prevents the action of the air from destroying some of the baser metal. The charcoal should be perfectly pure and in a finely divided state, for if adulterated with any gritty matter (and sometimes such is the case) a very indifferent working material is produced, the evil results of which show themselves in every stage of manufacture. These instructions with regard to melting the more infusible metals having been carried out, the zinc is taken with a long pair of tongs (Fig. 19), and held within the furnace, over the mouth of the crucible,

Fig. 19. Tongs for Melting.

until the temperature has almost reached the melting point, when it should be carefully dropped into the fused mass below, quickly stirred, so that it may become intimately mixed with the other metals, and at once withdrawn from the furnace and poured into a suitable ingot mould (Fig. 20).

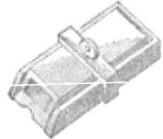

Fig. 20. Ingot Mould.

The ingot mould should be clean and smooth inside, slightly greased, and dusted over with fine vegetable charcoal; this latter substance prevents the metal from adhering to the sides of the mould. It is, perhaps, almost unnecessary to state that the ingot mould requires heating to a certain temperature before the melted composition is poured in, otherwise serious spouting takes place, resulting in a great loss of metal. On the other hand, the operator should be cautious not to over-heat it, as the same evil consequences may result.

The bar of metal upon cooling should be weighed, and the difference—as most meltings show a little—noted. This is *loss*, but it will be very little, if the above instructions have been strictly adhered to from the beginning of the operation. With the charcoal flux we have referred to, very nice and clean bars of metal can be produced. This flux is always floating upon the surface of the mixture, and, with a little dexterity in the pouring, it can be prevented from coming out of the crucible with the metal; its proper place is at the end of the pouring. When tin is employed, either in alloys or solders, its treatment is similar to that described for zinc; such alloys should not be kept too long in the furnace after they have become fused, as they rapidly become oxidized, especially if brought into contact with the air.

The waste in silver, and in fact of all alloys, is entirely dependent on the duration of the time of fusion. If it is prolonged after the addition of the fusible metals, the loss is greater in every case, than when once melted. The metals should be subjected to the heat of the furnace for the shortest possible period. The alloys of silver with zinc would lose more than the alloys of silver with tin, because zinc rapidly volatilises when heated above the temperature of its fusion, and this is especially the case when it enters into combination with silver and copper in the fused state; its vapours can be seen to rise and burn in the air, producing light and white flaky fumes, and, chemically speaking, forming the *protoxide* of zinc. With care and manipulative skill during the process of fusion, the proportion of waste can be reduced to a minimum; and when this is exactly ascertained an allowance can be made in the preparation of the mixture for the crucible. From the above remarks it will be apparent that when both tin and zinc form component parts of a mixture, either to be used as an alloy or as solder, the tin should be added to the other metals, and well stirred, so as to obtain an intimate mixture, before the addition is made of the zinc.

Scrap silver should be carefully sorted before undergoing the process of re-melting, and if possible all foreign substances removed. It may, if preferred to work it in that way, be melted into a separate bar, or otherwise used as an addition to a new mixture. When, however, it is separately melted, a flux, such as carbonate of soda, may be employed, on account of its cheapness, in small proportions to the charcoal flux already alluded to. In brittle and troublesome alloys we have found charcoal and a small quantity of borax extremely effective. Saltpetre is a very useful flux in dissolving impurities, but in some alloys its presence is injurious. Sandiver will remove iron or steel from the mixture. Corrosive sublimate destroys lead and tin. We have found the sub-carbonate of potash one of the best fluxes for silver, when matters have not been quite so straight as they should be in the working of the metal; it is used in melting the difficult alloy of 18-carat gold, and is considered a secret not generally known to the trade. Salammoniac is an excellent flux for producing clean and bright ingots and tough alloys. We invariably use it with all our alloys, mixed in small quantities with charcoal, and prefer it to all others.

Lemel, that is the filings and turnings produced during the process of manufacture, should have quite a separate method of treatment. It is best prepared for the crucible by passing it through a fine sieve, afterwards thoroughly burning it in an iron ladle, and then intimately mixing it with a flux of the following nature and proportions :—

ON THE MELTING OF SILVER.

Silver dust	24 parts
Carbonate of soda	4 ,,
Common salt	2 ,,
Sal-enixum	1 ,,
	31 parts.

The sal-enixum prevents the rising of the mixture in the crucible—which should be of the skittle shape (Fig. 21)—and keeps it from overflowing; it also possesses a refining capacity the same as salt-petre, and is much cheaper. The burning of the lemel has a great tendency to destroy all organic matter that would be likely to cause the mixture to overflow during the period of fusion; but if such a thing should be at all likely to take place, the addition of a little dried common salt would remedy the evil, a small quantity of which ought always to be provided for the purpose. The common carbonate of soda is also a cheap and useful flux to the silversmith. Five-sixths of the above flux should be well mixed with the stated proportion of lemel, then placed in the pot, and the one-sixth remaining placed upon the top of the mixture, when it may at once be transferred to the

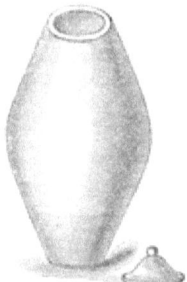

Fig. 21. Fire-clay Crucible for Lemel.

furnace. Great heat is required in this operation, and it also requires careful supervision to prevent, if possible, waste of material. When the mixture has become perfectly liquid, the heat of the furnace should not be allowed to decrease, but continued for half an hour longer, and if the use of it be not further required, the fire may then be allowed gradually to die out. The mixture will require repeated stirrings during the period of fusion, in order to dissolve such portions as might otherwise not come immediately under the action of the flux. When the operation of fusion has been completed, the crucible is withdrawn and allowed to cool, the solidification of the metal is then perfect, and it may be recovered by breaking the pot at the base, when it will fall out in a lump corresponding with the shape of the crucible. The lump of metal should then be carefully weighed, the loss ascertained—which always varies in proportion to the amount of organic matter contained therein; it may then be sold to the refiner, or exchanged for new metal.

In this process it will be observed that the crucible is broken every time a fusion takes place, consequently some little expense is incurred in providing crucibles for the purpose. To obviate which the following plan may be economically and successfully employed; and especially when the metal is sold to the refiner by assay, the method about to be described will be found most advantageous, for it should be borne in mind that the lump of metal from the previous fusion has to be again run down in another crucible and poured into an ingot mould before the refiner will consent to take his assay from it. In this latter process the whole work is performed in one fusion, and the expense of a new crucible thereby saved. The flux employed in the reduction of the metal is also considerably reduced. The plan is performed after the following manner:—

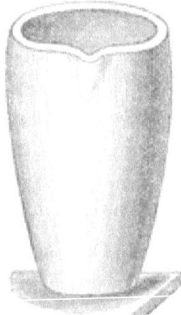

Fig. 22. Plumbago Crucible for Lemel.

Take a plumbago crucible of the shape shown in Fig. 22, and capable of holding the required mixture; put the lemel into it, and then place on the top one ounce of finely powdered carbonate of soda; this is all the flux the mixture requires, and it is then quite ready for the furnace. When the lemel has become properly fused, for facilitating which it is repeatedly stirred with a thin iron rod, it is withdrawn and poured into an ingot mould prepared for it as previously described. The flux and other organic matter, which always accumulates upon mixtures of this kind, is held back by the timely application of a thin piece of flat wood to the mouth of the crucible. After the withdrawal of the bar of metal from the ingot mould, it is cooled and weighed, and then it is quite ready for the operations of the refiner.

CHAPTER IX.

On the Working of Silver.

HAVING reached a most important and very interesting part of our subject, viz. the working of silver, and being desirous of making this treatise useful to the silver-worker in all the branches of his art, it is our intention to enlarge upon these processes—which are purely mechanical—and somewhat minutely to describe the various manipulations and arrangements required in the production of the wares of the silversmith.

After the removal of the bar of metal from the ingot mould, it should be plunged into a vessel of cold water, dried, and then carefully weighed. At this stage of the process it is ready for the operation of rolling. This process, so far as it concerns large ingots of the metal, is a distinct branch of the trade, and is carried on in separate premises established by certain firms for the purpose. These establishments are called "rolling-mills," the machinery used in them (which is powerful and costly) being moved by steam-power, the reduction of the bars of metal to their various sizes is soon effected. The very thin ribbon-shaped metal is produced by submitting it to the action of rollers of smaller dimensions, one after the other, until the desired thinness is obtained. The bars of metal are taken to these mills by a man whose special duty it is to watch over them during the processes of rolling and annealing, otherwise it would be very easy to have an ingot of gold or silver exchanged for one of base metal, the mill companies not being responsible for the material intrusted to their care for rolling; hence the necessity for the porter's services, to watch over his employer's interests. To prevent accidently exchanging the bars of metal, through their great similarity to each other, it is the usual thing for the men in charge of them to put a special mark upon the property of each person, previous to the process of annealing. This mark is applied by means of a piece of chalk or soap, and is not removable by heat. The annealing is performed in large iron muffles, heated to redness and kept in that condition by flues; the bars which require annealing being placed upon a piece of sheet-iron which slides into the muffle, and there they remain with the doors closed until they have become red-hot. It is more particularly during this operation that each person's property requires marking and watching, because of the number of bars admitted at one time into the muffle; and unless the greatest care be exercised at such a time some mistake is almost sure to occur.

A register is kept of the weight of the metal sent to the mill for the purpose of being rolled into the required shapes and sizes by the manufacturer, who afterwards works it up into different wares and utensils. The metal is also weighed on its admittance to the mill, by the clerk of the works, and again on its passage out, and a comparison of the weights registered; but in Birmingham, in some cases, this has been so irregularly performed that great discrepancies have actually taken place in the weights at times, and it has led to the establishment of another rolling-mill for gold and silver, in which the proprietors take upon themselves the whole responsibility and care of metals intrusted to their charge for the above purpose. The method pursued by them in respect to their business is as follows: A manufacturer sends a bar of metal to be rolled, carefully noting the exact weight and size to which it is to be reduced upon a proper *order head*. This weight is carefully tested at the mill, and if found correct, an invoice is given in exchange, upon which is entered the cost of rolling and the time when the work will be completed. The messenger then goes away, returning at the time stated to bring away the rolled metal.

The advantages this system presents over the others are obvious; the return of the full weight of the metal is guaranteed by responsible persons, the messenger is at liberty during the time occupied in rolling to follow his other duties, the weighing of the respective metals is far more accurately performed both in and out of the mill, besides greater satisfaction being given both to the manufacturer and the roller, the reciprocation of confidence between each, being among some of the additional advantages which might be enumerated. Messrs. Kemp, of Birmingham, deserve the thanks of the jewellery community for their enterprising efforts in the establishment of a system so admirably suited to the requirements of the trade.

The following table gives the charges at the present time for rolling bars of silver:—

Table of the Cost of Silver Rolling.

	oz.		oz.	£	s.	d.
Under	6			0	0	6
Above	6 and under		12	0	0	9
,,	12	,,	18	0	0	10
,,	18	,,	25	0	1	0
,,	25	,,	35	0	1	3
,,	35	,,	45	0	1	6
,,	45	,,	55	0	1	9
,,	55	,,	70	0	2	0
,,	70	,,	85	0	2	3
,,	85	,,	100	0	2	6
,,	100	,,	115	0	2	9
,,	115	,,	130	0	3	0

Above this 2s. 6d. per 100 ozs.

It is a usual thing at all rolling establishments to provide slitting-rolls for those who choose to avail themselves of that mode of cutting up their metal. These rolls are used for the purpose of cutting stout bars of metal into strips suitable for wire-drawing, thus dispensing with the older process of cutting with a pair of vice shears, which method was slow and somewhat uncertain in the production of good work. The slitting-rolls consist of circular barrels, after the manner of the "breaking-down" rolls, only of course much smaller in diameter, and with this exception, the slitting-rolls have square grooves cut into each barrel, the projecting portion of each corresponding with the hollow of the other, whereas the breaking-down rolls are perfectly smooth and plain. Rollers something similar to those we have described are used by wire-drawers to facilitate the speedy reduction of the metal, the difference being in the construction and action of the grooves. In the grooves of the latter, which are inserted farther apart, the hollows take a half-round shape, and unlike the slitting-rollers, during the revolution of the barrels, the grooves in this case directly meet each other, and thus produce a strip of wire almost round. It is almost needless to remark that wire-rolling requires some amount of practical knowledge to perform it properly. The manipulations indispensable to the art of silver working are so varied and so numerous that we are at a comparative loss which part of the process to consider first; however, if we follow the course of the workman with regard to the production of the various manufactures of his art, we shall perhaps not be far wrong in our desire to effect the purpose we have in view.

In commencing to enlarge upon these mechanical processes we may at once state that it is our intention to refrain from going into the whole art of wire-drawing, because that process has been somewhat minutely alluded to in our other work recently published in the interests of the goldsmiths; the details of which are there fully described.

The draw-plate, Fig. 23, which is the principal tool of the modern wire-drawer, was unknown in this country until the middle of the sixteenth century, when it was introduced by Christopher Schultz, a Saxon, from France. It was supposed to have been the invention of a native of that country named Archal. The draw-plate had been in use some years on the Continent previous to its introduction into England. The old method of making wire was upon the anvil, by means of the hammer; and those who manipulated in this art were termed wiresmiths at that period. The best form of draw-plate consists of a piece of steel about nine or ten inches long, one and a quarter to one and a half inch broad, and about half an inch thick, each containing a number of conical holes of various sizes, becoming smaller in succession until the last hole in the plate is reached, when another plate, corresponding in size, having smaller graduated holes, is employed, and the wire drawn through it; and so on, until the proper size has been obtained.

Fig. 23. Draw plate.

The drawing of stout pieces of wire is effected very readily by means of the draw-bench (Fig. 24), and the thinner pieces, by the application of draw-tongs (Fig. 25), held in the hands of the operator,

FINE WIRE-DRAWING.

and made to do service by swinging the body backwards. Very fine wire is now drawn by

Fig. 25. Draw-bench for Wire.

means of an apparatus called a *drum* (Fig. 26), revolving upon a perpendicular pin, the exterior of which receives the wire and prevents it from becoming entangled. When the end of the wire has finally passed through the draw-plate, the whole coil is carefully removed from the drum (which is made slightly conical in form for facili-

Fig. 25. Draw-tongs.

Fig. 27. Skeleton Frame or Swift used by wire-drawers.

Fig. 26. Drum used by wire-drawers.

tating the process) and placed upon a skeleton frame made to receive it (Fig. 27); it is then in proper form for its passage through the next hole of the draw-plate.

In the production of very fine wire, the metal, after passing a few times through the draw-plate, requires annealing, as its fibres become so condensed and hardened that it is impossible to repeat the operation without some risk of the wire breaking. For fine wire the annealing is repeated five or six times during its passage through the draw-plate; for stouter kinds the annealing need not be so frequent. This process produces a scale or oxide upon the surface of the wire, which should be removed before the continuation of the drawing takes place, which is generally done by an immersion for a time in very dilute sulphuric acid pickle; or its passage may be assisted through the draw-plate by the application of some lubricating substance, such as beeswax, or a mixture of beeswax and oil, which enables it the more readily to pass through it. In the progress of the wire-drawing the holes have a tendency to become enlarged; these are made smaller again, by repeated blows upon the front of the plate with a somewhat pointed hammer (Fig. 28), and then opened from the back with a tapered steel punch, such as is shown in the woodcut (Fig. 29). The hardening and tempering of the punch is of importance. A gauge-plate is used in all establishments for the purpose of determining the size of the wire. The hammering should not take place upon a hardened draw-plate, as it would fly to pieces: it is only those known as soft which should receive such treatment; and those, by a continual alteration of the holes, gradually become hard and require annealing at intervals.

Fig. 18. Knocking-up Hammer.

Draw-plates for wire-drawing purposes are mostly cylindrical in form, but they are employed in various degrees of fineness and in different shapes; such as oval, oblong, half-round, square, fluted, star, sexagon, triangular, and other complex sections, for the production of corresponding wires, all of which receive similar treatment to that above described.

The process of wire-drawing, in connection with the art of the silversmith, is more particularly employed in the manufacture of chains, in which branch a very large quantity of silver is consumed. Fig. 19. Round Steel Punch. This branch of the craft is almost a purely mechanical one, but, nevertheless, there are some designs in chains which require a considerable knowledge of art for the proper execution of them. It is, however, in "wrought" or hand-made work that true art is made to play so conspicuous a part; for it is here that perfect workmanship, together with great skill and taste, are required in the manufacture of an article. "Wrought" work was one of the earliest productions of the goldsmith and silversmith, and it still remains the true *artistic* method, although it has been superseded by others of a less expensive character; such as stamping, chasing, engraving, enamelling, casting, &c., to which the older processes of ornamentation and decoration by means of hammering have given place.

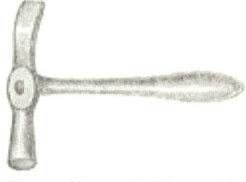
Fig. 30. Hammer for Wrought Work.

Wrought work is produced by hammering and soldering the various pieces or ornaments together; and one of the very first things to be attended to in the production of this kind of work is proportion, a knowledge of which is indispensable to true art-workmanship; for the piece of metal which is to be operated upon by the hammer should be of the proper size, so as to require none to be cut off afterwards. Every portion of a design should be wrought out of the piece of metal separately, and soldered in its proper place upon the article in process of manufacture. When circular forms have to be raised or flanged by the employment of the hammer, as in the case of a raised or flanged brooch "bezil," the *modus operandi* is as follows:—Take a piece of metal of the exact size and shape, turn the two ends together from the longitudinal direction, and unite them by soldering; when this is done, the circular band of metal is taken and flanged by means of the hammer and a miniature anvil, placed upon a stout piece of wood which the workman renders secure by placing between his knees, the pressure of which retains it steadily in its place during the various manipulations performed upon it; this kind of tool is termed a "sparrow-hawk"—a representation of it is given in Fig. 31. The work is effected by a series of blows dealt with the hammer in regular concentric circles, the bezil all the time gradually working round the pointed end of the sparrow-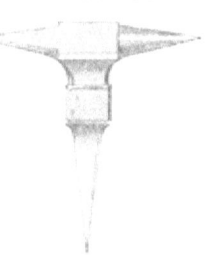

Fig. 31. Sparrow-hawk.

hawk. It requires great skill and practice to produce the proper shape, and to keep all parts of the metal of equal thickness. The bezils may be produced in this manner round or oval, as well as other complex shapes; the hammering taking place according to the shape required. When raised or ornamental brooch bezils, such as concave or convex patterns, are to be made, the means adopted in their execution are somewhat more complicated than the mode of flanging above alluded to. A tool called a "swage" is employed, which partakes of many forms, the pattern or ornamental device which the metal is required to take being the shape of the swage, or otherwise cut upon it. The metal is easily raised to take the proper design, by a very careful application of the hammering process.

Sometimes in silver-working the form of the object to be manufactured is of such a nature as not to allow of the use of the swage tool, and this is more particularly the case in the manufacture of plate. Such things, for instance, as cups or tankards which have raised ornamental surfaces, and which have to be executed after the vessel is roughly finished, require altogether a different tool for the effecting of such purposes. The one commonly employed in operations of this description consists of a bent piece of steel, upon one end of which is cut the device required; this end being turned up to the required height for raising the design, and the other end being bent in an opposite direction, which, when required for use, is secured in a vice. The workman, in executing the design upon the object in hand, places it upon the "snarling-iron" (for such the tool is called) at the part to be raised, and there holds it securely while another man strikes the piece of steel at the top of the angle, or just above where it is secured in the vice, the reaction of the steel wire then throws out the metal, in accordance with the device or pattern cut on the end of it. Designs are only roughly raised in this manner, the perfecting of them being performed by the application of various kinds of chasing tools. To prevent a change in the form of the object undergoing this operation, it is filled with a composition formed of pitch, resin, and brick-dust, in the following proportions:—

Pitch	4 parts.
Resin	4 ,,
Brick-dust	2 ,,
	10 parts.

The preparation of the cement is as follows:— Reduce the brick-dust to a very fine powder, and pass it through a fine sieve; then take the other ingredients and melt them in an iron ladle or other suitable vessel over a slow fire, stirring them well together; when this has taken place, the mixture will present a thin liquid appearance, which is the time for using the brick-dust. This should be added in small quantities at a time, and well stirred together, until the mass has become tolerably thick. It is then poured out either upon the floor, or into some suitable vessel provided for its reception. While undergoing the operation of

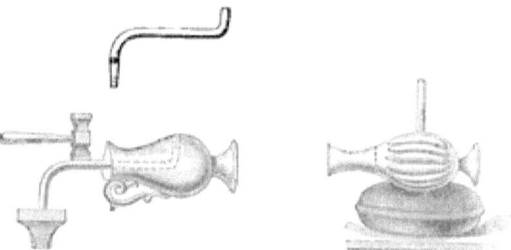

Figs. 32, 33. Snarling-tool, and its mode of application for raising.

chasing, the lower part of the object is preserved from injury, by being laid on a sand-bag. The illustrations, Figs. 32 and 33, represent the snarling-tool, and its mode of application to the work of the silversmith.

The progress of the silversmith's art, in conjunction with the researches and discoveries in the mode of working the precious metal during the last sixty years, have wrought a great change both in the style and manner of workmanship. Before the period referred to, the gold and silversmiths' trade was in its lowest possible condition; partly, no doubt, on account of the war then raging on the continent of Europe, and partly because the silversmith at that time was not allowed to manufacture articles of any standard inferior to that of the coinage of 11 ozs. 2 dwts. Until the peace of Waterloo, few people were busy but the gun-maker, and other smiths who were able to work at similar occupations; but with respect to most other trades, the men did all they were capable of, in order to earn their daily bread. If at that time the silver trade had been specially cultivated, the art, as regards its progress, would have met with many drawbacks, as compared with the present time; the knowledge of the workmen in the production of finished work was not equal to that to be found upon the best articles now manufactured. And although forbidden by law to work in inferior metal, they would have been incapable of effecting the beautiful surfaces which modern articles of inferior quality are made to present. The recent scientific discoveries, both chemical and mechanical, that have taken place during the last sixty or seventy years, have wrought a great change in the general conditions, as well as in the mode of the manufacture of silver wares.

We have said that previous to the year 1815 all was dark and obscure with the precious metal worker, but from that period the work gradually rose in artistic excellence, and the trade very slowly improved; the cause of this no doubt being due, in a great measure, to the security afforded as the result of peace, and with it a revival of the industrial occupations. With the increased industries of the nation arose the pleasures and pastimes of the people, and racing became a national sport. This kind of pleasure soon led to an increase in the work of the silversmith, in consequence of the demand for racing cups, which gave opportunities for the artistic excellence of design in their manufacture; and the silversmiths who made them soon acquired a prestige as Art-manufacturers. The demand for work of that and a similar kind led to the employment of regular designers and modellers, who gradually improved both the designs and the work in different parts of the country.

At the period of which we are speaking, polished or burnished silver goods were most in demand, the modern processes of surface finishing not being then understood. The introduction of the French style of work in filigree soon afterwards caused a demand for that class of work; and the attention of those in the trade was then turned in that direction for a time, and others springing up, the silversmith's and goldsmith's trade generally began to assume a position of importance. This kind of work required no polishing and very little artificial finish; besides being exceedingly light in weight and graceful in appearance. It required fine material for its manufacture. In England filigree work has been superseded by other processes, but in India, and in other parts of the East, it is still cultivated to perfection.

Silver and gold filigree is also manufactured in the Ionian Islands, in Switzerland, and in some parts of Germany and France, where labour is cheap. In the two latter countries it is made from a very inferior material to that used in India. Silver filigree work in this country was soon found not to answer all the requirements of modern society, so far as regarded its utility, durability, and cheapness; fashion therefore demanded something different. It is worthy of remark that while this class of jewellery in both gold and silver was so much in vogue for ladies' wear, the old-fashioned seals and keys had undergone a change, and the chasing of them in representation of filigree ornamentation had become the fashion for gentlemen's wear. The processes of the manufacture of filigree wire and its mode of application to the work of the artist, have been considered in a previous chapter, further detailed information is therefore rendered unnecessary.

When filigree work was no longer used, the fashion changed into "stamped" or "struck-up" ornament. Small pieces of metal were struck up by means of the hammer and punch, or by the use of the hand-press or stamp; in the former case a lead cake would be prepared, composed of a mixture of lead and tin, and upon it the various ornaments would be produced from the flat metal, corresponding with the pattern of the punch employed for the purpose; in the latter a small die (Fig. 34) would be employed with the pattern sunk upon it; this would have an aperture through it, the dimensions of the off-side being generally rather large, gradually becoming smaller towards the front surface, which takes the form, in general outline, of the desired pattern. When the necessary blanks have been cut out, another die and punch are used, by which they are raised to their proper shape. These tools should be firmly secured in the press (Fig. 35), otherwise they are likely to be soon destroyed.

Fig. 34. Die.

The small ornaments thus raised were variously arranged one upon another, until a design or pattern was formed, which in every way appeared very showy. Such articles suited the tastes of the people at that time, and still suits those who require good weight for their money. The same kind of thing existed at that period in chains, and being heavy-looking, and costly in appearance, they attracted attention and caused a demand. Thus with the continual changing of the fashions a new era for the goldsmiths and silver-smiths of England began. They were beginning to work in all sorts of qualities, with the manipulations and finish of which they were becoming now thoroughly conversant, and a demand springing up for goods for purposes of exportation, encouragement was given to the trade, which soon assumed the position of a thriving industry.

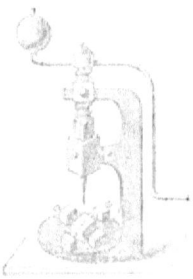

Fig. 17. Press.

The style of work that followed the "struck-up" patterns was that of plain and solid silver-work, well polished and whitened. This sprung up about the period when coloured gold became the fashion, and the mode of finishing it being somewhat similar, no doubt the demand arose as much from the introduction of colouring as from any other assignable cause. In the chain-maker's branch of the art, a great variety of new patterns came into existence at this period; chain bracelets also began to be introduced; and altogether the trade made rapid strides, and fast rose into a great commercial industry. This kind of work has remained more or less in fashion up to the present time, and vast quantities of silver chains of the plain and solid patterns are now being made in Birmingham.

The silver trade seems to be an exception to the general depression which now prevails in all the other branches of the jewellery trade; the fashion just now is for silver, which causes a greater demand than is usual for goods manufactured of that material. In a short time we believe this fashion will undergo a change, and then no doubt manufacturers who have taken advantage of it to make large stocks will have goods remaining upon their hands which they will not be able readily to dispose of, unless at a sacrifice; for it should be borne in mind, that to keep a large stock of silver goods in a saleable condition, and without a quick sale, considerable expense is entailed above the cost of making, to keep them in that condition, through their great liability to become tarnished.

After the introduction of plain and solid-looking work, it next became the fashion to have it chased over its entire surface. Following this, about the year 1825, came the beautiful process of enamelling, which added artistic beauty to the work, and brought out the harmonies of colour. About this time, too, there sprung up a great demand for the so-called "galvanic ring," which consisted of a lining of zinc and one of silver. The ring represented, in appearance, those large, plain, half-round rings which are now made in 18-carat gold, and which weigh from 7 to 10 dwts. each. It was then as now made of half-round shape, and sometimes with the addition of a buckle upon it. The silver was so drawn upon the zinc that the outer surface appeared entirely of silver, and a portion of the inner surface was made to show the zinc only, which was quite sufficient for the purpose required. When the ring was put on the finger the zinc, in conjunction with the silver, touched the flesh of the wearer, and was thus supposed to create a galvanic action, which it was alleged had a tendency to remove or prevent *rheumatism*. This kind of work had a good run at the time of its introduction, but like all the rest, the fashion lasted only for a while, when something else had to be brought to the front in the silver trade. The mode of the preparation of the wire was as follows: —A bar of silver would be rolled out until a certain thinness was attained, occasionally annealing it during the process; it was then cut into strips wide enough for the purpose required, again annealed, and subsequently doomed.

Fig. 36. Hammer for dooming.

The latter process was effected in this manner:—A block of hard wood, such as boxwood, would be made use of, having a round groove in one side of it, the metal to be doomed would be laid along the groove and a round piece of iron or steel held upon the upper surface with the left hand; a wooden mallet is then taken with the right hand, and by a skilful application of it to the piece of iron or steel, the metal is soon forced down in the groove and made to take the proper form for drawing. The flat strip of metal should be pointed; this may either be done before or after the dooming process, though it commonly takes place before. It is performed by taking away a small portion in a conical form, from one of the ends with a pair of hand-shears. A piece of zinc wire should be pro-

vided, corresponding in shape with that the ring is
to take; this is placed in the hollow of the silver
to be drawn, with the flat side outwards, so as to
correspond with the aperture in the plate through
which it has to be drawn. A draw-plate is then
taken, with holes of the half-round shape, and the
two metals carefully drawn through them. The
drawing through a succession of holes produces
an edge upon the silver coming against the flat
side of the aperture in the draw-plate which over-
laps the zinc and thus holds it securely in its
place.

A change in the style of work gradually took
place in the course of every few years, and thus it
was that hollow-work became the fashion. This
kind could be made in a variety of ways, and
being very light and showy, it appeared much
more expensive than it really was. It is therefore very easy to account for the changes which
have taken place in the manufacture of articles of
adornment and luxury, and for the encouragement
which the art has received. With the present
styles of the "plain," the "solid," the "filigree,"
the "stamped," the "mosaic," the "cameo," the
"repoussé," the "inlaid," the "enamelled," and a
variety of others, we can fearlessly say that silver-
working has of late years made rapid progress,

and attained to a higher standard than it ever before possessed.

The art of stamping and shaping articles of jewellery from sheets of the various metals came into general use just previous to the first Exhibition in 1851. These, which are made in considerable numbers, are produced by means

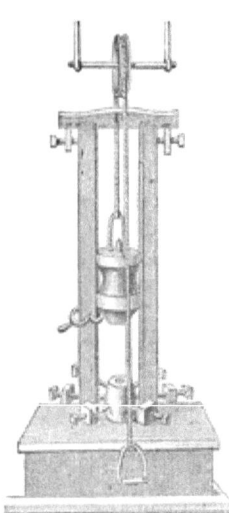

Fig. 37. Steel Die.

Fig. 38. Stamping Press.

of dies, having the shape of the pattern upon them, both at the top and bottom, made of hardened steel. Fig. 37 represents a bottom die for the use of the stamping press, and Fig. 38 represents the press. In raising the metal by stamping, the material undergoes the same bendings and extensions between the dies as if it were being manipulated by the hammer, and consequently it requires to be repeatedly annealed, otherwise it would crack and fall to pieces in a subsequent operation. The raising should be brought about gradually, and this is done by placing a number of sheets of metal between the dies, which prevents the top die from falling with too sudden an action upon the metal, which it would do, as it falls with a succession of forces if the process be repeated, and if its action be not arrested by the means we have pointed out. After every blow of the stamp one of these pieces is removed from the bottom, and a fresh one added at the top; the continual falling of the stamp gradually forces these plates, if placed in the manner we have indicated, to take the shape of the die. The exact form of the figure is effected by striking the plates singly between dies which exactly correspond. A very large quantity of work is now produced by the means we have stated, such as brooches, studs, locket-backs, earrings, rings, and an endless variety of other things; moreover, by the cultivation of this art a considerable amount of the labour formerly bestowed by hand upon the work is now saved, as the stamping in many instances is so complete, almost taking the form of a finished article after that process has been performed, that the workman has only to arrange the parts and supply the ornamentation when required, to render the article complete.

Works of art are also produced by other methods; as an example, we will take the process of "spinning or burnishing into form," which consists in spinning the metal to the desired shape in a lathe, by means of burnishing tools, specially made for the purpose. This process is employed in the production of large bangle bracelets with plain surfaces and other similar works. The metal to be operated upon should be soft and malleable, otherwise the process is very difficult to perform. The disc, or other form of metal, is taken and fixed in the lathe with the aid of holdfasts, a chuck or mould of the desired pattern being provided, upon which the disc is turned by the tools referred to. The metal, as in the other processes, is *gradually* spun into the required form. In most cases the mould is exactly the shape of the interior of the article required to be made, and under these circumstances it would be made up in several pieces together with a key-piece; so that when this latter is taken away, there is no difficulty in removing the rest, and leaving the article free. It is of importance, during the spinning, to keep the edges free from notches, but should these occur, it would be better to touch them a little with a turning tool. The metal for spinning into a bangle bracelet should be of the form of a flat circular band,

soldered of course; it would then be secured upon
a properly shaped mould, composed of several
pieces, in the manner above described; this would
then be placed in the lathe, and the application of
the spinning tools would soon bring about the
desired form. After the removal of the spun piece
of metal, the workman trims the edges up a little,
then saws it into two pieces, and at once proceeds
to the operations of snapping and jointing, which
are delicate processes to perform properly in work
of this kind, and require the services of a skilled
and competent workman.

Having now described some of the processes in
the working of silver, and alluded to the various
articles which are produced by *wire-drawing*;
raising with the hammer; *stamping*; *spinning*;
chasing, &c.; we shall next direct attention to those
processes which immediately come after the putting
together and soldering the article; and foremost
of these is *polishing*. We trust that the
foregoing details in reference to this part of the
subject will convey some idea of the art of silver-
working.

Polishing is an important process with all precious
metal workers. It is applied for the production
of *surface* to their wares, and in proportion
to the smoothness required upon the work, so

should be the fineness of the material employed in effecting it. The polishing powders are *emery, powdered pumice, crocus, rottenstone, putty of tin,* and *rouge.* In the best work, scratches are removed with a smooth and rather soft dark grey stone (Water-of-Ayr stone); it is then polished in the lathe with a stiff brush, and the application of a little fine polishing mixture. We have placed the materials for polishing in their respective order of smoothness or fineness, beginning with emery, which is the coarsest. A very good mixture for ordinary work consists of equal portions of emery, pumice, and crocus, with oil added to the consistence of a thick paste. Good work does not want much polishing, for the beauty of it depends *more* on its being executed by a well-trained workman; whereas rough and badly executed work requires much polishing, and for this the coarser powders are preferable, or a mixture of them; but for the smoother work the finer powders should be employed.

The Water-of-Ayr stone employed for polishing is usually obtained in the form of small square sticks, and is used with a small quantity of water to the surface of the work, in a similar manner to filing. The stone is softer than the material upon which it operates (and, in fact, so are all the materials for polishing, and therefore wears away, producing a mud-like substance upon the article, which should be repeatedly removed in order to ascertain the progress made. This may be done with a piece of clean rag, or tissue-paper. When the work is polished at the lathe it will gradually become enveloped in grease, &c., which should be removed occasionally, to show when the process has been carried far enough. The polishing of silver work is a branch of the trade commonly performed by girls. It is hard work for them, as the metal possesses a very soft nature; it therefore pulls hard against the brush which holds the polishing mixture. The lathe employed is the ordinary polishing lathe with a horizontal spindle, and is worked with a common foot-treadle; steam-power is used by some firms for moving these lathes, but it is by no means the usual custom at present.

After the completion of the polishing process, the work is well washed out in a prepared solution, to remove the mixture which adheres to it; a solution of soda is found to answer the purpose best, both from its cheapness and effectiveness. It should be used hot, with the addition of a little soap, and with a stiff brush the dirt is soon removed. The quantity of soda used to a given proportion of water differs in the trade, and there is no set rule to go by; it depends, more or less, upon the adhesiveness of the polishing mixture. We have found about two ounces of it to a quart of water amply sufficient for the purpose.

CHAPTER X.

Enriching the Surfaces of Silver.

BY the application of the processes about to be described, the finishing touches in their relation to articles or wares of silver manufacture are effected. These processes, as adopted by the trade, are various, almost every firm having a specially prepared mixture and mode of employing it. We shall refer only to those which, from their practical utility, are likely to be of service to those workmen who have to do with this particular metal. The branch of the art of which we are now treating comes only into operation when every other process of workmanship has been completed; and some of these processes must be executed in a perfect manner in order to arrive at the highest possible results in this one. The best and richest surface is produced when the metal to be operated upon is good in quality, and the workmanship of a fair order, so far as regards smoothness, and freedom from surplus solder-marks.

One of the oldest methods for producing a pure snowy whiteness upon articles of silver was as follows:—Take an iron or copper annealing pan (the latter is much to be preferred), place the work upon it in proper order, so that it may be heated all over alike. It should, previous to this, be immersed in a thick solution of borax, or otherwise brushed over with it. After the work has been properly arranged upon the pan for annealing, it must be sprinkled over with fine charcoal dust; the pan is then placed in the muffle upon a bright clear fire without blaze, and when the work has assumed a degree of heat approaching to cherry redness, it is withdrawn and allowed to cool. When this has taken place, it is removed and boiled out in a very weak solution of sulphuric acid, commonly called oil of vitriol. If the right colour was not then produced, the process was repeated as many times as circumstances permitted, though usually two or three times was found to be amply sufficient. The annealing process required great attention, for the work being in contact with borax, if slightly overheated, it was liable to become melted, therefore the operation was a delicate one to perform, and was only intrusted to such workmen as were experienced in the art. Small delicate articles were commonly treated with the mouth blow-pipe and gas-jet, and were placed upon a pumice-stone, or some other suitable substance capable of withstanding the power of burning. According to the inferiority of the silver alloy, is the difficulty of producing a good white surface on wares of such standards. Fine silver requires very little whitening, generally one process suffices to effect a good colour; but inferior standards require half a dozen or more to bring up the proper degree of whiteness; and those ranging below 9 oz. 12 dwts. to the lb. Troy cannot be whitened at all by the means we have described, but require the application of the modern chemical process, known as electro-plating.

The East Indian silversmiths never touch their manufactures with any kind of abrasive substance, from the most delicate, to the more strongly made article. But then it should be remembered, that in India the natives work from the pure material, a point which they rigidly adhere to; whereas we are compelled in this country to manipulate in all sorts of qualities; and some of these require no little trouble and difficulty to bring back to the surface the snow-white appearance of the pure metal. In the former case it is effected without any difficulty whatever—in fact, the metal scarcely undergoes any change throughout the whole of the manipulations to which it is subjected in the various processes of manufacture. The Indian mode of procedure is as follows:—Some juicy lemons are cut into slices; the silver articles are briskly rubbed with these for a short time, and subsequently covered with them, being placed in a suitable vessel for a few hours for the completion of the process. For very delicate articles of jewellery the natives cut a large lime nearly in two halves, into which they insert the work; the halves are then tightly closed up again, and placed aside for a few hours; when the article is removed, it is well rinsed in clean water, and consigned to a vessel of nearly boiling soap-suds, where it is well brushed, again rinsed in fresh hot water, and finally dried on a metal plate placed over hot water; the process is rendered complete by a little gentle rubbing with wash-leather if the work be of a plain nature. Green tamarind pods are also employed by them for the purpose of whitening silver, in the same manner as just described; they are great detergents both of gold and silver manufactures, and are largely employed by artisans in the East for the removal of oxides and fire-marks.

Another process for the whitening of silver goods is performed in the following manner:—Take the work, which must be cleanly prepared, and

WHITENING SILVER GOODS.

give it a coating of the following mixture:—Finely powdered vegetable charcoal four parts, saltpetre one part; the ingredients should be well mixed with a little water, and may be applied to the surface of the metal either by brushing over with a soft brush, or by dipping the work into it. The work is then placed upon the annealing pan and submitted to the heat of the mufile, until the wet powder has become perfectly dry and ceased to fly about; it is then withdrawn from the mufile, allowed to cool, and afterwards boiled out in a solution of potash prepared for the purpose, in the proportion of about one ounce of bi-sulphate of potash to twenty ounces of water. The boiling out is done in a copper pan (Fig. 39), and if the work be put through the above process two or three times a beautiful dead-white colour is the result. It is then washed in a hot solution of soda, soap, and water, or if preferred bright, scratched, or burnished, and the process is finally completed by drying it in fine boxwood sawdust, which should be made hot, but not allowed to char or burn in any way, as it would produce a stain upon the work very difficult to remove, and thus the finish would be considerably impaired.

Fig. 39. Boiling-out Pan.

In large manufactories the process of whitening silver goods is repeatedly required to be performed, and where such is the case, the above methods are found not only tedious and expensive, but occupy much unnecessary time and labour; to dispense with a portion of which, the custom of covering the work with a chemical preparation was accordingly departed from, and yet it was made to show its former brilliancy. To effect this object the liquid for boiling it in was differently prepared, which only required to be made of a proper strength to do all that the surface mixture had done before. The following is the method adopted in preparing the cleansing liquid. Boiling out mixture:—To one pound of smoking salts, add two ounces of cream of tartar; well shake the ingredients together, so that they may be thoroughly incorporated. The smoking salts employed for this purpose are not the ordinary *spirits of salts* of commerce, but a preparation of the common oil of vitriol; therefore the one should not be taken for the other; the spirits of salts would turn the work black, whereas, if the proper ingredient were procured, a fine dead matt or blanched surface would be the result of its application. The mixture employed for boiling the work in consists of the proportion of one ounce of the above preparation to about thirty ounces of water. The silver articles simply require to be annealed, allowed to cool, and then boiled for a minute or so in this solution, when the desired result will be attained; if, however, the exact colour be not obtained the first time, the process should be repeated a second, and if necessary, a third time; the right colour will then be produced, if the articles are not made of a too inferior standard.

The mode we have ourselves adopted for the colouring or whitening of silver goods is somewhat different, and still more simple than even the above. We will proceed to give the details of the process. A mixture of very dilute sulphuric acid is first provided, in the proportion of one ounce to forty ounces of water, and well mixed together; the work, after being heated to a good red-heat, is boiled in this, which soon removes the oxide from the surface, and shows the fine white colour of the pure silver. For fine silver work, such as Indian filigree, one process will generally suffice, for English standard quality two, and for low qualities three, but these latter must not by any means be too low; if so, no colouring can take place by the method just described. Objects of delicate workmanship are usually annealed by the gas; being placed on a pumice-stone of light material, the flame of the gas is blown with the mouth blow-pipe, in such a manner that the object gradually becomes heated all over alike; and the work should be well heated, as this facilitates the process of oxidation, and subsequently that of whitening. The oxidation takes place at the expense of the copper in the silver alloy, and this is only effected by raising the articles to a very high temperature, which produces the oxidation of the copper coming in contact with the air, and which necessarily exists upon the surface of the alloyed goods. Whitening silver goods then is nothing more than the removal of the base alloy from the surface, leaving the pure metal behind with its full rich colour. Therefore to be clear, the process of annealing in contact with cold air oxidizes the copper upon the surface, and the pickling mixture so dissolves and removes it, that it gradually undergoes a process of refining, and is ultimately made to represent the finest material in all its purity.

Sometimes silver work is to be seen having a brown colour upon it; this is produced when the acid employed for cleansing has been too strong; it can only be remedied by another annealing and boiling out in a much more diluted mixture. There are various other methods employed in the trade for the purpose of whitening silver work of the best quality; and although annealing is always a part of the process, other ingredients, such as salt and tartar, permanganate of potash, cyanide of potassium, alum, &c., have been severally used for the cleansing or whitening mixture. They may be useful in their application to plated work (articles that have received a coating of pure metal by means of the electro-metallurgical process), for cleansing purposes only, but for all practical purposes the process to which we have called special attention is to be much preferred.

Common articles of silver cannot be whitened by annealing and boiling out in a diluted acid; a thin film of pure silver must be deposited upon their surface by the process of electro-deposition, or by the action of some chemical preparation in which fine silver forms the principal ingredient. Such preparation, however, as the latter can be used only to plain surfaces, therefore they are not applicable to all kinds of work. They are composed of the following chemical ingredients:—1st, chloride of silver 1 part, cream of tartar 1 part; 2nd, chloride of silver 1 part, common salt 1½ parts; 3rd, chloride of silver 1 part, prepared chalk 1 part, pearl-ash 1 part; 4th, chloride of silver 1 part, alum 1 part, common salt 2 parts. The chloride of silver is easily prepared by precipitating it from the nitrate with a solution of common salt or hydrochloric acid. The various mixtures should be worked up with water into a thin paste, and applied to the work by rubbing with a soft cork or piece of wash-leather, or by thoroughly stirring it about in the mixture until it has acquired the requisite degree of whiteness. For the purpose of silvering watch and clock faces, &c. these mixtures may be used with advantage and entire success.

Other solutions are sometimes employed for similar purposes and are very useful; being simple in their preparation and easy of management. We have selected the following as being the most practical:—Take one ounce of the *nitrate* of silver and dissolve it in one quart of pure distilled water, or if this cannot be procured, water which has been boiled, by which it loses some of its impurity. When the nitrate of silver has become thoroughly dissolved, throw into the mixture a little powdered hyposulphite of soda, this will precipitate the silver, and when it has taken place, a further addition of hyposulphite of soda should be made, which will eventually re-dissolve the precipitate, and the solution is then ready for use. To produce a good mixture, the salt of soda should be added slightly in excess. The solution is used by simply dipping a sponge in it and rubbing it over the surface of the articles to be coated, and this is continued until they have assumed the desired colour.

For improving the colour of silver and electroplated wares, the following mixture has been strongly recommended:—Nitrate of silver 4 pennyweights, cyanide of potassium 5 ounces, and water 1 quart; the ingredients should be well mixed together, and applied by means of a soft brush or sponge to the surface of the work. In using this cyanide solution, the operator should be careful to guard against a too frequent contact with it, as it is decidedly injurious to the hands, especially if there be any abrasion of the skin; it being one of the deadliest poisons known. Sufficient details of the process of silver whitening and cleansing having now been given to assist the workman who manipulates in this particular metal, and to enable him to select a form of recipe in every way adapted to the kind of work in hand, we shall now proceed to the modern process of *electro-plating*, and give a practical description of it in its applicability to the trade of the silversmith.

This art is decidedly of modern origin, as far as concerns its employment for commercial purposes. The invention is supposed to be due to the electrical and chemical researches of Mr. Spencer, of this country, and Professor Jacobi, of Russia, both of whom claim to have found out the art of depositing one metal upon another, somewhere about the same period. Of course it was left to others to apply the invention to the industrial arts, and it was not until after the discovery of the *Constant Battery*, by Professor Daniell, about half a century ago, that the art began gradually to extend in the direction of commercial pursuits. The Messrs. Elkington, of Birmingham, were the first to employ it in their manufactures, with a success which their enterprise thoroughly merited. This took place about the year 1840, and since that time the art of electro-plating and gilding has wonderfully developed, in its application to the various manufactures of the country. Its progress would be a subject highly interesting, were we to trace the general details of it, but the part of it we are considering being the practical mode of its employment in manufactures, we shall at once direct our attention to it, by giving a complete description of the process; so that the ordinary silversmith may be enabled to employ it in his business with safety and advantage.

The first thing to be considered in electro-plating is what *Battery* to employ, which will be the most simple, inexpensive, and effective one.

When the battery is only occasionally required for use we prefer the Smee before any other. It is a small portable apparatus, and consists of a high, but narrow, glass or stoneware jar, in the form of a cylinder, capable of holding about two quarts; inside this jar is fitted a thin plate of platinized silver fitted to a frame with two zinc plates, one on each side of it, the zinc plates being held to the frame by means of a binding screw. Strong copper wires are firmly secured to these screws, which serve as the positive and negative poles of the battery. Those parts of the plates which are not exposed to the action of the acid solution may be advantageously coated with sealing-wax varnish or melted paraffin wax, to protect them from the destructive influences of the battery acid, and to prevent it from creeping upwards, which destroys the connections. The jar is filled with water acidulated with sulphuric acid, in the proportion of 1 of acid to 20 of water; the frame containing the plates is then lowered into the solution, and the battery is ready for use. In the above form of battery for occasional use we have one simple in construction, easy of management, of fair constancy, and when once prepared very inexpensive, merely requiring a little free acid at times to keep up the strength of the current. Two cells of this form of battery, each holding two quarts of mixture, will be found sufficient for all ordinary purposes. The zincs should be well amalgamated, and not touch the bottom of the cells. The connections should be regularly examined, and kept perfectly free from corrosion, which would stop the passage of the current. For plating small delicate articles of jewellery one cell of the above form will be found powerful enough for the purpose.

The battery that we prefer and have of late years employed, for regular continuous working, is the Bunsen, consisting as before of a cylindrical glass or stoneware jar of the same size and dimensions, fitted with a well amalgamated *cylinder* of zinc and a copper wire secured to it; a porous cell is placed in the centre, and a bar or rod of carbon is put into this cell with a copper wire also secured to it. The porous cell is filled with a mixture of equal parts of nitric and sulphuric acids, or sulphuric acid alone; we prefer the latter, as it does not give off such fumes as does the other acid; a little of the more powerful acid, however, is sometimes required to be added in order to increase the action, as with this acid alone it sometimes becomes slow. The outer cell is filled with a mixture of 1 part of sulphuric acid to 20 parts of water, and the connections being in proper order the battery is then ready for use. In action this form of battery is regular and continuous, it lasts a long time upon one charge, and is therefore inexpensive in use; if the two cells are coupled for power or intensity, an unusual quantity of work may be got through in a given time. This cell is admirably suited to the work of the manufacturing silversmith, and to those who prefer doing their own plating.

The amalgamation of the zinc is effected as follows :—The cylinders are best treated by putting some mercury into a coarse flannel bag, dipped repeatedly into muriatic acid and applied to the surface of the zinc, both inside and out; and when they present the bright characteristic appearance of mercury they are sufficiently operated upon, and may be rinsed and set aside to drain. The zinc plates may be advantageously amalgamated by placing some mercury in a shallow dish with a little muriatic or sulphuric acid, a hare's foot or a piece of cloth tied to the end of a stick is then dipped into the mercury and acid, and rubbed over the plates until they are sufficiently protected with mercury, when they should be rinsed in clean water and set aside to drain. If possible the process of amalgamation should always be conducted in the open air, as the fumes which are given off, if breathed, are highly injurious. The best possible way to amalgamate rods of zinc is by pouring mercury into the melted metal just before casting it into rods, in the proportion of 1½ oz. of mercury to the pound of zinc. This makes the rods exceedingly brittle, and they should therefore be handled with care. The mercury should not be added to the zinc when the latter is at too high a temperature, and the best manner of testing this is by the application of a piece of paper to the molten metal, when if it takes fire, the temperature is still too high; it should be allowed to cool until the paper refuses to ignite, then and not till then is the proper time for the addition of the mercury.

The copper conducting wires and binding screws must be cleaned when they become much corroded; if not they add resistance to the current, and it will become considerably diminished, or cease altogether. The cleaning may be effected by simply annealing and then plunging them while still hot into dilute sulphuric acid pickle, or dipping them into nitric acid for about an instant.

The zincs should be taken from the battery liquids when not required for use; and the porous cells should be removed every night and their contents poured into a large jug kept for the purpose. The porous cells should be placed in clean water to prevent the salts of the battery liquid from crystallizing in the pores, which would crack and spoil them for future use; the carbons should also be placed in water; and when required for use again these arrangements should be reversed, when the battery will work as well as ever.

The solution for electro-plating articles of jewellery is the next part of the subject we have to consider, of which there are many, containing various proportions of the metal employed in silver depositing. The following is one of the best we have employed: take pure silver and dissolve it in a mixture of nitric acid and water:—

Fine silver	5 dwts.
Nitric acid	4 drms.
Water .	2 drms.

The silver should be put into a small Florence flask, so as to allow the mixture of acid and water to cover it thoroughly; this mixture on being added to the metal soon promotes a chemical action, and the silver becomes gradually dissolved. If the acid employed has been weak, it will necessitate a further addition of it to complete the dissolution of the silver, or the removal of the flask to some other and warmer place, such as a sand-bath, but care should be taken not to apply too much heat. As the chemical action proceeds, red fumes are formed in the flask; and the action should be allowed to go on until these cease to rise, when the silver should by that time have become dissolved. The mixture then consists of a solution of nitrate of silver, and should be carefully poured into a suitable porcelain or Wedgwood capsule; this is then heated upon a sand-bath until a scum or pellicle appears upon the surface, when it should at once be transferred from the sand-bath to a suitable place for cooling. During the last operation the mixture begins to form itself into crystals, and the liquid which appears reluctant to crystallize should be poured away from those already formed, into another capsule, and again heated until it has sufficiently evaporated to crystallize. When the whole of the liquor has finally undergone this process, the crystals of nitrate of silver must be removed to another vessel, and about one pint of cold water added, the whole being then well stirred until they have become thoroughly dissolved. A solution of cyanide of potassium is next prepared in water, in the proportion of about one ounce of cyanide to the pint of water; some of this solution is then added to the one containing the nitrate of silver. It must, however, be added very cautiously, for precipitation soon takes place, and if too much be used, the precipitate becomes again dissolved. For this reason it is advisable to take a little of the solution from the vessel, in a wine-glass or test tube, and to add a few drops of the prepared solution of cyanide, in order to ascertain its exact state. If the application of this solution produces no effect upon the nitrate of silver, the operation of precipitation is complete.

The liquid above the sediment should next be carefully poured away to avoid any waste of silver; when this is done fresh water should be added, well stirred with the sediment, and allowed to settle; it is then again poured off, and the process repeated until the precipitate has become thoroughly washed. Now add sufficient cyanide of potassium to dissolve the precipitate and a little more, and make up two quarts of solution with fresh clean water. It is better to filter the solution before using it.

The solution may be made by means of the battery, and, if preferred, the above mode of chemically preparing it may be dispensed with. The following is the most simple method by the battery process:—Dissolve in two quarts of water about half an ounce, and no more, of best black cyanide; this should be done in an oval, or still better, oblong stoneware vessel, placed in an iron one of the same shape containing water. The stone jar should not be allowed to touch the bottom or sides of the iron one, a space being left for holding the water. When the cyanide has become dissolved, fill a porous cell with some of the solution, place this cell in the other vessel containing the cyanide; the solution should be about the same height in both vessels. Now put a piece of sheet copper, secured to the end of the wire issuing from the zinc of the battery, into the porous cell, and place in the larger vessel containing the cyanide solution about one ounce of sheet silver, properly secured to the wire issuing from the carbon of the battery. In a short time the solution in the larger vessel will have acquired the right proportion of silver (5 dwts. to the two quarts) for use; when this has been effected, the porous cell should be removed and its contents thrown away. These solutions are both worked hot, at a temperature of not exceeding 120° Fahr. with the battery we have described.

The solutions are heated by means of gas-jets, and the articles are plated by being suspended to the wire proceeding from the zinc of the battery. To the wire proceeding from the carbon is to be attached the piece of sheet silver which dissolves and keeps up the strength of the solution. The piece of silver or anode being lowered into the solution, upon the immersion of the work, an almost instantaneous deposit of fine silver takes place, the thickness of which depends entirely upon the period of immersion.

When a solution begins to plate of an inferior kind through the acquisition of organic matter, it will be better to abandon it altogether and make a new one, rather than to waste valuable time in repeated attempts at improvement, which seldom can be effected in solutions that have been employed for all kinds of work. The silver may be recovered from such solutions by means of the battery, by precipitation, and by evaporation; the first process, however, we have not always found successful, the solution in some cases refusing to give up its silver to the action of the battery. It is put into operation as follows:—The anode which supplies the solution with silver is replaced by one of platinum, on which the cyanide solution has no action whatever; a piece of clean sheet copper should be hung upon the zinc wire of the battery, and the battery kept in action until the whole of the silver held in the solution has become deposited upon it; at which stage it may be removed, and the exhausted solution thrown into the waste water tub. The piece of copper containing the silver may be used again in the place of the silver anode until it has become dissolved, or it may be removed by any other means, if preferred. In the event of the above plan failing, the process of precipitation or evaporation should be resorted to. If the former one be adopted, the solution should be poured into a large open vessel, and considerably diluted with water; sulphuric acid should then be carefully poured in, a little at a time, until it produces no effervescence. The sulphuric acid precipitates the silver, and the fumes which it creates are highly deleterious to health, therefore the process ought to be performed in the open air, and not in ill-ventilated workshops. When the sulphuric acid produces no effect upon the solution, it should be allowed to stand for a while for the precipitate to subside, when the water above (which should be clear) may be drawn off, the precipitate well washed, to free it from the acid, dried, and fused in a crucible with a little potash or soda. If the latter plan be adopted, the solution may be placed in a cast-iron kettle or saucepan, and then heated upon a gas-jet or stove, until evaporation takes place, after which the sediment should be removed and fused in a crucible, as before.

The finishing of silver work requires some little knowledge and skill to perform it properly; and

FINISHING SILVER WORK.

we think that a few observations bearing upon it will be of service to those for whom this manual is written. After either of the processes of whitening or plating, the work has to be scratched, unless required to be left a *dead* white, then this process does not take place; the scratching removes from the surface the dull white colour produced by the above processes, and effects a characteristic bright and uniform colour to the work of the silversmith. Scratching is done at the lathe (Fig. 40) by the application of a very fine brass-wire brush of circular form running upon the spindle; a solution of weak ale runs from a barrel with a tap to it, placed upon the framework of the lathe so as to enable the beer running from it to fall upon the brush during the whole time of its rotary action, and this assists the brush the more easily to glide over the surface of the work submitted to it. A large quantity of silversmith's work receives no other treatment than this, after the whitening processes have taken place. Silver chains are burnished by means of a polished steel

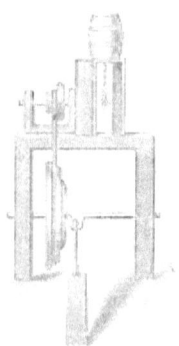

Fig. 40. Scratch-brush Lathe.

jack chain, and the application of a little soft soap and hot water, or otherwise scratch-brushed. The beautiful frosted surfaces to be seen upon silver lockets, and other work of a similar nature, are all produced by means of the scratch-brush.

Burnishing is another mode of finishing silver work. It produces a polished surface, which reflects like a mirror, and gives the greatest lustre; it removes marks left by the polishing mixtures, and produces a darker surface than the other modes of finishing. The tools employed for this process are extremely variable, and well adapted to the different kinds of work to which they are applied; they are of two kinds, one being formed of hard stone, and the other of polished hardened steel; they vary with regard to shape, some being straight with rounded points, or with curved and blunted edges, others with large rounded surfaces, &c. Stone burnishers are made of blood-stone, which is mounted in a wooden handle with a brass ferrule, which firmly secures the stone to it, in which state it is used. Steel burnishers are likewise fixed in wooden handles, which enable them to be firmly grasped by the operator. Throughout the whole process of burnishing, the tool should be repeatedly moistened with a solution of soap and water; which causes it to glide more easily over the surface of the work, prevents it from becoming too much heated, and generally facilitates its action. In consequence of the great friction which the burnishing tool undergoes, it soon loses its bite, when it slips over the work as if it were greasy; its effectiveness must therefore be restored from time to time by rubbing it upon the leather which the workman has beside him for the purpose. It generally consists of a piece of buff leather, impregnated with a little crocus. In very small articles only steel burnishers are used, as they are finer in make, and by their greater variety of form, are exceedingly well adapted to all kinds of work; in this class of work, if any soap-suds should adhere to the article they may be removed by the application of a little tissue paper. Large pieces of work are rubbed with a piece of old linen, or washed in a warm solution of soap and water, rinsed, and dried in boxwood sawdust, which finally completes the process.

Silver work may be oxidized by any of the following processes:—

1.

Sal ammoniac	2 parts.
Sulphate of Copper	2 „
Saltpetre	1 part.

Reduce the above ingredients to a fine powder,

and dissolve it in a little acetic acid. If the article is to be entirely oxidized, it may be dipped for a short time into the boiling mixture; if only in parts, it may be applied with a camel-hair pencil, the article and the mixture both being warmed before using.

II.

Platinum	1 part.
Hydrochloric acid	2 parts.
Nitric acid	1 part.

Dissolve the platinum in the mixture of acid, evaporate to crystallization, and when cold, dissolve again in a little sulphuric ether. Apply the mixture with a camel-hair pencil to the parts required to be blackened.

III.

Saltpetre	2 parts.
Common Salt	1 part.
Spirits of Salts	1 ,,

Reduce the salts to powder, and place it in a black-lead crucible along with the acid, boil up, and then dip the articles into the mixture for a short time, or otherwise apply it to the parts required to be oxidized.

These mixtures will give the various tints of oxidation to silver work if properly treated; but if other tints be desired, the following chemical substances may be employed according to taste:—For slate-coloured surface, dip the articles into a boiling solution of sulphuret of potassium. Strong hydrosulphate of ammonia produces a dark tint of oxidation, and if diluted with much water a light tint is produced. Nitric acid produces a light surface. The fumes of sulphur produce a beautiful blue-coloured surface. This operation should be conducted in a closed box, and all parts not to be blackened should be coated with a suitable resist varnish. After any of these processes the articles may either be scratched, or otherwise burnished.

CHAPTER XI.

Imitation Silver Alloys.

The undermentioned white alloys have their various uses in the industrial and mechanical arts, some being employed as common silver, whilst others are manufactured as near as possible in imitation of it, and used as a substitute, for many purposes. In melting the alloys in which nickel and several other compounds enter into combination, unless very great care be exercised, it is a difficult matter to maintain the true and definite proportion of each metal of which the alloy proper is composed, owing to the loss of the more fusible metals by volatilization, if allowed to remain too long in the furnace. The best method of preparing the compound for the crucible, is to mix the copper and nickel together. The latter is produced from the pure oxide of nickel; therefore it is taken in this form and placed in the crucible with the copper at the commencement of the operation. When these ingredients are well melted, and incorporated by stirring, add the zinc or other fusible metal required to make up the compound, previously heating it thoroughly over the mouth of the crucible, to prevent the chilling of the already molten metal which it contains. When silver forms a component part in any of these alloys it should be added at the beginning of the process along with those of a high degree of fusibility, and reduced under the protection of a suitable flux; charcoal being the best for the purpose. This flux also tends to preserve the fusible metals, upon their addition to the melted compound in the pot, from too suddenly flying away in the shape of fumes. The best zinc of commerce should be employed in these alloys, which is sold under the name of spelter.

Common silver alloy—

	oz.	dwts.	grs.
Fine silver	1	0	0
Shot copper	0	17	0
Nickel	0	13	0
	2	10	0

Another—

	oz.	dwts.	grs.
Fine silver	1	0	0
Shot copper	1	0	0
Nickel	0	15	0
	2	15	0

IMITATION SILVER ALLOYS.

Common silver alloy—

	oz.	dwts.	grs.
Fine silver	1	0	0
Shot copper	1	3	0
Nickel	0	17	0
	3	0	0

Another—

	oz.	dwts.	grs.
Fine silver	1	0	0
Shot copper	1	6	0
Nickel	0	19	0
	3	5	0

Another—

	oz.	dwts.	grs.
Fine silver	1	0	0
Shot copper	1	9	0
Nickel	1	1	0
	3	10	0

Another—

	oz.	dwts.	grs.
Fine silver	1	0	0
Shot copper	1	12	0
Nickel	1	3	0
	3	15	0

Common silver alloy—

	oz.	dwts.	grs.
Fine silver	1	0	0
Shot copper	1	15	0
Nickel	1	5	0
	4	0	0

Another—

	oz.	dwts.	grs.
Fine silver	1	0	0
Shot copper	2	2	12
Nickel	1	7	12
	4	10	0

Another—

	oz.	dwts.	grs.
Fine silver	1	0	0
Shot copper	2	10	0
Nickel	1	10	0
	5	0	0

Another—

	oz.	dwts.	grs.
Fine silver	1	0	0
Shot copper	0	16	0
Nickel	0	10	12
Spelter	0	3	12
	2	10	0

IMITATION SILVER ALLOYS.

Common silver alloy—

	oz.	dwts.	grs.
Fine silver	1	0	0
Shot copper	0	19	0
Nickel	0	12	0
Spelter	0	4	0
	2	15	0

Another—

	oz.	dwts.	grs.
Fine silver	1	0	0
Shot copper	1	2	0
Nickel	0	15	0
Spelter	0	3	0
	3	0	0

Chinese silver—

	oz.	dwts.	grs.
Shot copper	1	0	0
Spelter	0	6	0
Nickel	0	4	0
Cobalt	0	3	18
Silver	0	0	18
	1	14	12

Imitation silver—

	oz.	dwts.	grs.
Shot copper	1	0	0
Nickel	0	6	12
Spelter	0	4	18
	1	11	6

ALLOYS.

Imitation silver—

	oz.	dwts.	grs.
Shot copper	1	0	0
Spelter	0	12	0
Nickel	0	8	0
	2	0	0

Another—

	oz.	dwts.	grs.
Shot copper	1	0	0
Spelter	0	8	0
Nickel	0	4	0
	1	12	0

Another—

	oz.	dwts.	grs.
Shot copper	1	0	0
Spelter	0	10	0
Nickel	0	10	0
	2	0	0

Another—

	oz.	dwts.	grs.
Shot copper	1	0	0
Nickel	0	8	8
Spelter	0	6	16
	1	15	0

IMITATION SILVER ALLOYS.

White alloy—

	oz.	dwts.	grs.
Shot copper	1	0	0
Tin	0	10	6
Brass	0	2	12
Arsenic	0	0	18
	1	13	12

Clark's patent alloy—

	oz.	dwts.	grs.
Shot copper	1	0	0
Nickel	0	3	18
Spelter	0	1	22
Tin	0	0	12
Cobalt	0	0	12
	1	6	16

White alloy—

	oz.	dwts.	grs.
Shot copper	1	0	0
Tin	0	10	0
Arsenic	0	1	0
	1	11	0

Alloy with platinum—

	oz.	dwts.	grs.
Fine silver	1	0	0
Platinum	0	5	0
	1	5	0

Alloy with palladium—

	oz.	dwts.	grs.
Fine silver	1	0	0
Palladium	0	5	0
	1	5	0

The platinum and palladium of which the last two alloys are composed, although very difficult to use in combination with any other metal, readily unite in any proportions with silver; and it has been found that such alloys are not so easily tarnished as the ordinary ones, or even as fine silver itself. These various alloys serve to effect the several purposes for which they are employed in manufactures; wires prepared from any of them will supply the place of silver, as brooch tongs, stems for pins, catches and joints, &c. for articles of common quality and cheap workmanship. They are also employed for preparing the ground for "electro-plate," for which they are very serviceable. When, however, these alloys are employed by the regular silversmith, care should be taken not to get the scraps of metal in any way mixed with those of the better material, otherwise difficulties will soon begin to present themselves, which will materially interfere with the regular and proper working of the best silver alloys; and in fact, with all qualities that have originally been prepared free from nickel. Those prepared from nickel are much more infusible than those made without it; consequently, if a piece of the nickel alloy, either by accident or design, gets intermixed with the other quality, in a subsequent melting, it will be found to float upon the surface of the molten metal for some considerable time, and thus retard the process. Alloys prepared in imitation of silver are harder and much more difficult to work than those of the true metal; therefore it can easily be imagined what alteration the latter undergo upon the addition of some of the former compounds. The hardness and toughness which these alloys possess admirably adapt them for such purposes as we have described.

CHAPTER XII.

Economical Processes.

IN all silversmiths' establishments, the economical or waste-saving processes, as they are termed, require special and careful attention, so that the actual working loss, or that portion of it which is entirely irrecoverable by the manufacturer, may be reduced to the lowest possible degree. It may not be known to the general reader, or to the beginner in the precious metal trades, that there always takes place in the working up of the metal a loss of material, a portion of which the manufacturer is unable to recover, however cautious may be the means employed for that purpose. In the best regulated workshops, this loss will amount at the lowest estimate to about $2\frac{1}{2}$ per cent. of the whole quantity worked up in the establishment. If the actual loss can be reduced to within the above limit it is considered very low, and highly satisfactory. Taking into consideration the loss that is occasioned in precious metal working, and from calculations that we have made from experience, we have long since arrived at the conclusion, that it cannot possibly be estimated under 10 per cent. of the total work daily performed; and this opinion is based upon experiments, the *raw* material being weighed before the process of melting and after the articles were completed, a fair calculation of course being made for unfinished work. This was including every description of manufacture; in some branches of the trade the working loss is not quite so great, but then there are others in which it is exceedingly heavy, so that the estimated loss in the jewellery trades cannot be safely put at a lower percentage than we have quoted.

It will thus be seen that the *real* loss, such as manufacturers are unable to recover by the means already known to them, amounts to one-fourth part of the total working loss of the establishment. This is easily accounted for: in the first place, a little takes place in the melting of the various alloys, the re-melting of scrap metal, the reduction of lemel, &c.; then there are the sundry manipulations of working; the passage of the metal through various acids, and the processes of finishing, each of which detaches small particles of metal, too small to be visible to the naked eye, but all of which go to form a portion of the loss which the manufacturer never recovers. The unrecovered metal may be judiciously proportioned as follows:—A portion of it works itself into the wood-work of the flooring of the shops, lathes, boards, and other parts of workshop appliances; then there is the refiner's profit—as purchases of the sweep, polishings, and other refuse of precious metal workers. Instances can be recorded in which shrewd business-men have actually taken up the floors of their workshops and recovered a vast quantity of metal which was supposed to be lost for ever; and instances are well remembered in which two jewellers, upon removing into more extensive premises, availed themselves of the opportunity, not only of removing the boards which formed the flooring of the premises they were about to leave, but also those of the tenants they were about to succeed. In one case, metal of the value of £80 was recovered, and in the other it reached the large amount of £150. The two jewellers referred to, of course, were too un-English to refund the proceeds to the late tenants, who, when they became aware of it, if ever they did, would be, no doubt, wiser if sadder men.

To prevent the precious metal from finding its

way into such places as these, it is advisable to have the floors well protected with sheet zinc or iron, in which case not the least particle could be lost in this manner. The extra cost of laying the floors would soon be amply repaid, by an extra quantity of the working loss being recovered; and if other equally effective precautions were adopted in the waste-saving processes by precious metal workers, the *real* loss, which they cannot avoid suffering, might even yet be reduced to the lowest possible point. Iron or zinc covered floors may be protected from wear, by laying over the surface small square grates of perforated iron, and these, being removable, may be readily taken up at stated periods, for sweeping the refuse from the floors; once a month will be found often enough to do this. The gratings should, however, be swept over lightly every day in order to remove the dust and particles of metal that may accumulate upon the surface into the perforations, and also for the removal of waste paper and other rubbish, continually accumulating in workshops.

Floors containing no such waste-saving precautions, are commonly swept over once, and sometimes twice each day, the refuse arising therefrom being carefully passed through a very fine sieve, all extraneous matter removed, and the residue remaining in the sieve being well sorted for the detection of all the precious metal visible to the naked eye. The whole refuse matter is then thoroughly burned in a muffle provided specially for the purpose, and finally reduced to a fine powder in a cast-iron mortar. When it has reached this stage of the process, it is quite ready for the particular kind of treatment it next receives at the hands of the refiner. Grinding by large stone rollers is now fast superseding this mode of pulverising jewellers' waste and refuse. When the latter plan is adopted, the refuse should be swept from the floors every morning, carefully looked through, and then transferred to a barrel (having the top removed, which may be used as a lid), where it can be well kept together, and hidden from view until the time arrives for its further treatment.

The waste which accumulates in the processes of polishing, lapping, &c., is greater than that already referred to, consequently, it cannot be too carefully looked after, in every stage, where a large manufacturing trade is being carried on in various branches. It is advisable in the practice of true economy, for the polishing, lapping, and scratching boxes to be repeatedly cleaned out, and the contents removed out of the temptation of every one, by being placed in a box, well lined with either sheet lead or zinc, which ensures the perfect safety of the material placed therein from all irregularities in the workshop. This kind of waste on being prepared for sale is again placed in a very strong wrought-iron box, made of a suitable size to fit the muffle, and having a thick close lid to it. After the work of the day has been completed, the fire in the furnace or muffle is made up, the dampers are closed, and then the iron box containing the refuse is at once passed in and allowed to remain there till morning, when every particle of matter will have become thoroughly burned; a slight pulverization after this process readily reduces it to a fine powder; further operations then cease, and the product is in all probability in a fine state of division, and fit for the subsequent operations of the refiner and assayer, whose special business it is to attend to these arrangements of precious metal workers.

The next process we have to consider is one which includes the whole of the liquid substances variously employed in silver-working establishments, such as the pickling solutions, washing-out waters, whitening mixtures, and waste or spent solutions of every kind. The whitening solutions or mixtures, when in use, should be kept apart from the ordinary cleansing liquids, as after they have been in use for a time, they become saturated with copper taken off the work during the whitening processes; if the solution is then set aside for some time the copper eventually crystallizes out from the liquor, which may be poured into the waste-water tub, and the remaining crystals of sulphate of copper, for such it then is, may be removed and preserved.

In small establishments one large tub, to form the receptacle for all spent or used-up liquids, will be found sufficient; but in large places several will be required. In the former case the water is only drawn off at the beginning of every fresh week, which allows plenty of time for the precipitation of the silver without any disturbance taking place in the mixture between the close of one week and the commencement of another; whereas in large concerns it requires to be drawn off continually unless other vessels are provided for its reception during a long period. Attempts have been made to recover the silver from these solutions by simply filtering the liquid through a coarse piece of felt or flannel; or by providing a false bottom in the tub or other vessel containing the waste waters, arranged in the following manner:—A tolerably large tub would be employed, being about one-fourth filled with coarse deal sawdust, next would be placed the false bottom perforated with numerous small holes, and upon this would be firmly secured a piece of felt, so as to exactly fill up the space in that part of the tub, which then serves to act as the filterer of all solutions poured in above. The liquid after passing through the piece of felt proceeds through the perforations in the false bottom into the sawdust beneath, where it is allowed to run away by means of a small hole or tap at the bottom. But the use of either of these processes, if adopted on a large scale, where the waste products amounted to some hundreds per annum, would be wretchedly bad economy and tend to a serious loss of valuable metal; the boiling sulphuric acid, used in cleansing the work and for other purposes, has the power of dissolving minute particles of silver as well as those of the baser metal which always enters into the composition used in the production of the work of the silversmith; therefore, that portion of the metal which has become dissolved and entered into the chemical state, requires to be brought back to its original form before it can be saved by such means as those just described. To illustrate this more clearly, we will take the process of gold-colouring If workmen were to notice the rinsing waters employed in this process, subsequently allowing the vessels containing the rinsing to stand for a very short time, upon pouring away the surplus water, a white curdy precipitate will at once be observed at the bottom. This is the silver removed from the surface of the gold alloy, which has been precipitated by the muriatic acid and the common salt employed in the colouring mixture, into the form of *chloride of silver*. Now in this proceeding there is no gold to be seen in any of the vessels, but it is a well-known fact that a portion has been removed during the process from the surface of the gold articles. Where is it? Why, it has become dissolved, and is therefore held invisible in the solution, in consequence of the colouring mixture forming the well-known solvent for gold, *aqua-regia*. This is exactly the case with a portion of silver in the silversmith's solutions; small particles are continually being dissolved by the mixtures employed, and are thus held in solution past the power of filtering, unless some chemical ingredient be added to it, which acts as a re-agent upon the metal sought to be recovered. From what we have seen in the colour water, which always contains a little silver, it is evident that both muriatic acid and common salt will do this work for us. We prefer common salt, on account of its cheapness, besides being easily procurable.

The best mode of treatment for the silversmith's waste waters, after being collected together by pouring into the receptacle specially provided for that purpose, is to prepare a saline solution for the precipitation of the silver. This may be made by mixing together common salt and tepid water, in the following proportions:—

    Common salt   .   .   .   .   3 oz.
    Tepid water   .   .   .   .   1 pt.

The water need only be sufficiently warm to dissolve the salt, and the proportions given do not require to be strictly adhered to; in fact any quantity, if properly mixed, will do to effect the purpose required, and we merely give these as a guide for the process. In small establishments where only one tub is employed, the above proportion of saline solution may be added (every Saturday after the completion of the day's work) to the waste water; the whole should then be stirred slowly in a circular direction, and allowed to settle until Monday morning, when all the surplus water may be drawn off and poured away. In larger establishments the accumulation of waste water is greater, therefore several collecting vessels should be employed, and the mixture for precipitation may be added to them at other times than those stated, if required, and in accordance with workshop regulations. The sediment produced in the collecting vessels after the supernatant water has all been drawn off, may be removed, dried by heat in a strong iron pan, and subsequently sold to the refiner.

CHAPTER XIII.

Licences and Duties.

MANUFACTURING silversmiths, and all persons trading in silver wares of more than five pennyweights each, are compelled to take out a licence; articles under that weight being exempt. The licence has to be taken out annually, and costs £2 6s. for manufacturing or trading in articles under thirty ounces in weight, and £5 15s. for articles of thirty ounces and upwards. It should be taken out on the 6th day of July in each year at the Excise Office. This Act of the Legislature was passed in the year 1803, 43 George III. c. 69, and is not the only one which refers to the subject we are now considering. There are other conditions besides the compulsory *Plate Licence*, as it is called, to which manufacturing silversmiths are subject, such as the supervision of the assay offices, in the case of certain descriptions of goods; and the payment of duty on all such goods. At the present time all hall-marked silver articles have to pay a duty of 1s. 6d. per ounce, calculated not on their gross weight, but on five-sixths of the weight, the other sixth being allowed for waste in finishing the articles, as they are sent to the Hall in a half-finished state. The duty is paid at the Assay Office at the time the goods are sent to be marked. Some dissatisfaction just now exists in a portion of the trade with regard to the above duty, as it is considered excessive, besides having a tendency to discourage the manufacture of silver wares; be this as it may with respect to a certain description of goods, on the bulk of the trade it can have no injurious effect whatever. The duty is paid only on manufactured *plate* and such other articles as are requested to be hall-marked; besides which the trade in this particular department of manufacture has never been very extensive, being confined to a few firms of eminence only.

Before going into the general details of this question, it will be as well, perhaps, if we give a short history of the imposts that have existed in the silver trade for some time back. The first impost that we can find recorded took the shape of a *duty*, and was levied as far back as the year 1720, by 6 George I. c. 11, which placed a tax of 6d. per ounce on all silver plate manufactured in

Great Britain, which should be assayed or marked. The officers of the Excise were to collect the tax, but the great difficulty of ascertaining the number of ounces worked up, which the provisions of the Act did not clearly set forth, soon rendered it ineffectual, and it was consequently repealed by the statute 31 George II. c. 32, and a licence then substituted had to be taken out by manufacturers and dealers in plate. The licence at this period amounted to forty shillings, and had to be renewed annually. In 1759, 32 George II. c. 14, it was increased to £5 per annum, for every person trading in silver wares of thirty ounces and upwards; wares in one piece not exceeding five pennyweights in weight being exempted.

The next change that took place was in the year 1784, 24 George III. c. 53, when a duty was again imposed of 6d. per ounce on silver plate. It was also enacted that the assay masters should stamp the work with the additional mark of the "King's head," as well as the others already ordered by the various Acts of the Legislature. The mark of the King's head represented that of the reigning sovereign, and showed that the duty had been paid on the work. The present mark, therefore, is the Queen's head.

By an Act passed in the year 1797, 37 George

III. c. 90, the duty on silver ware was increased to one shilling per ounce, but the Act which subjected silver wares to a duty of 6*d*. per ounce (24 George III. c. 53) has not been repealed, and is therefore in existence to this very day; by its provisions, however, the duty has been increased from time to time, until it has reached the amount at which it now stands.

The present annual licences of £2 6*s*. and £5 15*s*. respectively, were enacted in the year 1803 by an Act of 43 George III. c. 69, and by these regulations every person making or trading in silver wares, or otherwise dealing in the raw material, is compelled to take out an annual licence, or render himself liable to a penalty of £50.

Another Act was passed in reference to the duty on silver goods in the year following, 1804, 44 George III. c. 98, whereby it was increased to 1*s*. 3*d*. per ounce. And in the year 1815, 55 George III. c. 185, the Act was further extended to 1*s*. 6*d*. per oz. calculated in the manner we have described at the beginning of this chapter. To sum up, therefore, the silver *duties* in their several forms, bearing upon the trade at the present time, we find them as follows:—

Manufacturers of silver wares under 5 dwts. in weights.—*Exempted from all duties.*

Vendors and dealers in silver wares under 5 dwts. in weight.—*Exempted from all duties.*

Manufacturers of silver wares under 30 oz. in weight.—*A plate licence of £2 6s. annually.*

Vendors and dealers in silver wares under 30 oz. in weight.—*A plate licence of £2 6s. annually.*

Manufacturers of silver wares of more than 30 oz. in weight.—*A plate licence of £5 15s. annually.*

Vendors and dealers in silver wares of more than 30 oz. in weight.—*A plate licence of £5 15s. annually.*

Bullion dealers, refiners, and assayers.—*A plate licence of £5 15s. annually.*

Manufacturers of plate.—*A duty of 1s. 6d. per ounce.*

Hall-marked goods.—*A duty of 1s. 6d. per ounce.*

Manufactured plate includes silver wares, such as spoons, forks, snuff-boxes, tea-sets, &c., and other articles used by the rich, and upon which the duty is compulsory; the duty on hall-marked goods, refers to all articles—with the exception of watch-cases, which are free—marked at the request of intended purchasers, which then pay duty on the manufacture of them. It will be observed from these remarks, that the silver trade generally is not at all affected by the *duty tax;* the wares manufactured by the trade at large not coming directly under the compulsory provisions of the law bearing upon this subject. It has been said that the silver trade ministers to luxury, and no doubt that portion of it which manufactures costly articles of plate for the wealthy does so; but we fail to see exactly, that the same remark applies to that vast and increasing commercial industry which has sprung up of late years, and which bids fair to become one of the staple trades of the country. The duty-bearing articles are generally purchased by the classes of society who can well afford to pay the little extra which the duty imposes, and as the tax affects only that section of the silver trade which manufactures the article of luxury, it is not at all likely that the general trade would be increased by its entire removal. The duty, no doubt to most persons, may seem excessive, when calculated upon the percentage system; such for instance, as a tax of 20 per cent. upon spoons and forks; or one of 15 per cent. upon chains; or of $12\frac{1}{2}$ per cent. upon tea-sets, &c.; this appears unjustly oppressive, and undoubtedly affects the *silver-plate* manufacturer more vitally than any one else.

To the ordinary silversmith this question of duty is not likely to be of much importance; the agitation therefore commenced against it, may be expected to confine itself to those persons more directly affected, and whose interests would be advanced by its abolition.

The question of licences is one of far greater importance to the trade generally than that of duties, every manufacturer and dealer being compelled to procure a licence before he can carry on his business. If more direct action were taken in regard to this particular question, we believe that the whole trade would enter into it; for it resolves itself into this:—Why should the silversmith or goldsmith pay for a licence for the purpose of manufacturing and dealing, any more than the coppersmith, or the manufacturer of electro-plate, both of whom escape scot-free? We believe this to be an unjust tax, and that it ought not to be levied upon one particular trade any more than another. We have also distinctions made in the general class of silversmiths: we have those who may trade without any licence at all; those who may trade with a 46s. licence; and those who may trade with 115s. licence, that is, those who work or sell under 5 dwts., those who work or sell under 30 oz., and those who work or sell at any weight. Now this way of arranging the matter is very unsatisfactory to the trade generally; and any one of the first two traders to whom we have referred, is liable at any moment to be summoned before a criminal court for an infringement of the law, if he should happen to sell an article slightly over the weight for which he is duly licensed. At the present time a raid is being made upon the goldsmiths with reference to this particular question, and a number have already been summoned for infringing their licences in this manner. However, there appears to be some doubt with respect to the Act of Parliament bearing upon the subject, as in most of the cases the defendants have gained a verdict, the line of defence on their behalf being, that the clause of the act which bore upon the cases referred to, meant the weight in fine metal, *i.e.* "pure gold," of which the article was composed, and not that of the gross weight of the article sold. It was urged by those engaged in the various cases on the side of the defendants, that, for a 46s. licence, the vendor could sell an article in which the gold did not exceed two ounces, without any regard to the quality and weight made by alloy, and on this plea the magistrates granted them a verdict. In the higher courts we believe such verdicts would be reversed, for we firmly believe that the framers of the act meant no such thing, however defective may have been the legality of the points raised. The clause of the act to which we have alluded is No. 5, and runs as follows:—" All articles sold, or offered for sale, or taken in pawn, or delivered out of pawn, and alleged to be composed wholly, or in part, of gold or silver, are for the purposes of the above act to be deemed to be composed of gold or silver respectively; and if upon the hearing of any information for any offence against this act, any question shall arise touching the *quantity* of gold or silver contained *in any article*, the *proof of such quantity* shall be upon the defendant." The Excise authorities argue that this clause means that the absolute or gross weight of an article sold as gold must not exceed two ounces, and one sold as silver must not exceed thirty ounces, gross weight. If this view of the meaning of the act be eventually taken, and we believe it will, it will certainly operate to a greater extent against makers and vendors of gold articles than it will against silversmiths.

That part of the *clause* referring to the quantity of gold or silver contained in a given article, we believe has reference to articles containing jewels, &c., in their construction, which renders it exceedingly difficult to get at their exact weight, when the work is finally completed with these jewels properly affixed upon it, and not to the amount of fine material any article may contain by assay. The last part of the clause we have marked in italics, "proof of such quantity shall be upon the defendant," fully bears out these observations, because he is supposed to know the gross weight of any special article before the addition to it of any jewels.

We have been led to make these few remarks, in order to point out the gross anomalies which exist in the trade with respect to these licences, and to show the necessity of a reform taking place in a trade singled out from all the others, and made to pay a tax for the privilege of being allowed to make, or sell, articles in which gold or silver forms a component part. Therefore, if any action is to be taken in the matter, it must not be confined (if it is to be successful) to one particular branch of this important trade, but all must unite, and every influence should be brought to bear upon it in as forcible a manner as possible. The electro-plate manufacturer, and the dealer in *his* wares, ought in all common fairness to the trade, to be put upon the same footing as the silversmith, if this licence is to be still continued. In electro-plating establishments, thousands of ounces of silver are being annually used on the surface of such wares as are manufactured there; and if such decisions as those lately given at the Thames and other police courts, with reference to the Act of Parliament on the subject of gold and silver wares are upheld, we fail to see how the manufacturers of silver-plated articles, who are continually making and selling them, containing as they do, more silver than the general public would suppose, are to escape much longer these new interpretations of the Act of Parliament, and avoid being called upon to take out a licence in the same manner as the silversmiths. This is a tax in which the holder gets no direct return, and is levied in an unfair manner by the establishment of various grades of silversmiths, so that it gives a just cause for grievance. If the tax is to be upheld at all, why not make it equal by the establishment of one uniform rate for all trades alike?

CHAPTER XIV.

Useful Information for the Trade.

Silversmith's Alloy.

Copper, 1 oz.; nickel, 3 dwts. 12 grs; bismuth, 6 grs.; zinc, 2 dwts. 12 grs.; soft iron, 12 grs.; tin, 12 grs. This compound is said to form a fusible and malleable metal, that can be easily worked by the silversmith; it is also said to resist oxidation through atmospheric influences.

Silver Wares.

Never scratch-brush silver ware with a solution of soap and water; neither should it be washed with the solution if it can be avoided, as it gives it the colour of pewter; better to scratch in weak ale, or if plain, rub it with a piece of wash-leather and prepared chalk.

Cleaning Plate.

Carbonate of ammonia, 1 oz.; water, 4 oz.; Paris white, 16 oz.; well mix the ingredients together, and apply to the surface of the plate by means of a piece of soft leather or sponge.

Imitation Silver.

Fine silver, 6 dwts.; nickel, 6 dwts.; copper, 8 dwts. This alloy will cost about 1s. 9d. per ounce.

Another Recipe.

Fine silver, 5 dwts.; nickel, 6 dwts.; copper, 9 dwts. Cost about 1s. 6d. per ounce.

Removing Gold from Silver Articles.

Silver articles which have been gilt, may be brought back to their original colour, by simply covering them with a thick solution of borax, and then well annealing them. After this process if the articles are boiled for a short time in one of the whitening mixtures and scratched, they will present a beautiful white and uniform surface.

Oxydizing Silver.

A beautiful deep black colour, possessing great lustre, may be given to finished silver work by boiling it in the following preparation for some time:—Bromine, 5 grs.; bromide of potassium, 5 dwts.; water, 10 oz. The boiling should be effected in a stoneware pipkin, and generally from two to five minutes will suffice for the purpose. The work is finished after the proper colour has been attained, by well rubbing with a soft piece of wash-leather and a little best jeweller's rouge. It is better to make the work as bright as possible before submitting it to this mixture; for this reason it is preferable to thoroughly buff all plain surfaces on a piece of felt by the application of the lathe, as by that means a characteristic brightness is imparted.

Dipping Mixture.

Brass or metal goods may be cleaned and their oxides removed by dipping into the undermentioned liquid for a few seconds only:—Oil of vitriol, five parts; water, five parts; nitric acid, two and a half parts; spirits of salts, two drachms. Well mix the several ingredients together, and immerse the work in the solution cold. The mixture improves after a quantity of work has been dipped into it.

Silver Powder for Copper.

Chloride of silver, two parts; cream-of-tartar, two parts; alum, one part. Mix with water to the consistence of a paste, and apply with a soft leather or sponge; when sufficiently whitened, well polish.

Powder for Silver.

Chloride of silver, 1 oz.; sal ammoniac, 2 oz.; sandiver, 2 oz.; white vitriol, 2 oz.; bichloride of mercury, 5 dwts. Make into a paste with water and rub the articles over with it; then expose them to a good heat upon a clear fire, in order to run the silver and evaporate the mercury, after which process dip in very weak sulphuric acid to clean.

To Protect the Polish of Metals.

Melt one part by weight of best wax paraffin and when sufficiently cooled, add three parts of petroleum. Well mix together, and apply to the polished articles by means of a soft brush. The protecting film is required to be only very thin, therefore too much should not be put on.

Silver Stripping Mixture.

Sulphuric acid, six parts; nitric acid, one part. Take a large black-lead crucible or pipkin, and heat the mixture in it; when this is done, put in the work required to be stripped, occasionally withdrawing it to ascertain the progress made. The large proportion of sulphuric acid allows of the dissolution of the silver, and does not sensibly corrode or interfere with copper, or any of its alloys, if kept quite free from water; therefore be careful not to introduce wet articles into the mixture. After finally withdrawing the work, it should be well rinsed, annealed, and then boiled out.

Stripping Silver.

Put some strong oil of vitriol in a similar vessel to those above described, apply heat, and during the process add a few crystals of saltpetre. When the solution has become hot enough the work should be immersed in it, and be moved about or agitated until the silver is dissolved from the surface. The articles should not be allowed to remain too long in the solution, and if it does not remove the silver quickly, more saltpetre should be added from time to time until the desired end be attained.

Soft Solder.

Pure tin, two parts; lead, one part. Melt and well incorporate together; when this is done pour into strips for use.

Soldering Fluid.

Muriatic acid (spirits of salts), three parts; metallic zinc, one part; or as much as the acid will take up. When dissolved and all effervescence ceases, allow it to settle, then decant the clear solution from the sediment at the bottom of the vessel in which it has been made, and it is ready for use. If a small quantity of water be added to the mixture at this stage, say one-sixth, it will answer quite as well for some purposes. For soldering iron and steel, a very small portion of sal ammoniac is of great advantage to the mixture for promoting toughness.

Dissolving fine silver.—Nitric acid, two parts; water, one part.
Dissolving silver alloys.—Nitric acid, one part; water, two parts.
Dissolving copper.—Nitric acid, one part; water, four parts.
Dissolving soft solder.—Perchloride of iron, one part; water, four parts.
Dissolving silver solder.—Nitric acid one part; water four parts.
Dissolving sealing-wax.—Place for a time in a solution of spirits of wine.

Resist Varnish.

Dissolve resin, or copal, in essence of turpentine, or boiled linseed oil; to give it different shades of colour, add red lead, chrome yellow, or Prussian blue.

Plate Powder.

Whitening, two parts, white oxide of tin, one part, calcined hartshorn, one part. Reduce to a powder and well mix together; apply as usual.

Electro-plating Soft Solder.

Take nitric acid, 1 oz.; water, 2 oz.; copper about 1 oz. in small flat pieces; when the copper has all dissolved and effervescence has ceased, the solution is ready for use. To apply it, take up a few drops by means of a camel-hair pencil and apply it to the desired part, then touch it with a bright piece of steel, and there will be instantaneously a film of copper deposited. If the copper has not spread all over the desired part, the process should be repeated, when deposition in the plating bath will take place with perfect success.

Another Recipe.

Take sulphate of copper (that which accumulates in the whitening mixture), one ounce; water, six ounces. Reduce the sulphate of copper to a fine powder and dissolve it in the water. Treat according to the directions given in the previous one. A good mixture for effecting the same result may be made by dissolving verdigris in vinegar.

Testing Silver Wares.

Take nitric acid, six ounces; water, two ounces; bichromate of potash, one ounce. Reduce the salt of potash to a powder and well mix it with the acid and water. The solution is used cold, and should be placed in a stoppered glass bottle, the stopper having a long dropper extending into the mixture, which acts as the agent for conveying the liquid from the bottle to the article to be tested. The surface of the article should be perfectly clean, and to make certain what kind of metallic substance you are testing, it is advisable to rub a file over some obscure part of the surface and to apply the liquid to that part. The test liquid should be used, by means of the glass stopper, to the filed part, and immediately removed by a sponge damped with cold water. If the article consists of pure silver, there will appear a clean blood-red mark, which is less deep and lively in proportion to the quality of the metal. Upon platinum the test liquid has no action whatever; on German silver at first a brown mark appears, but this is removed by the sponge and cold water; on Britannia metal a black mark is produced; and on all the various metals an entirely different result takes place to that on silver; therefore the test is a simple one, and may be advantageously employed for the detection of any fraud in relation to the precious metal.

Another Test.

Water, 2 oz.; sulphuric acid, 2 drs.; chromate of potash, 4 dwts. This mixture is applied in the same way as before and produces a purple colour of various depths, according to the quality of the silver. No other metallic element exhibits the same colour with this preparation.

Perchloride of Iron.

Take spirits of salts, 8 oz.; crocus powder (jeweller's polishing material), 1 oz.; well mix them together and keep in solution. In preparing the mixture for the dissolution of soft solder, &c., take 1 oz. of it, and add to it 3 ozs. of boiling water.

Aluminium Alloy.

Copper, 18 dwts; aluminium, 2 dwts.

New Alloy.

Zinc, 10 dwts; soft iron, 1 dwt. This alloy is said by the inventor, to be remarkable for its whiteness and tenacity.

Removing Gold from Silver Wares.

Sometimes the process of annealing and boiling-out fails to effect the removal of the gold from articles which have been thickly gilt, in which case the work should be submitted to the action of the following chemical preparation:—Sulphuric acid, 6 ozs.; muriatic acid, 1 oz.; nitric acid, ½ oz. This mixture should be heated in a black-lead crucible or earthen vessel, and the work immersed until the dissolution of the gold takes place, carefully watching it during the progress of the operation. The gold may also be removed by using a strong solution of oil of vitriol, to which has been added a fair proportion of common salt.

Silver Plating Fluid.

Nitrate of silver, 1 oz.; cyanide of potassium, 2 ozs.; water, 12 ozs. Put the cyanide and the nitrate of silver into the water; shake them well together until they become thoroughly dissolved, then let the mixture stand till it becomes thoroughly clear. It is then ready for use. If preferred, a little prepared chalk may be used as an additional ingredient.

Plate-cleaning Powder.

Take of the finest rouge, and prepared chalk, equal parts, well mix and use dry by means of soft leather.

Solder for Aluminium.

Spelter, 18 dwts.; aluminium, 1 dwt. 6 grs.; copper, 18 grs. To be employed for soldering the *pure* white metal, and not the so-called aluminum bronze, that being commonly soldered with bath-metal solder.

CHAPTER XV.

Foreign Silver Standards.

TABLE showing the various standards of the silver work manufactured in the principal countries :—

Countries.	Silver per oz.			Thousandth parts.	Remarks.
	oz.	dwts.	grs.		
France	0	18	23	948-1000	Old Standard.
,,	0	19	0	950-1000	1st ,,
,,	0	18	0	900-1000	Coinage.
,,	0	16	0	800-1000	2nd Standard.
Germany	0	19	0	950-1000	1st ,,
,,	0	18	0	900-1000	2nd ,,
,,	0	16	0	800-1000	3rd ,,
,,	0	15	0	750-1000	4th ,,
Austria	0	19	0	950-1000	1st ,,
,,	0	18	0	900-1000	2nd ,,
,,	0	16	0	800-1000	3rd ,,
,,	0	15	0	750-1000	4th ,,
Geneva	0	19	0	950-1000	1st ,,
,,	0	17	12	875-1000	2nd ,,
,,	0	16	0	800-1000	3rd ,,
Holland	0	17	12	875-1000	Old Standard.
,,	0	18	16	933-1000	1st ,,
,,	0	16	16	833-1000	2nd ,,
Belgium	0	19	0	950-1000	1st ,,
,,	0	18	0	900-1000	2nd ,,
,,	0	16	0	800-1000	3rd ,,
Spain	0	14	18	738-1000	Lowest ,,
Portugal	0	16	21	844-1000	One only.

Countries.	Silver per oz.			Thousandth parts.	Remarks.
	oz.	dwts.	grs.		
Neuchatel .	0	16	0	800–1000	One only.
Russia . .	0	16	19	830–1000	1st Standard.
,,	0	15	0	750–1000	2nd ,,
Italy . . .	0	19	0	950–1000	1st ,,
,,	0	18	0	900–1000	2nd ,,
,,	0	16	0	800–1000	3rd ,,
China . .	0	19	14½	980–1000	About.
Norway . .	0	16	19	830–1000	One only.
Sweden . .	0	16	19	830–1000	,,
Denmark .	0	16	19	830–1000	,,

In France, all articles manufactured as silver are subject to *Government control* and pay duty, but this is very slight compared with the English duty, amounting only to one *franc* per *hectogramme* which is equal to about threepence per ounce. This is exclusive of the charge for testing and marking; the state of the articles sent for this purpose with regard to the state of manufacture is, moreover, very different from the custom in this country. Here they are sent in their rough or half-manufactured state, and this seems better suited to the particular processes through which they have to pass; whereas in France they may be tested and marked in their whole or finished state; and, if thought requisite, this operation may be performed while the goods are on their way to their final destination, by calling at the Control Office for that purpose.

The Continental silversmiths, especially the French workmen, exhibit much ingenuity, original thought, and refined taste, in the execution of their work; and the natural capacity for design which they possess enables them to produce articles of a very high order and artistic character. The construction of some of their productions is exceedingly ornamental and decorative, and in some instances this is even carried to excess, as may be seen from some very elaborate articles which they manufacture.

To them belongs the credit of being producers of the most artistic and best decorative work in the whole world. They set the *fashions* and work them out with a will to be only found in a people so enthusiastic as the French. Their jewellery is very elegant, light, and showy; some of which is prepared so thin as regards material, that it has to be supported underneath by a wax composition, which, however, gives increased strength to all articles so manipulated. With regard to articles of *vertu*, the French workmen certainly far excel those of any other country: they are more original, and bring into play greater ingenuity in the various processes which they employ in their manufactures. Still with all this ingenuity and skill, their works of art in this department are not durable, being very *tinsilfied*; in wear their shape and form soon undergo a change, and eventually they soon get destroyed. In this branch of art the French workman might learn something to his advantage from the English style of work, which is the most durable of any nation in the world. French silver plate and jewellery of the best manufacture partake of the first standard; all other kinds are of the lowest standard.

In Germany all silver manufactures are placed under *Imperative* control, and lower standards than those given in the table, under their respective heads, cannot be worked. The German style is similar to that of the French, but the former manufacture an unusually large quantity of filigree articles, very light in construction, tasteful, and cheap; and the possession of these advantages enables them to export to England and other countries their wares at a cheap rate. They are commonly sold by weight, and not so much per article; in many cases the charge does not exceed 12s. 6d. per ounce. In filigree work the Germans cannot equal the taste and variety displayed in Indian workmanship. In India the natives have definite designs, but the Germans are too fond of a variety of colours in their wares, which do not always harmonize with their particular kind of work.

In Austria silver manufactures are commonly ornamented by enamel, niello, &c., which gives them a very pleasing appearance. They are usually light and showy, and something after the style of French work. The laws affecting the Austrian silver workers are the same as those of Germany.

The English style of work is strong and solid; and is undoubtedly superior to that of all Continental manufacturers as regards substantial workmanship, careful manipulation, and durability. It is, moreover, capable of a higher finish, and possesses more evenness of surface, together with a combination of strength, that admirably suits it for articles and utensils for daily use, and which causes it to be preferred before that of any other nation; and while France, Germany, and other countries may exhibit greater ingenuity, to England belongs the credit of producing the best *finished* and the most *durable* work of any nation in the world.

INDEX.

ACIDS, vegetable, 10
    Action of acids on copper, 44
    of silver under heat, 8
Acts of the Legislature, 189
    on licences, 186
    clause on, 193, 194
Advantages of scorification, 20
Air in furnace, 33
Alkalies, caustic, 10
Allowed, remedy in fineness, 72
Alloy, 41
    Clark's patent, 172
    commonly used, 63
    for cupel quantity, 35
    for hall-marking, 62
    for plate, 71
    for silver-wares, 72
    French, for coinage, 69
    French, for plate, 69
    French, for silver-ware, 69
    German, for coinage, 71
    instructions in preparing, 70
    new, 205
    Nos. 1 to 8, 64—67
    of the highest quality, 62
    silver dissolving, 202
    standard, 61
    white, 172

Alloy, with copper, 68
    with palladium, 173
    with platinum, 172
Alloys of common silver, 167—170
    characteristics of, 173, 174
    imitation, 166—173
    imitation, uses of, 173
    of nickel, 46
    of silver, 42
    of tin with gold, 49
    of tin with silver, 49
    silversmith's, 40, 197
Aluminium alloy, 205
    solder, 206
Amalgam, 41
Amalgamation of zinc, 153
America, 11
American supply of silver, 12
Ancient method of assaying, 37
    workers in tin, 48
Ancients, 6
Annealing silver, 109
Anthracite, 21
Art in soldering, 90
    in the silver trade, 122
Articles, hand-made, 54
    of silver common, 147

INDEX.

Art of soldering, 74
Arts, metals employed in, 41
Assay crucible, 16
    charge for, 17
    English system, 39
    fluxes, 16
    of silver ores, 16
    scorification, 19
    weighing of, 30
Assayer's muffle, 28
Assaying, borax, use of, in, 22
    Dr. Lamborn on, 38
    of silver ores, 16
Austrian style of work, 211

BATTERY, Bunsen's, 152
    constant, 150
    exciting mixture, 151
    for plating, 150
    solution, 151
Bean-shot copper, 44
Best crucibles, 95
Birmingham, 52
Black cyanide, 157
Blowpipes, 89
Boiling-out mixture, 144
    pan, 143
    pickle, 93
Bone-ash, 32
    cupel, 33
Borax, 22
    sprinkle, 92
Breaking-down rollers, 112
Brightening, 29
British Isles, 11
Brown colour on silver goods, 146
Burning of lemel, 104
    of polishings, 179, 180
Burnished silver work, 124
Burnishing silver work, 161, 162

CALCULATED alloys, various, 80
Calculating the qualities of silver, 64
Carbonate of soda, 16, 102
Casting-mould, 18
Cause of inferior work, 74
Caustic alkalies, 10
Cement for chasers, 121
Chain bracelets, 128
Chain solder, 85
Characteristics of imitation alloys, 173, 174
    of metals, 41
Charcoal, 99
Charge and flux for crucible, 23
    for assay, 17
    for scorification assay, 20
Chief places for filigree, 53
    of filigree manufacture, 8
    uses of silver, 9
Chinese filigree, 56
    silver, 170
Chloride of silver, 183
Christianity and tin, 48
Clark's alloy, 172
Cleaning plate, 198
    powder for plate, 206
Coinage, 69
    alloys for, 71
    English, 61
    French, 69
    German, 71
Collecting-vessels, 184
Colour-improving, 149
Common articles of silver, 147
    easy solder, 85
    silver alloy, 167—173
    silver solder, 84
    solder, 85
    solders, 84
Composition for solder, 81

INDEX.

Conducting-wires, 154
Connections for soldering, 77
Constant battery, 150
Continental cheap labour, 54
    method of assaying, 22
    silversmiths, 208
Copper, 42
    action of acids on, 44
    bean-shot, 44
    characteristics of, 43
    chemical name, 44
    dissolving, 202
    for alloying, 68
    powder for, 199
    protoxide of, 44
    solder with, 76
Cost of silver alloys, 64, 67
    of silver-rolling, 112
Cronstedt, 45
Crucible, dimensions, 16
    for lemel, 106
    mixture for, 104
    pouring lemel from, 107
    weighing metal for, 95
Crucible assay, 16
    fluxes for, 16
    process of, 19
Crucibles, 95
    best to employ, 95
    action with fluxes, 96
    testing soundness, 97
Cupel, defects in, 33
    mode of manufacture, 26
    mould, 27
    quantity of alloy for, 35
    tongs, 28
    withdrawal of silver, 34
Cupellation, 26
    of silver ores, 31
    purity of silver, 37
Cup-fusing, 19
Currents of air to furnace, 33

Cyanide solution, 156
    black, 157

DEFECTS in bone-ash cupel, 33
Density of nickel, 45
    of silver, 7
    of tin, 48
Dimensions of crucible, 16
Dipping-mixture, 199
Directions on melting, 94
    in preparing solders, 88
Discoverer of electro-plating, 149
Dissolving silver, 202
    copper, 202
    impurities, 103
    soft-solder, 202
    silver solder, 202
    sealing-wax, 202
    tin, 48
Dissolution of silver, 9
Dr. Lamborn, 38
Drawbacks to hall-marking, 63
Draw-bench, 114, 115
Drawing fine wire, 116
Draw-plate, 114
Draw-tongs, 115
Drossy solders, 88
Drum for wire-drawing, 115
Ductility of nickel, 45
    of silver, 6
    of tin, 49
    of zinc, 48

EAST Indian silversmiths, 141
Easy solders, 79
    for chains, 85
    silver solder, 80
    solder, 81
    solder, for filigree work, 84
    solder, common, 85
Economical processes, 175
Economy, 1

INDEX

Elucidation, technical, 2
Electrolysis, 96
Electro-plating, 147
　　processes of, 143
　　methods of, 208
Electro-metallurgy, 52
Employed metals, 2
Enamelling, 131
English alloys commonly used, 84
English and Foreign soldiers, 2
　　coinage, 68
　　forges, workers, 63
　　hall-marking, 63
　　standard in silver, 60
　　style of work, 211
　　test in of assay, 70
Etching the surfaces of silver, 133
Exciting mixture for battery, 151
Experts, Government, 73

FILIGREE manufacture, 8
　　method of making, 57
　　of China and Japan, 56
　　of Norway and Sweden, 56
　　silver work, 127
　　wire, how, 54
　　work, 8, 10, 32
　　working, 56
Filed filigree, 70
Finishing of twisted wire, 54
Flux, an exchange for crucible, 23
　　for soldering, 77
　　repairing, 101
Flux for assay, 16
　　employed on crucibles, 96
　　employed in melting, 97
Foreign silver currency, 13
　　silver standards, 207, 8
　　workmen, 2
French alloy for silver ware, 69
　　of for coinage, 69
　　alloy for plate, 70

French, duty, 208
　　standards, 69
　　style of work, 211
Fusibility of nickel, 75
　　of tin, 75
　　of silvers of lines, 80
Fusing-cup, 15

GALVANIC ring, 126
　　German coinage, 71
　　　standards, 72
　　　style of work, 210
Gold alloyed with tin, 44
　　mode of soldering, 88
　　removing from silver, 105, 205
Goods, silver, bronze colour of, 146
Government experts, 73
Gravity, specific, of zinc, 47
Great Britain, 51
Guarantee mark, 73

HALL-MARKING, alloy for, 62
　　drawbacks, 63
Hand-made articles, 54
Hard silver solders, 79
　　solder, best, 81
Hardest silver solder, 78
　　silver solder, 79
Hardness of silver, 8
Hawksparrow, 144
Heating power of silver, 7
Hollow silver work, 131

IMITATION silver alloys, 166, 173
　　alloys, characteristics of, 173
　　alloys, uses of, 173
　　silver, 166, 147
Improving colour of electro-plate, 142
Impurities, dissolving, 103
Indian filigree workers, 8

INDEX.

Indian filigree silversmiths, 141
    mode of whitening, 142
Industrial arts, 41
Inferior plating solution, 159
Ingot mould, 100
Instructions in preparing alloys, 68
Irregularities in rolling-mills, 110

JAPANESE filigree, 56
    Jewellery trade, state of, 12

LAW on silver wares, 73
    Lead, 103
Legislature, Acts of, 186
Lemaille solder, 91
Lemel, 104
    burning, 104
    crucible, 106
    melting, 104—106
    pot for, 104
    pouring from crucible, 107
Licence question, 191
Licences, 190
Litharge, 17
Loss, working, 175
    real, 175
    total working, 176

MAKING filigree, 56
    Malleability of nickel, 45
    of silver, 6
    of tin, 49
    of zinc, 48
Maltese filigree, 55
Manner of removing litharge, 35
Manufacture of cupels, 26
    inferior, 73
    of filigree, 53
    of silver wares, 72
Mark, guarantee, 72
Marking, hall, 62

Marking, hall, drawbacks of, 63
Material, bad working, 98
Mechanical uses of silver, 52
Medium solders, 82
    silver solder, 79
Melting, crucible for, 99
    directions on, 94
    fluxes employed, 96
    imitation alloys, 166
    points of metals, 51
    solders, 86
    tongs for, 100
Mercury, 15
Metal, fusible, 98
    pure, 56
Metallic elements, table of, 50
Metals, 41
    their characteristics 41
Method of assaying, 22
    for whitening, 139
    of calculating qualities, 64
    of preparing filigree, 59
Mills, rolling, 110
    Kemp's, 111
Mine, richest, 12
Mining, 11
Mixing metals for melting, 97
Mixture, boiling-out, 144
    dipping, 199
    for washing-out, 138
    stripping, 200
Mixtures for whitening, 147
    for battery, 152
    nitrate of silver, 148
Modes of melting lemel, 105
    of preparing ring, 130
    of whitening, Indian, 142
    of whitening, our, 145
Molten metal, 99
    lemel, 103
Mould-casting, 18
Mould cupel, 27

INDEX.

Mod'd ingot, 100
Muffle assayers, 28

NATIVE silver, 11
   Necessity for pure metal, 56
New alloy, 205
   method for filigree, 59
Nickel, 45
Nitrate of silver, 8
   of silver, mixture, 148
Nitre, 10
Norway filigree, 59

OLD method of filigree, 57
   Oldest method of whitening, 140
On the melting of silver, 94
   working of silver, 108
Ores of silver, 9
Our mode of whitening, 145
Oxidizing silver work, 163

PALLADIUM alloy, 173
   Pallion solder, 89
Parliament, Acts of, 190
Perchloride of iron, 205
Physical properties of metals, 51
Plain solid work, 127
Plate, 4
   alloy for, 70
   cleaning powder, 206
   electro, 46, 150
   French, 70
   manufacture, 190
   powder, 202
Plating, battery for 150
   discoverer of, 149
   electro, 150
   fluid silver, 206
   soft solder, 201
   solution, 157
Plating solutions, recovery of silver, 160

Platinum alloy, 172
Plumbago, crucible for melting, 99
Polished silver, 7
Polishing, 135
   lathe, 137
Polishings, burning of, 179
Pouring off lemel, 107
Powder for silver, 200
Precious metal, 1
Precipitation of silver, 183
Preparation for assay, 17
   of bone-ash, 32
   of plating solution, 155
   of solders, 87
Present state of silver trade, 128
Press, 127
   stamping, 132
Price of silver, 9
Principal alloys of silver, 42
   metals, 51
Process, scorification, 18
   advantages of, 20
   details of, 23
   of silver recovery, 180—183
Producing various shades, 165
Production of surface, 135
Protect polish of metals, 200
Protoxide of copper, 44
   of zinc, 102
Pure silver, 3
Purity of silver, 37

QUALITIES used by silversmiths, 64
Quantity of alloy for cupel, 35
Quick-running solder, 85

RAISED work, 120
Raising, 122
Recovery of silver from waste, 160
   of silver from waste waters, 183, 185

Refining surface of silver, 146
Remarks on silver solders, 80
Remedy in fineness, 72
Removal of litharge, 35
Removing gold from silver, 198
   gold from silver wares, 205
Resist varnish, 202
Ring, galvanic, 129
   preparing wire for, 130
Rollers, slitting, 112
   breaking-down, 112
Rolling, silver, 108
   mills, 110
   silver, 112
   wire, 113

SAL-AMMONIAC, 103
   Saving waste, 177
Scientific name for tin, 49
Scorification process, 18
   assay, 20
Scorifier, 19
   special form, 19
Scrap silver, 102
Scratch-brushing, 161
   brush lathe, 161
Scriptural testimony, 37, 38
Sealing-wax, dissolving, 202
Sediment, 185
Separation of silver, 21
Shades, 165
Shop floors, 177
Shot-copper for alloying, 44
Silver a precious metal, 1
   action under heat, 8
   alloy, dissolving, 202
   alloy for coinage, 72
   alloy, standard, 61
   alloyed with tin, 49
   alloys, Chinese, 170
   alloys, common, 167, 172
   alloys, imitation, 167, 172

Silver alloys, No. 1, 64
   No. 2, 64
   No. 3, 65
   No. 4, 65
   No. 5, 66
   No. 6, 66
   No. 7, 67
   No. 8, 67
   American supp'y, 12
   and aqua-regia, 8
   and mercury, 15
   annealing, 103
   articles, 194
   articles, common, 147
   assay, 14
   British, chief sources, 13
   British yield, 11
   burnishing, 162
   characteristics of, 5
   chief alloy of, 30
   chloride, 183
   commercial, 9
   currency, 6
   currency, foreign, 13
   density of, 7
   dissolution of, 9
   dissolving, 202
   ductility of, 6
   easily tarnished, 129
   European supplies, 12
   filigree work, 125
   for filigree work, 5
   fusibility of, 7
   goods, brown colour, 146
   hardness of, 8
   heating power of, 7
   imitation, 198
   known to the ancients, 6
   law on, 73
   lead and tin in, 103
   malleability of, 6
   mechanical uses of, 32

INDEX. 219

Silver, method of calculating, 63
    mining, 11
    native, 11
    nitrate of, 8, 148
    ores, 9
    ores, assay of, 16
    oxidizing, 163, 198
    plating fluid, 206
    polished, 7
    powder, 199, 200
    powder for copper, 199
    precipitating, 183
    principal alloys, 42
    pure, 3
    purity of, after cupellation, 37
    recovery of, 160
    recovery, 177, 178
    rolling, 109
    rolling, table of cost, 112
    solders, 81
    solder, dissolving, 202
    solder, easy, 82
    solder, hardest, 79
    solder, medium, 82
    solder, zinc in, 46
    solders, fusibility of, 80
    standards, foreign, 207
    stripping mixture, 200
    surface, improving, 139
    tarnished, 7
    test for, 6
    trade, art in, 123
    uses of, 9
    various qualities, 52
    ware, 69, 195
    ware, French, 69
    ware, German, 71
    wares, alloys for, 72
    wares, removing gold, 205
    wares, testing, 203
    weighing, 30
    whitening of, 140

Silver work, burnished, 124
    work, hollow, 131
    yield of, 13
Silversmiths, 63
    alloys, 49, 197
    continental, 209
    East Indian, 141
    working, 2
Skittle-pot, 25
    for lemel, 104
Slitting-rollers, 112
Snarling-tools, 122
Soda, carbonate of, 16, 102
Soft solder, 90, 202
    dissolving, 202
    plating, 202
Solder, composition for, 81, 93
    best hard, 81
    common, 83, 85
    common easy, 86
    dish, 89
    easy, 79, 82, 86
    filed, 76
    for aluminium, 206
    for chains, 85
    for filigree, 84, 91
    hard, 77
    Lemaille, 91
    medium, 76, 82
    paillon, 88
    quick running, 85
    very common, 87
    with arsenic, 86
    with copper and silver, 76
    with zinc, 76
Soldering, art of, 74, 90
    alloy, dissolving, 202
    connections, 77
    mode of, 88
    fluid, 201
    flux, 77
Solders containing tin, 73

INDEX.

Solders, drossy, 88
   for enamelling, 84
   melting of, 83
   preparations of, 87
   remarks on, 80
   tin in, 49
Solid plain work, 127
Solution for battery, 151
   cyanide, 156
   for plating, 157, 158
   for precipitation, 184
   inferior, 159
   No. 1, 163
   No. 2, 164
   No. 3, 164
Soundness of crucibles, 97
Spain, 11
Sparrow-hawk, 119
Special soldering flux, 92
Specific gravity of zinc, 47
Spelter, 46
   used by jewellers, 47
Spinning, 134, 135
Sprouting, 29
Stamped work, 126
Stamping-press, 132
Standard alloy for hall-marking, 62
   alloys of the highest quality, 62
Standards, English, 60
   French, 70
   German, 71
State in which silver is found, 14
State of silver trade, 128
State of the jewellery trade, 12
Stone, Water-of-Ayr, 136
Strength of solution, 152
Stripping silver, 201
Style of work, Austrian, 211
   English, 211
   French, 209

Style of work, German, 210
   Indian, 210
Surface, refining of silver, 145
Swedish filigree, 56
System of assaying, 39.

TABLE of cost of silver-rolling, 112
   of metallic elements, 50
   of various duties, 90
Tarnishing of silver, 7
   of zinc, 47
Tax or licence, 196
Technical education, 2
Test for pure silver, 6
Testing crucible, 97
   silver wares, 203
Testimony, Scriptural, 37, 38
Test-ring, 31
Tin, 48
   alloyed with gold, 49
   alloyed with silver, 49
   ancient workers, 48
   and Christianity, 48
   density of, 48
   dissolving, 48
   ductility of, 49
   fusibility of, 48
   in solders, 49, 76
   malleability of, 49
   scientific name, 50
   tenacity of, 49
   vapours, 49
Tongs, draw, 115
Tongs for melting, 100
Total working loss, 176
Trade, silver, state of, 128
   useful information for, 197
Treatment, economical, 1
   in furnace, 18
   of waste, 179

INDEX.

Treatment of waste liquids, 180
Twisting wires, 58

UNJUSTLY assessed tax, 195
    Uses of silver, 9
      borax, 22
      for imitation alloys, 173
      of lathe, 58
      silver, mechanical, 52

VAPOURS of tin, 49
    Various qualities of silver, 52
      duties, table of, 190
      metals, mixing, 95
Varnish, resist, 1

WARES, ornamental, 4
    law on, 73
    removing gold from, 205
    silver alloy for, 72
    silver, 197
    testing purity, 203
Washing-out mixture, 138
Waste, saving, 178
    liquids, treatment of, 180
    treatment of, 181
    waters, 182—183
    water, precipitation in, 184
Water-of-Ayr stone, 139
Weighing of silver assay, 30
Whitening, old method, 140
    Indian mode of, 142
    our mode of, 145
    powder, 147
Wire for filigree, 59
    rolling, 112
    drawer's drum, 115
    drawer's punch, &c., 117
    drawing, fine, 117

Wires, conducting, 154
Withdrawal from cupel, 34
Work, Austrian style, 211
    burnishing, 162
    English, style, 211
    filigree, 5, 40, 125
    French duty on, 208
    French style, 209
    German style, 210
    hollow, 131
    Indian style, 210
    silver, burnishing, 124
    solid, 127
    stamped, 132
Workers, Indian, 5
Working filigree, 56
    loss, 175
    material, bad, 98
    silversmiths, 2
    total, 176
Workmen, English and Foreign, 2
Workmanship, process of, 55
Wrought work, 118

YIELD of silver, 11, 13

ZINC, 46
    a fusible metal, 98
    amalgamation, 153
    annealing, 47
    ductility of, 48
    gravity of, 47
    in silver solder, 46, 76
    malleability of, 48
    on floors, 178
    tarnishing of, 47
    tenacity of, 48

BY THE AUTHOR OF
"THE SILVERSMITH'S HANDBOOK."

Just published, crown 8vo, cloth, price 7s. 6d.

THE
PRACTICAL GOLD-WORKER;
OR, THE

GOLDSMITH'S & JEWELLER'S INSTRUCTOR.

THE ART OF ALLOYING, MELTING, REDUCING, COLOURING, COLLECTING, AND REFINING.

THE PROCESSES OF MANIPULATION, RECOVERY OF WASTE, CHEMICAL AND PHYSICAL PROPERTIES OF GOLD, WITH A NEW SYSTEM OF MINING ITS ALLOYS; SOLDERS, ENAMELS, AND OTHER USEFUL RULES AND RECIPES, ETC.

"A good, sound, technical educator, and will be generally accepted as an authority. It gives full particulars for mixing alloys and enamels, is essentially a book for the workshop, and exactly fulfils the purpose intended."—*Horological Journal.*

"The best work yet printed on its subject for a reasonable price. There can be no doubt that the more the work is referred to and tested the better it will be appreciated, and we have no doubt that it will speedily become a standard book, which few will care to be without."—*Jeweller and Metalworker.*

"A thoroughly practical treatise on the different uses and applications of gold &c., as a guide to workmen and apprentices it must prove of great value. In fact there is such a valuable amount of information contained in so very small a compass, that we have no doubt this work will meet with the general appreciation it unquestionably so well deserves."—*Watchmaker and Jeweller.*

"The information is thoroughly practical, and will, no doubt, prove useful to the artisan as well as interesting to the general reader."—*Academy.*

"It is essentially a practical manual, intended primarily for the use of working jewellers, but is well adapted to the wants of amateurs and apprentices, containing, as it does, trustworthy information that only a practical man can supply."—*English Mechanic.*

"The writer not only aims at removing obstacles from the path of the inexperienced craftsman, but on every possible point he supplies information for the purpose of aiding in his advancement and efficiency. There are many processes shown which are entirely new, and which have, nevertheless, been tested by experience, and several secrets which have been hitherto jealously guarded. We think it will prove a boon to that class for whom it is mainly intended."—*Birmingham Daily Gazette.*

"The treatise is a thorough one in every respect, dealing practically with the intricacies and difficulties of the goldworker's art in all its various branches and stages."—*Liverpool Albion.*

"This convenient little book appears to be very full, and, at the same time, remarkably concise and practical, and will doubtless become a manual of reference and a guide to the jeweller's workshop."—*Morning Advertiser.*

CROSBY LOCKWOOD & CO., 7, STATIONERS' HALL COURT, E.C.

LONDON, July, 1877.

A Catalogue of Books
INCLUDING MANY
NEW & STANDARD WORKS
IN
ENGINEERING, ARCHITECTURE,
AGRICULTURE, MATHEMATICS, MECHANICS,
SCIENCE, &c. &c.

PUBLISHED BY

CROSBY LOCKWOOD & CO.,
7, STATIONERS'-HALL COURT, LUDGATE HILL, E.C.

ENGINEERING, SURVEYING, &c.

Humber's New Work on Water-Supply.
A COMPREHENSIVE TREATISE on the WATER-SUPPLY of CITIES and TOWNS. By WILLIAM HUMBER, Assoc. Inst. C.E., and M. Inst. M.E. Author of "Cast and Wrought Iron Bridge Construction," &c. &c. Imp. 4to. Illustrated with 50 Double Plates, 2 Single Plates, Coloured Frontispiece, and upwards of 250 Woodcuts, and containing 400 pages of Text, elegantly and substantially half-bound in morocco. Price 6l. 6s.

List of Contents:
I. Historical Sketch of some of the means that have been adopted for the Supply of Water to Cities and Towns.—II. Water and the Foreign Matter usually associated with it.—III. Rainfall and Evaporation.—IV. Springs and the water-bearing formations of various districts.—V. Measurement and Estimation of the Flow of Water.—VI. On the Selection of the Source of Supply.—VII. Wells.—VIII. Reservoirs.—IX. The Purification of Water.—X. Pumps.—XI. Pumping Machinery.—XII. Conduits.—XIII. Distribution of Water.—XIV. Meters, Service Pipes, and House Fittings.—XV. The Law and Economy of Water Works.—XVI. Constant and Intermittent Supply.—XVII. Description of Plates.—Appendices, giving Tables of Rates of Supply, Velocities, &c. &c., together with Specifications of several Works illustrated, among which will be found: Aberdeen, Bideford, Canterbury, Dundee, Halifax, Lambeth, Rotherham, Dublin, and others.

OPINIONS OF THE PRESS.
"The most systematic and valuable work upon water supply hitherto produced in English, or in any other language."—*Engineer's Text-book,* Nov. 3, 1876.
"Mr. Humber's work is characterised almost throughout by an exhaustiveness much more distinctive of French and German than of English technical treatises."—*Engineer. Published,* Dec. 15, 1876.
"We can congratulate Mr. Humber on having been able to give so large an amount of information on a subject so important as the water-supply of cities and towns. The plates, fifty in number, are mostly drawings of executed works, and alone would have commanded the attention of every engineer whose practice may lie in this branch of the profession."—*Iron,* Dec. 2, 1876.

Humber's Great Work on Bridge Construction.

A COMPLETE and PRACTICAL TREATISE on CAST and WROUGHT-IRON BRIDGE CONSTRUCTION, including Iron Foundations. In Three Parts—Theoretical, Practical, and Descriptive. By WILLIAM HUMBER, Assoc. Inst. C.E., and M. Inst. M.E. Third Edition, revised and much improved, with 115 Double Plates (20 of which now first appear in this edition), and numerous additions to the Text. In 2 vols. imp. 4to, price 6l. 16s. 6d. half-bound in morocco.

"A very valuable contribution to the standard literature of civil engineering. In addition to elevations, plans, and sections, large scale details are given, which very much enhance the instructive worth of these illustrations. No engineer would willingly be without so valuable a fund of information."—*Civil Engineer and Architect's Journal.*

"Mr. Humber's stately volumes lately issued—in which the most important bridges erected during the last five years, under the direction of our most eminent engineers, are drawn and specified in great detail."—*Engineer.*

"A book—and particularly a large and costly treatise like Mr. Humber's which has reached its third edition may certainly be said to have established its own reputation."—*Engineering.*

Strains, Formulæ & Diagrams for Calculation of.

A HANDY BOOK for the CALCULATION of STRAINS in GIRDERS and SIMILAR STRUCTURES, and their STRENGTH; consisting of Formulæ and Corresponding Diagrams, with numerous Details for Practical Application, &c. By WILLIAM HUMBER, Assoc. Inst. C.E., &c. Second Edition. Fcap. 8vo, with nearly 100 Woodcuts and 3 Plates, price 7s. 6d. cloth.

"The arrangement of the matter in this little volume is as convenient as it well could be. . . . The system of employing diagrams as a substitute for complex computations is one justly coming into great favour, and in that respect Mr. Humber's volume is fully up to the times."—*Engineering.*

"The formulæ are neatly expressed, and the diagrams good."—*Athenæum.*

"Mr. Humber has rendered a great service to the architect and engineer by producing a work especially treating on the methods of delineating the strains on iron beams, roofs, and bridges by means of diagrams."—*Builder.*

Barlow on the Strength of Materials, enlarged.

A TREATISE ON THE STRENGTH OF MATERIALS, with Rules for application in Architecture, the Construction of Suspension Bridges, Railways, &c.; and an Appendix on the Power of Locomotive Engines, and the effect of Inclined Planes and Gradients. By PETER BARLOW, F.R.S. A New Edition, revised by his Sons, P. W. BARLOW, F.R.S., and W. H. BARLOW, F.R.S., to which are added Experiments by HODGKINSON, FAIRBAIRN, and KIRKALDY; an Essay (with Illustrations) on the effect produced by passing Weights over Elastic Bars, by the Rev. ROBERT WILLIS, M.A., F.R.S. And Formulæ for Calculating Girders, &c. The whole arranged and edited by W. HUMBER, Assoc. Inst. C.E., Author of "A Complete and Practical Treatise on Cast and Wrought-Iron Bridge Construction," &c. 8vo, 400 pp., with 19 large Plates, and numerous woodcuts, 18s. cloth.

"The book is undoubtedly worthy of the highest commendation."—*Mining Journal.*

"The best book on the subject which has yet appeared. . . . We know of no work that so completely fulfils its mission."—*English Mechanic.*

"The standard treatise upon this particular subject."—*Engineer.*

Iron and Steel.

'IRON AND STEEL': a Work for the Forge, Foundry, Factory, and Office. Containing Ready, Useful, and Trustworthy Information for Ironmasters and their Stocktakers; Managers of Bar, Rail, Plate, and Sheet Rolling Mills; Iron and Metal Founders; Iron Ship and Bridge Builders; Mechanical, Mining, and Consulting Engineers; Architects, Contractors, Builders, and Professional Draughtsmen. By CHARLES HOARE, Author of 'The Slide Rule,' &c. Eighth Edition. Revised throughout and considerably enlarged. With folding Scales of "Foreign Measures compared with the English Foot," and "fixed Scales of Squares, Cubes, and Roots, Areas, Decimal Equivalents, &c." Oblong, 32mo, leather elastic-band, 6s.

"We cordially recommend this book to those engaged in considering the details of all kinds of iron and steel works. . . . . It has been compiled with care and accuracy. . . . . Many useful rules and hints are given for lessening the amount of arithmetical labour which is always more or less necessary in arranging iron and steel work of all kinds, and a great quantity of useful tables for preparing estimates of weights, dimensions, strengths of structures, costs of work, &c., will be found in Mr. Hoare's book."—*Naval Science.*

Weale's Engineers' Pocket-Book.

THE ENGINEERS', ARCHITECTS', and CONTRACTORS' POCKET-BOOK (LOCKWOOD & CO.'s; formerly WEALE'S). Published Annually. In roan tuck, gilt edges, with 10 Copper-Plates and numerous Woodcuts. Price 6s.

"A vast amount of really valuable matter condensed into the small dimensions of a book, which is, in reality, what it professes to be—a pocket-book. . . . . We cordially recommend the book."—*Colliery Guardian.*

"It contains a large amount of information peculiarly valuable to those for whose use it is compiled. We cordially commend it to the engineering and architectural professions generally."—*Mining Journal.*

Iron Bridges, Girders, Roofs, &c.

A TREATISE on the APPLICATION of IRON to the CONSTRUCTION of BRIDGES, GIRDERS, ROOFS, and OTHER WORKS; showing the Principles upon which such Structures are Designed, and their Practical Application. Especially arranged for the use of Students and Practical Mechanics, all Mathematical Formulæ and Symbols being excluded. By FRANCIS CAMPIN, C.E. Second Edition revised and corrected. With numerous Diagrams. 12mo, cloth boards, 3s.

"Invaluable to those who have not been educated in mathematics."—*Colliery Guardian.*
"Remarkably accurate and well written."—*Artisan.*

Mechanical Engineering.

A PRACTICAL TREATISE ON MECHANICAL ENGINEERING: comprising Metallurgy, Moulding, Casting, Forging, Tools, Workshop Machinery, Mechanical Manipulation, Manufacture of the Steam Engine, &c. &c. With an Appendix on the Analysis of Iron and Iron Ore, and Glossary of Terms. By FRANCIS CAMPIN, C.E. Illustrated with 91 Woodcuts and 28 Plates of Slotting, Shaping, Drilling, Punching, Shearing, and Riveting Machines—Blast, Refining, and Reverberatory Furnaces—Steam Engines, Governors, Boilers, Locomotives, &c. 8vo, cloth, 12s.

6 WORKS IN ENGINEERING, SURVEYING, ETC.,

Pioneer Engineering.

PIONEER ENGINEERING. A Treatise on the Engineering Operations connected with the Settlement of Waste Lands in New Countries. By EDWARD DOBSON, Assoc. Inst. C.E., Author of "The Art of Building," &c. With numerous Plates and Wood Engravings. Crown 8vo, 10s. 6d. [*Just published.*

"A most useful handbook to engineering pioneers."—*Iron,* Dec. 2, 1876.
"The author's experience has been turned to good account, and the book is likely to be of considerable service to proper explorers."—*Building News.*
"Promises a great deal, and fulfils most of its promises. . . . Of use to the colonial pioneering surveyor and engineer."—*Scotsman.*

New Iron Trades' Companion.

THE IRON AND METAL TRADES' COMPANION: Being a Calculator containing a Series of Tables upon a new and comprehensive plan for expeditiously ascertaining the value of any goods bought or sold by weight, from 1s. per cwt. to 112l. per cwt., and from one farthing per pound to one shilling per pound. Each Table extends from one pound to 100 tons; to which are appended **Rules** on Decimals, Square and Cube Root, Mensuration of Superficies and Solids, &c.; also Tables of Weights of Materials, and other Useful Memoranda. By THOMAS DOWNIE. Strongly bound in leather, 396 pp., price 9s.

"A most useful set of tables, and will supply a want, for nothing like them before existed."—*Building News,* Dec. 8, 1876.
"We have tested the calculations in various old hand-books, and always found them correct."—*Engineer,* Dec. 1, 1876.
"Will save the possessor the trouble of making numerous laborious calculations. Although specially adapted to the iron and metal trades, the tables contained in this handy little companion will be found useful in every other trade in which any article is bought and sold by weight."—*Railway News,* Dec. 2, 1876.

Sanitary Work.

SANITARY WORK IN THE SMALLER TOWNS AND IN VILLAGES. Comprising:—1. Some of the more Common Forms of Nuisance and their Remedies; 2. Drainage; 3. Water Supply. A useful book for Members of Local Boards and Rural Sanitary Authorities, Health Officers, Engineers, Surveyors, Builders, and Contractors. By CHARLES SLAGG, Assoc. Inst. C.E. Crown 8vo, cloth, price 5s. [*Just published.*

"Mr. Slagg has brought together much valuable information, and has a happy facility of expression; and he has been industrious in collecting data."—*Athenæum.*
"This is a very useful book, and may be safely recommended. . . . The author, Mr. Charles Slagg, has had practical experience in the works of which he treats. There is a great deal of work required to be done in the smaller towns and villages, and this little volume will help those who are seeking to do it."—*Builder.*

Steam Engine.

STEAM AND THE STEAM ENGINE, Stationary and Portable, an Elementary Treatise on. Being an Extension of Mr. John Sewell's Treatise on Steam. By D. KINNEAR CLARK, C.E., M.I.C.E., Author of "Railway Locomotives," &c. With Illustrations. 12mo, cloth, 4s.

"Every essential part of the subject is treated of competently, and in a popular style."—*Iron.*

Strains.

...: Horse Power, Motion, Toothed Wheel
Driving Bands, Angular Forces, &c.
With 73 Diagrams. 12mo, cloth...

Metallurgy of Iron.

A TREATISE ON THE METALLURGY OF IRON: containing Outlines of the History of Iron Manufacture, Methods of Assay, and Analyses of Iron Ores, Processes of Manufacture of Iron and Steel, &c. By H. BAUERMAN, F.G.S., Associate of the Royal School of Mines. With numerous Illustrations. Fourth Edition, revised and much enlarged. 12mo, cloth boards, 5s. 6d.

"Carefully written, it has the merit of brevity and conciseness, as to less important points, while all material matters are very fully and thoroughly entered into."—*Standard.*

Trigonometrical Surveying.

AN OUTLINE OF THE METHOD OF CONDUCTING A TRIGONOMETRICAL SURVEY, for the Formation of Geographical and Topographical Maps and Plans, Military Reconnaissance, Levelling, &c., with the most useful Problems in Geodesy and Practical Astronomy, and Formulæ and Tables for Facilitating their Calculation. By LIEUT-GENERAL FROME, R.E., late Inspector-General of Fortifications, &c. Fourth Edition, Enlarged, thoroughly Revised, and partly Re-written. By CAPTAIN CHARLES WARREN, R.E., F.G.S. With 19 Plates and 115 Woodcuts, royal 8vo, price 16s. cloth.

8 WORKS IN ENGINEERING, SURVEYING, ETC.,

Practical Tunnelling.

PRACTICAL TUNNELLING: Explaining in detail the Setting out of the Works, Shaft-sinking and Heading-Driving, Ranging the Lines and Levelling under Ground, Sub-Excavating, Timbering, and the Construction of the Brickwork of Tunnels with the amount of labour required for, and the Cost of, the various portions of the work. By FREDERICK WALTER SIMMS, M. Inst. C.E., author of "A Treatise on Levelling." Third Edition, Revised and Extended, with additional chapters illustrating the Recent Practice of Tunnelling as exemplified by the St. Gothard, Mont Cenis, and other modern works, by D. KINNEAR CLARK, M. Inst. C.E. Imp. 8vo, cloth, with 21 Folding Plates and numerous Wood Engravings, price 30s. [*Just published.*

"It is the only practical treatise on the great art of tunnelling. Mr. Clark's work brings the exigencies of tunnel enterprise up to our own time. The great length of modern tunnels has led to a new dexterity in the art, which the last generation was ignorant of, namely, the difficulty of ventilation. In Mr. Clark's supplement we find this branch of the subject has been fully considered. Mr. Clark's additional chapters on the Mont Cenis and St. Gothard Tunnels contain minute and valuable experiences and data relating to the method of excavation by compressed air, the leading operations, rock-boring machinery, services of enlargement, ventilation in course of construction by compressed air, labour and cost, &c."—*Building News, Dec. 8, 1876.*

"The estimation in which Mr. Simms' book on tunnelling has been held for over thirty years cannot be more truly expressed than in the words of the Late Professor Rankine:—'The best source of information on the subject of tunnels is Mr. F. W. Simms' work on "Practical Tunnelling."'—*The Architect, Dec. 9, 1876.*

Levelling.

A TREATISE on the PRINCIPLES and PRACTICE of LEVELLING; showing its Application to Purposes of Railway and Civil Engineering, in the Construction of Roads; with Mr. TELFORD'S Rules for the same. By FREDERICK W. SIMMS, F.G.S., M. Inst. C.E. Sixth Edition, very carefully revised, with the addition of Mr. LAW'S Practical Examples for Setting out Railway Curves, and Mr. TRAUTWINE'S Field Practice of Laying out Circular Curves. With 7 Plates and numerous Woodcuts. 8vo, 8s. 6d. cloth. *** TRAUTWINE on Curves, separate, price 5s.

"One of the most important text-books for the general surveyor, and there is scarcely a question connected with levelling for which a solution would be sought but that would be satisfactorily answered by consulting the volume."—*Mining Journal.*

"The text-book on levelling in most of our engineering schools and colleges."—*Engineer.*

The High-Pressure Steam Engine.

THE HIGH-PRESSURE STEAM ENGINE; an Exposition of its Comparative Merits, and an Essay towards an Improved System of Construction, adapted especially to secure Safety and Economy. By Dr. ERNST ALBAN, Practical Machine Maker, Plau, Mecklenberg. Translated from the German, with Notes, by Dr. POLE, F.R.S., M. Inst. C.E., &c. &c. With 28 fine Plates, 8vo, 16s. 6d. cloth.

"A work like this, which goes thoroughly into the examination of the high-pressure engine, the boiler, and its appendages, &c., is exceedingly useful, and deserves a place in every scientific library."—*Steam Shipping Chronicle.*

Hydraulics.

HYDRAULIC TABLES, CO-EFFICIENTS, and FORMULÆ for finding the Discharge of Water from Orifices, Notches, Weirs, Pipes, and Rivers. With New Formulæ, Tables, and General Information on Rain-fall, Catchment-Basins, Drainage, Sewerage, Water Supply for Towns and Mill Power. By JOHN NEVILLE, Civil Engineer, M.R.I.A. Third Edition, carefully revised, with considerable Additions. Numerous Illustrations. Cr. 8vo, 14s. cloth.

"Undoubtedly an exceedingly useful and elaborate compilation."—*Iron.*
"Will prove alike valuable to students and engineers in practice; its study will prevent the annoyance of avoidable failures, and assist them to select the readiest means of successfully carrying out any given work connected with hydraulic engineering."—*Mining Journal.*

Strength of Cast Iron, &c.

A PRACTICAL ESSAY on the STRENGTH of CAST IRON and OTHER METALS. By the late THOMAS TREDGOLD, Mem. Inst. C.E., Author of "Elementary Principles of Carpentry," &c. Fifth Edition, Edited by EATON HODGKINSON, F.R.S.; to which are added EXPERIMENTAL RESEARCHES on the STRENGTH and OTHER PROPERTIES of CAST IRON. By the EDITOR. The whole Illustrated with 9 Engravings and numerous Woodcuts. 8vo, 12s. cloth.

*** HODGKINSON'S EXPERIMENTAL RESEARCHES ON THE STRENGTH AND OTHER PROPERTIES OF CAST IRON may be had separately. With Engravings and Woodcuts. 8vo, price 6s. cloth.

Steam Boilers.

A TREATISE ON STEAM BOILERS: their Strength, Construction, and Economical Working. By ROBERT WILSON, late Inspector for the Manchester Steam Users' Association for the Prevention of Steam Boiler Explosions, and for the Attainment of Economy in the Application of Steam. Fourth Edition. 12mo, cloth boards, 328 pages, price 6s.

"We regard Mr. Wilson's treatise as the best work on boilers which has come under our notice, and we consider that all boiler makers and boiler owners should give it a place in their libraries."—*Engineering.*
"The best treatise that has ever been published on steam boilers."—*Engineer.*
"A valuable contribution to the subject of steam boiler literature . . . . The book is full of hints which the proprietor of a steam boiler would find it to his advantage to know."—*Iron and Coal Trades Review.*

Tables of Curves.

TABLES OF TANGENTIAL ANGLES and MULTIPLES for setting out Curves from 5 to 200 Radius. By ALEXANDER BEAZLEY, M. Inst. C.E. Printed on 48 Cards, and sold in a cloth box, waistcoat-pocket size, price 3s. 6d.

"Each table is printed on a small card, which, being placed on the theodolite, leaves the hands free to manipulate the instrument—no small advantage as regards the rapidity of work. They are clearly printed, and compactly fitted into a tough case for the pocket—an arrangement that will recommend them to all practical men."—*Engineer.*
"Very handy; a man may know that all his day's work at last fall on two of these cards, which he puts into his own card case, and leaves the rest behind."—*Athenæum.*

Earthwork.

EARTHWORK TABLES, showing the Contents in Cubic Yards of Embankments, Cuttings, &c., of Heights or Depths up to an average of 80 feet. By JOSEPH BROADBENT, C.E., and FRANCIS CAMPIN, C.E. Cr. 8vo, oblong, 5s. cloth.

"Creditable to both the authors and the publishers.... The way in which accuracy is attained, by a simple division of each cross section into three elements, two of which are constant and one variable, is ingenious."—*Athenæum*.
"Likely to be of considerable service to engineers."—*Building News*.
"Cannot fail to come into general use."—*Mining Journal*.
"These tables, which are clearly printed and neatly arranged for reference, will be found to facilitate the accurate determination of the quantities of earthwork in making out estimates."—*English Mechanic*.

Surveying (**Land and** Marine).

LAND AND MARINE SURVEYING, In Reference to **the** Preparation **of** Plans for Roads and Railways, Canals, Rivers, Towns' Water Supplies, Docks and Harbours; with Descriptions and Use of Surveying Instruments. By W. DAVIS HASKOLL, C.E., Author of "The Engineer's Field Book," "Examples of Bridge and Viaduct Construction," &c. Demy 8vo, price 12s. 6d. cloth, with 14 folding Plates, and numerous Woodcuts.

"A most useful and well arranged book for the aid of a student.... We can strongly recommend it as a carefully-written and valuable text-book."—*Builder*.
"Mr. Haskoll has knowledge and experience, and can so give expression to it as to make any matter on which he writes, clear to the youngest pupil in a surveyor's office."—*Colliery Guardian*.
"A volume which cannot fail to prove of the utmost practical utility.... It is one which may be safely recommended to all students who aspire to become clean and expert surveyors."—*Mining Journal*.

Engineering Fieldwork.

THE PRACTICE OF ENGINEERING FIELDWORK, applied to Land and Hydraulic, Hydrographic, and Submarine Surveying and Levelling. Second Edition, revised, with considerable additions, and a Supplementary Volume on **WATERWORKS, SEWERS, SEWAGE, and IRRIGATION.** By W. DAVIS HASKOLL, C.E. Numerous folding Plates. Demy 8vo, 2 vols. in one, cloth boards, 1l. 1s. (published at 2l. 4s.)

Mining, Surveying and Valuing.

THE MINERAL SURVEYOR AND VALUER'S COMPLETE GUIDE, comprising a Treatise on Improved Mining Surveying, with new Traverse Tables; and Descriptions of Improved Instruments; also an Exposition of the Correct Principles of Laying out and Valuing Home and Foreign Iron and Coal Mineral Properties; to which is appended M. THOMAN'S (of the Crédit Mobilier, Paris) TREATISE on COMPOUND INTEREST and ANNUITIES, with LOGARITHMIC TABLES. By WILLIAM LINTERN, Mining and Civil Engineer. 12mo, strongly bound in cloth boards, with four Plates of Diagrams, Plans, &c., price 10s. 6d.

"Contains much valuable information given in a small compass, and which, as far as we have tested it, is thoroughly trustworthy."—*Iron and Coal Trades Review*.
"The matter, arrangement, and illustration of this work are all excellent, and make it one of the best of its kind."—*Standard*.

PUBLISHED BY CROSBY LOCKWOOD & CO.

Fire Engineering
[illegible]

Manual of Mining Tools
[illegible]

Common Sense for Gas-Users
[illegible]

Gas and Gasworks
[illegible]

Waterworks for Cities and Towns
[illegible]

Coal and Coal Mining
[illegible]

Field-Book for Engineers.

THE ENGINEER'S, MINING SURVEYOR'S, and CONTRACTOR'S FIELD-BOOK. By W. DAVIS HASKOLL, Civil Engineer. Third Edition, much enlarged, consisting of a Series of Tables, with Rules, Explanations of Systems, and Use of Theodolite for Traverse Surveying and Plotting the Work with minute accuracy by means of Straight Edge and Set Square only; Levelling with the Theodolite, Casting out and Reducing Levels to Datum, and Plotting Sections in the ordinary manner; Setting out Curves with the Theodolite by Tangential Angles and Multiples with Right and Left-hand Readings of the Instrument; Setting out Curves without Theodolite on the System of Tangential Angles by Sets of Tangents and Offsets; and Earthwork Tables to 80 feet deep, calculated for every 6 inches in depth. With numerous wood-cuts, 12mo, price 12s. cloth.

"A very useful work for the practical engineer and surveyor. Every person engaged in engineering field operations will estimate the importance of such a work and the amount of valuable time which will be saved by reference to a set of reliable tables prepared with the accuracy and fulness of those given in this volume."—*Railway News*.

"The book is very handy, and the author might have added that the separate tables of sines and tangents to every minute will make it useful for many other purposes, the genuine traverse tables existing all the same."—*Athenæum*.

"The work forms a handsome pocket volume, and cannot fail, from its portability and utility, to be extensively patronised by the engineering profession."—*Mining Journal*.

"We strongly recommend Mr. Haskoll's 'Field Book' to all classes of surveyors."—*Colliery Guardian*.

"We know of no better field-book of reference or collection of tables than Mr. Haskoll's."—*Artizan*.

Earthwork, Measurement and Calculation of.

A MANUAL on EARTHWORK. By ALEX. J. S. GRAHAM, C.E., Resident Engineer, Forest of Dean Central Railway. With numerous Diagrams. 18mo, 2s. 6d. cloth.

"As a really handy book for reference, we know of no work equal to it; and the railway engineers and others employed in the measurement and calculation of earth work will find a great amount of practical information very admirably arranged, and available for general or rough estimates, as well as for the more exact calculations required in the engineers' contractor's offices."—*Artizan*.

Harbours.

THE DESIGN and CONSTRUCTION of HARBOURS: A Treatise on Maritime Engineering. By THOMAS STEVENSON, F.R.S.E., F.G.S., M.I.C.E. Second Edition, containing many additional subjects, and otherwise generally extended and revised. With 20 Plates and numerous Cuts. Small 4to, 15s. cloth.

Mathematical and Drawing Instruments.

A TREATISE ON THE PRINCIPAL MATHEMATICAL AND DRAWING INSTRUMENTS employed by the Engineer, Architect, and Surveyor. By FREDERICK W. SIMMS, M. Inst. C.E., Author of "Practical Tunnelling," &c. Third Edition, with numerous Cuts. 12mo, price 3s. 6d. cloth.

Bridge Construction in Masonry, Timber, & Iron.

EXAMPLES OF BRIDGE AND VIADUCT CONSTRUCTION OF MASONRY, TIMBER, AND IRON; consisting of 46 Plates from the Contract Drawings or Admeasurement of select Works. By W. DAVIS HASKOLL, C.E. Second Edition, with the addition of 554 Estimates, and the Practice of Setting out Works, illustrated with 6 pages of Diagrams. Imp. 4to, price 2*l*. 12*s*. 6*d*. half-morocco.

"One of the very few works extant descending to the level of ordinary routine, and treating on the common every-day practice of the railway engineer. . . . A work of the present nature by a man of Mr. Haskoll's experience, must prove invaluable to hundreds. The tables of estimates appended to this edition will considerably enhance its value."—*Engineer*.

Mathematical Instruments, their Construction, &c.

MATHEMATICAL INSTRUMENTS: THEIR CONSTRUCTION, ADJUSTMENT, TESTING, AND USE; comprising Drawing, Measuring, Optical, Surveying, and Astronomical Instruments. By J. F. HEATHER, M.A., Author of "Practical Plane Geometry," "Descriptive Geometry," &c. Enlarged Edition, for the most part entirely rewritten. With numerous Wood-cuts, 12mo, cloth boards, price 5*s*.

Drawing for Engineers, &c.

THE WORKMAN'S MANUAL OF ENGINEERING DRAWING. By JOHN MAXTON, Instructor in Engineering Drawing, Royal Naval College, Greenwich, formerly of R.S.N.A., South Kensington. Third Edition, carefully revised. With upwards of 300 Plates and Diagrams. 12mo, cloth, strongly bound, 4*s*. 6*d*.

"Even accomplished draughtsmen will find in it much that will be of use to them. A copy of it should be kept for reference in every drawing office."—*Engineering*.
"Indispensable for teachers of engineering drawing."—*Mechanics' Magazine*.

Oblique Arches.

A PRACTICAL TREATISE ON THE CONSTRUCTION of OBLIQUE ARCHES. By JOHN HART. Third Edition, with Plates. Imperial 8vo, price 8*s*. cloth.

Oblique Bridges.

A PRACTICAL and THEORETICAL ESSAY on OBLIQUE BRIDGES, with 13 large folding Plates. By GEO. WATSON BUCK, M. Inst. C.E. Second Edition, corrected by W. H. BARLOW, M. Inst. C.E. Imperial 8vo, 12*s*. cloth.

"The standard text-book for all engineers regarding skew arches, is Mr. Buck's treatise, and it would be impossible to consult a better."—*Engineer*.

Pocket-Book for Marine Engineers.

A POCKET BOOK FOR MARINE ENGINEERS. Containing useful Rules and Formulæ in a compact form. By FRANK PROCTOR, A.I.N.A. Second Edition, revised and enlarged. Royal 32mo, leather, gilt edges, with strap, price 4*s*.

"We recommend it to our readers as going far to supply a long-felt want."—*Naval Science*.
"A most useful companion to all marine engineers."—*United Service Gazette*.
"Scarcely anything required by a naval engineer appears to have been forgotten.—*Iron*.

Grantham's Iron Ship-Building, enlarged.

ON IRON SHIP-BUILDING; with Practical Examples and Details. Fifth Edition. Imp. 4to, boards, enlarged from 24 to 40 Plates (21 quite new), including the latest Examples. Together with separate Text, 12mo, cloth limp, also considerably enlarged. By JOHN GRANTHAM, M. Inst. C.E., &c. Price 2l. 2s. complete.

"A thoroughly practical work, and every question of the many in relation to iron shipping which admit of diversity of opinion, or have various and conflicting personal interests attached to them, is treated with sober and impartial wisdom and good sense. . . . As good a volume for the instruction of the pupil or student of iron naval architecture as can be found in any language."—*Practical Mechanics' Journal.*

"A very elaborate work. . . . It forms a most valuable addition to the history of iron shipbuilding, while its having been prepared by one who has made the subject his study for many years, and whose qualifications have been repeatedly recognised, will recommend it as one of practical utility to all interested in shipbuilding."—*Army and Navy Gazette.*

"Mr. Grantham's work is of great interest. . . . It is also valuable as a record of the progress of iron shipbuilding. . . . It will, we are confident, command an extensive circulation among shipbuilders in general. . . . By order of the Board of Admiralty, the work will form the text-book on which the examination in iron ship-building of candidates for promotion in the dockyards will be mainly based."—*Engineering.*

Weale's Dictionary of Terms.

A DICTIONARY of TERMS used in ARCHITECTURE, BUILDING, ENGINEERING, MINING, METALLURGY, ARCHÆOLOGY, the FINE ARTS, &c. By JOHN WEALE. Fifth Edition, revised and corrected by ROBERT HUNT, F.R.S., Keeper of Mining Records, Editor of "Ure's Dictionary of Arts," &c. 12mo, cloth boards, price 6s.

"A book for the enlightenment of those whose memory is treacherous or education deficient in matters scientific and industrial. The additions made of modern discoveries and knowledge are extensive. The result is 570 pages of concentrated essence of elementary knowledge, admirably and systematically arranged, and presented in neat and handy form."—*Iron.*

"The best small technological dictionary in the language."—*Architect.*

"A comprehensive and accurate compendium. Author, editor, and publishers deserve high commendations for producing such a useful work. We can warmly recommend such a dictionary as a standard work of reference to our subscribers. Every ironmonger should procure it—no engineer should be without it—builders and architects must admire it—metallurgists and archæologists would profit by it."—*Ironmonger.*

"The absolute accuracy of a work of this character can only be judged of after extensive consultation, and from our examination it appears very correct and very complete."—*Mining Journal.*

"There is no need now to speak of the excellence of this work: it received the approval of the community long ago. Edited now by Mr. Robert Hunt, and published in a cheap, handy form, it will be of the utmost service as a book of reference scarcely to be exceeded in value."—*Scotsman.*

Steam.

THE SAFE USE OF STEAM: containing Rules for Unprofessional Steam Users. By an ENGINEER. Third Edition. 12mo, Sewed, 6d.

N. B.—*This little work should be in the hands of every person having to deal with a Steam Engine of any kind.*

"If steam-users would but learn this little book by heart, and then hand it to their stokers to do the same, and see that the latter do it, boiler explosions would become sensations by their rarity."—*English Mechanic.*

PUBLISHED BY CROSBY LOCKWOOD & CO.

ARCHITECTURE, &c.

Construction.

THE SCIENCE of BUILDING: An Elementary Treatise on the Principles of Construction. By E. WYNDHAM TARN, M.A., Architect. With 47 Wood Engravings. Demy 8vo. 8s. 6d. cloth.

"A very valuable book, which we strongly recommend to all students."—*Builder.*
"No architect and student should be without this hand-book."—*Architect.*
"An able digest of information which is only to be found scattered through various works."—*Engineering.*

Beaton's Pocket Estimator.

THE POCKET ESTIMATOR FOR THE BUILDING TRADES, being an easy method of estimating the various parts of a Building collectively, more especially applied to Carpenters' and Joiners' work, priced according to the present value of material and labour. By A. C. BEATON, Author of 'Quantities and Measurements.' 33 Woodcuts. Leather. Waistcoat-pocket size. 2s.

Beaton's Builders' and Surveyors' Technical Guide.

THE POCKET TECHNICAL GUIDE AND MEASURER FOR BUILDERS AND SURVEYORS: containing a Complete Explanation of the Terms used in Building Construction, Memoranda for Reference, Technical Directions for Measuring Work in all the Building Trades, &c., &c. By A. C. BEATON, Author of 'Quantities and Measurements.' With 19 Woodcuts. Leather. Waistcoat-pocket size. 2s.

Villa Architecture.

A HANDY BOOK of VILLA ARCHITECTURE; being a Series of Designs for Villa Residences in various Styles. With Detailed Specifications and Estimates. By C. WICKES, Architect, Author of "The Spires and Towers of the Mediæval Churches of England," &c. First Series, consisting of 30 Plates; Second Series, 31 Plates. Complete in 1 vol. 4to, price 2l. 10s. half morocco. Either Series separate, price 1l. 7s. each, half morocco.

"The whole of the designs bear evidence of their being the work of an artistic architect, and they will prove very valuable and suggestive to architects, students, and amateurs."—*Building News.*

House Painting.

HOUSE PAINTING, GRAINING, MARBLING, AND SIGN WRITING: a Practical Manual of. With 9 Coloured Plates of Woods and Marbles, and nearly 150 Wood Engravings. By ELLIS A. DAVIDSON, Author of 'Building Construction,' &c. Second Edition, carefully revised. 12mo, 6s. cloth boards.

"Many persons in the trade may profit by a study of the chapters on the 'Principles of Decorative Art,' and of what we may call the 'lessons' on drawing suitable for sign painters, writers, and decorators. These chapters will be of considerable value to the painter's apprentices, while his journeymen will certainly be interested if not benefited by their perusal. The book is freely illustrated, and has some coloured plates of woods and marbles. It contains a mass of information of use to the amateur and of value to the practical man."—*English Mechanic.*

"Deals with the practice of painting in all its parts, from the grinding of colours to varnishing and gilding."—*Architect.*

"Carefully and lucidly written, and entirely reliable."—*Builders' Weekly Reporter.*

A Book on Building.

A BOOK ON BUILDING, CIVIL AND ECCLESIASTICAL. By Sir EDMUND BECKETT, Bart., LL.D., Q.C., F.R.A.S., Author of "Clocks and Watches and Bells," &c. Crown 8vo, cloth, with Illustrations, price 7s. 6d.

"A book which is always amusing and nearly always instructive Sir E. Beckett will be read for the raciness of his style. We are able very cordially to recommend all persons to read it for themselves. The style throughout is in the highest degree condensed and epigrammatic."—*Times*, Dec. 8, 1876.

"We commend the book to the thoughtful consideration of all who are interested in the building art."—*Builder*, Dec. 2, 1876.

"There is hardly a subject connected with either building or repairing on which sensible and practical directions will not be found, the use of which is probably destined to prevent many an annoyance, disappointment, and unnecessary expense."—*Daily News*, Nov. 28, 1876.

Architecture, Ancient and Modern.

RUDIMENTARY ARCHITECTURE, Ancient and Modern. Consisting of VITRUVIUS, translated by JOSEPH GWILT, F.S.A., &c., with 23 fine copper plates; GRECIAN Architecture, by the EARL of ABERDEEN; the ORDERS of Architecture, by W. H. LEEDS, Esq.; The STYLES of Architecture of Various Countries, by T. TALBOT BURY; The PRINCIPLES of DESIGN in Architecture, by E. L. GARBETT. In one volume, half-bound (pp. 1,100), copiously illustrated, 12s.

*** *Sold separately, in two vols., as follows:—*

ANCIENT ARCHITECTURE. Containing Gwilt's Vitruvius and Aberdeen's Grecian Architecture. Price 6s. half-bound.

N.B.—*This is the only edition of VITRUVIUS procurable at a moderate price.*

MODERN ARCHITECTURE. Containing the Orders, by Leeds; The Styles, by Bury; and Design, by Garbett. 6s. half-bound.

The Young Architect's Book.

HINTS TO YOUNG ARCHITECTS. By GEORGE WIGHTWICK, Architect, Author of "The Palace of Architecture," &c. &c. New Edition, revised and enlarged. By G. HUSKISSON GUILLAUME, Architect. Numerous illustrations. 12mo, cloth boards, 4s.

"Will be found an acquisition to pupils, and a copy ought to be considered as necessary a purchase as a box of instruments."—*Architect*.

"Contains a large amount of information, which young architects will do well to acquire, if they wish to succeed in the everyday work of their profession.—*English Mechanic*.

Drawing for Builders and Students.

PRACTICAL RULES ON DRAWING for the OPERATIVE BUILDER and YOUNG STUDENT in ARCHITECTURE. By GEORGE PYNE, Author of a "Rudimentary Treatise on Perspective for Beginners." With 14 Plates, 4to, 7s. 6d. boards.

Builder's and Contractor's Price Book.

LOCKWOOD & CO.'S BUILDER'S AND CONTRACTOR'S PRICE BOOK for 1877, containing the latest prices of all kinds of Builders' Materials and Labour, and of all Trades connected with Building, &c., &c. The whole revised and edited by FRANCIS T. W. MILLER, Architect and Surveyor. Fcap. 8vo, strongly half-bound, price 4s.

Handbook of Specifications.

THE HANDBOOK OF SPECIFICATIONS; or, Practical Guide to the Architect, Engineer, Surveyor, and Builder, in drawing up Specifications and Contracts for Works and Constructions. Illustrated by Precedents of Buildings actually executed by eminent Architects and Engineers. Preceded by a Preliminary Essay, and Skeletons of Specifications and Contracts, &c., &c. By Professor THOMAS L. DONALDSON, M.I.B.A. With A REVIEW OF THE LAW OF CONTRACTS. By W. CUNNINGHAM GLEN, of the Middle Temple. With 33 Lithographic Plates, 2 vols., 8vo, 2l. 2s.

"In these two volumes of 1,100 pages together, forty-four specifications of executed works are given, including the specifications for parts of the new Houses of Parliament, by Sir Charles Barry, and for the new Royal Exchange, by Mr. Tite, M.P. Donaldson's Handbook of Specifications must be bought by all architects."—*Builder*.

Taylor and Cresy's Rome.

THE ARCHITECTURAL ANTIQUITIES OF ROME. By the late G. L. TAYLOR, Esq., F.S.A., and EDWARD CRESY, Esq. New Edition, thoroughly revised, and supplemented under the editorial care of the Rev. ALEXANDER TAYLOR, M.A. (son of the late G. L. Taylor, Esq.), Chaplain of Gray's Inn. This is the only book which gives on a large scale, and with the precision of architectural measurement, the principal Monuments of Ancient Rome in plan, elevation, and detail. Large folio, with 130 Plates, half-bound, price 3l. 3s.

*** Originally published in two volumes, folio, at 18l. 18s.

Specifications for Practical Architecture.

SPECIFICATIONS FOR PRACTICAL ARCHITECTURE: A Guide to the Architect, Engineer, Surveyor, and Builder; with an Essay on the Structure and Science of Modern Buildings. By FREDERICK ROGERS, Architect. With numerous Illustrations. Demy 8vo, price 15s., cloth. (Published at 1l. 10s.)

*** A volume of specifications of a practical character being greatly required, and the old standard work of Alfred Bartholomew being out of print, the author, on the basis of that work, has produced the above. He has also inserted specifications of works that have been erected in his own practice.

The House-Owner's Estimator.

THE HOUSE-OWNER'S ESTIMATOR; or, What will it Cost to Build, Alter, or Repair? A Price-Book adapted to the Use of Unprofessional People as well as for the Architectural Surveyor and Builder. By the late JAMES D. SIMON, A.R.I.B.A. Edited and Revised by FRANCIS T. W. MILLER, Surveyor. With numerous Illustrations. Second Edition, with the prices carefully revised to 1875. Crown 8vo, cloth, price 3s. 6d.

"In two years it will repay its cost a hundred times over."—*Field*.
"A very handy book for those who want to know what a house will cost to build, alter, or repair."—*English Mechanic*.
"Especially valuable to non-professional readers."—*Mining Journal*.

Useful Text-Book for Architects.

THE ARCHITECT'S GUIDE: Being a Textbook of Useful Information for Architects, Engineers, Surveyors, Contractors, Clerks of Works, &c., &c. By FREDERICK ROGERS, Architect, Author of 'Specifications for Practical Architecture,' &c. With numerous Illustrations. Crown 8vo, 6s. cloth. [*Just Published.*

CARPENTRY, TIMBER, MECHANICS.

Tredgold's Carpentry, new and cheaper Edition.
THE ELEMENTARY PRINCIPLES OF CARPENTRY: a Treatise on the Pressure and Equilibrium of Timber Framing, the Resistance of Timber, and the Construction of Floors, Arches, Bridges, Roofs, Uniting Iron and Stone with Timber, &c. To which is added an Essay on the Nature and Properties of Timber, &c., with Descriptions of the Kinds of Wood used in Building; also numerous Tables of the Scantlings of Timber for different purposes, the Specific Gravities of Materials, &c. By THOMAS TREDGOLD, C.E. Edited by PETER BARLOW, F.R.S. Fifth Edition, corrected and enlarged. With 64 Plates (11 of which now first appear in this edition), Portrait of the Author, and several Woodcuts. In 1 vol., 4to, published at 2*l*. 2*s*., reduced to 1*l*. 5*s*., cloth.

"'Tredgold's Carpentry' ought to be in every architect's and every builder's library, and those who do not already possess it ought to avail themselves of the new issue."—*Builder.*

"A work whose monumental excellence must commend it wherever skilful carpentry is concerned. The Author's principles are rather confirmed than impaired by time, and, as now presented, combine the surest lore with the most interesting display of progressive science. The additional plates are of great intrinsic value."—*Building News.*

Grandy's Timber Tables.
THE TIMBER IMPORTER'S, TIMBER MERCHANT'S, and BUILDER'S STANDARD GUIDE. By RICHARD E. GRANDY. Comprising:—An Analysis of Deal Standards, Home and Foreign, with comparative Values and Tabular Arrangements for Fixing Nett Landed Cost on Baltic and North American Deals, including all intermediate Expenses, Freight, Insurance, &c., &c.; together with Copious Information for the Retailer and Builder. Second Edition. Carefully revised and corrected. 12mo, price 3*s*. 6*d*. cloth.

"Everything it pretends to be: built up gradually, it leads one from a forest to a treenail, and throws in, as a makeweight, a host of material concerning bricks, columns, cisterns, &c.—all that the class to whom it appeals requires."—*English Mechanic.*

"The only difficulty we have is as to what is NOT in its pages. What we have tested of the contents, taken at random, is invariably correct."—*Illustrated Builder's Journal.*

Tables for Packing-Case Makers.
PACKING-CASE TABLES; showing the number of Superficial Feet in Boxes or Packing-Cases, from six inches square and upwards. Compiled by WILLIAM RICHARDSON, Accountant. Oblong 4to, cloth, price 3*s*. 6*d*.

"Will save much labour and calculation to packing-case makers and those who use packing-cases."—*Grocer.*   "Invaluable labour-saving tables."—*Ironmonger.*

Nicholson's Carpenter's Guide.
THE CARPENTER'S NEW GUIDE; or, BOOK of LINES for CARPENTERS: comprising all the Elementary Principles essential for acquiring a knowledge of Carpentry. Founded on the late PETER NICHOLSON'S standard work. A new Edition, revised by ARTHUR ASHPITEL, F.S.A., together with Practical Rules on Drawing, by GEORGE PYNE. With 74 Plates, 4to, 1*l*. 1*s*. cloth.

Dowsing's Timber Merchant's Companion.

THE TIMBER MERCHANT'S AND BUILDER'S COMPANION; containing New and Copious Tables of the Reduced Weight and Measurement of Deals and Battens, of all sizes, from One to a Thousand Pieces, and the relative Price that each size bears per Lineal Foot to any given Price per Petersburgh Standard Hundred; the Price per Cube Foot of Square Timber to any given Price per Load of 50 Feet; the proportionate Value of Deals and Battens by the Standard, to Square Timber by the Load of 50 Feet; the readiest mode of ascertaining the Price of Scantling per Lineal Foot of any size, to any given Figure per Cube Foot. Also a variety of other valuable information. By WILLIAM DOWSING, Timber Merchant. Third Edition, Revised and Corrected. Crown 8vo, 3s. cloth.

"Everything is as concise and clear as it can possibly be made. There can be no doubt that every timber merchant and builder ought to possess it."—*Hull Advertiser.*

Timber Freight Book.

THE TIMBER IMPORTERS' AND SHIPOWNERS' FREIGHT BOOK: Being a Comprehensive Series of Tables for the Use of Timber Importers, Captains of Ships, Shipbrokers, Builders, and all Dealers in Wood whatsoever. By WILLIAM RICHARDSON, Timber Broker. Crown 8vo, cloth, price 6s.

Horton's Measurer.

THE COMPLETE MEASURER; setting forth the Measurement of Boards, Glass, &c., &c.; Unequal-sided, Square-sided, Octagonal-sided, Round Timber and Stone, and Standing Timber. With just allowances for the bark in the respective species of trees, and proper deductions for the waste in hewing the trees, &c.; also a Table showing the solidity of hewn or eight-sided timber, or of any octagonal-sided column. Compiled for the accommodation of Timber-growers, Merchants, and Surveyors, Stonemasons, Architects, and others. By RICHARD HORTON. Third edition, with considerable and valuable additions, 12mo, strongly bound in leather, 5s.

"Not only are the best methods of measurement shown, and in some instances illustrated by means of woodcuts, but the erroneous systems pursued by dishonest dealers are fully exposed. . . . The work must be considered to be a valuable addition to every gardener's library.—*Gazette.*

Superficial Measurement.

THE TRADESMAN'S GUIDE TO SUPERFICIAL MEASUREMENT. Tables calculated from 1 to 200 inches in length, by 1 to 108 inches in breadth. For the use of Architects, Surveyors, Engineers, Timber Merchants, Builders, &c. By JAMES HAWKINGS. Fcp. 3s. 6d. cloth.

Practical Timber Merchant.

THE PRACTICAL TIMBER MERCHANT, being a Guide for the use of Building Contractors, Surveyors, Builders, &c., comprising useful Tables for all purposes connected with the Timber Trade, Marks of Wood, Essay on the Strength of Timber, Remarks on the Growth of Timber, &c. By W. RICHARDSON. Fcap. 8vo, 3s. 6d., cloth. [*Just published.*

The Mechanic's Workshop Companion.

THE OPERATIVE MECHANIC'S WORKSHOP COMPANION, and THE SCIENTIFIC GENTLEMAN'S PRACTICAL ASSISTANT. By WILLIAM TEMPLETON. Twelfth Edition, with Mechanical Tables for Operative Smiths, Millwrights, Engineers, &c.; and an Extensive Table of Powers and Roots, &c., &c. 11 Plates. 12mo. 5s. bound.

"As a text-book of reference, in which mechanical and commercial demands are judiciously met, TEMPLETON'S COMPANION stands unrivalled."—*Mechanics' Magazine.*

"Admirably adapted to the wants of a very large class. It has met with great success in the engineering workshop, as we can testify; and there are a great many men who, in a great measure, owe their rise in life to this little work."—*Building News.*

Engineer's Assistant.

THE ENGINEER'S, MILLWRIGHT'S, and MACHINIST'S PRACTICAL ASSISTANT; comprising a Collection of Useful Tables, Rules, and Data. Compiled and Arranged, with Original Matter, by WILLIAM TEMPLETON. 5th Edition. 18mo, 2s. 6d. cloth.

"So much varied information compressed into so small a space, and published at a price which places it within the reach of the humblest mechanic, cannot fail to command the sale which it deserves. With the utmost confidence we commend this book to the attention of our readers."—*Mechanics' Magazine.*

"A more suitable present to an apprentice to any of the mechanical trades could not possibly be made."—*Building News.*

Designing, Measuring, and Valuing.

THE STUDENT'S GUIDE to the PRACTICE of MEASURING, and VALUING ARTIFICERS' WORKS; containing Directions for taking Dimensions, Abstracting the same, and bringing the Quantities into Bill, with Tables of Constants, and copious Memoranda for the Valuation of Labour and Materials in the respective Trades of Bricklayer and Slater, Carpenter and Joiner, Painter and Glazier, Paperhanger, &c. With 43 Plates and Woodcuts. Originally edited by EDWARD DOBSON, Architect. New Edition, re-written, with Additions on Mensuration and Construction, and useful Tables for facilitating Calculations and Measurements. By E. WYNDHAM TARN, M.A., 8vo, 10s. 6d. cloth.

"We have failed to discover anything connected with the building trade, from excavating foundations to bell-hanging, that is not fully treated upon."—*The Artizan.*

"Altogether the book is one which well fulfils the promise of its title-page, and we can thoroughly recommend it to the class for whose use it has been compiled. Mr. Tarn's additions and revisions have much increased the usefulness of the work, and have especially augmented its value to students."—*Engineering.*

Plumbing.

PLUMBING; a text-book to the practice of the art or craft of the plumber. With supplementary chapters upon house-drainage, embodying the latest improvements. By WILLIAM PATON BUCHAN, Sanitary Engineer. 12mo. cloth, with about 300 Illustrations. Price 3s. 6d. Just published.

"There is no other manual in existence of the plumber's art; and the volume will be welcomed as the work of a practical master of his trade."—*Public Health.*

"The chapters on house-drainage may be usefully consulted, not only by plumbers, but also by engineers and all engaged or interested in house-building."—*Iron.*

"A book containing a large amount of practical information, put together in a very intelligent manner, by one who is well qualified for the task."—*City Press.*

MATHEMATICS, &c.

Gregory's Practical Mathematics.

MATHEMATICS for PRACTICAL MEN; being a Commonplace Book of Pure and Mixed Mathematics. Designed chiefly for the Use of Civil Engineers, Architects, and Surveyors. Part I. PURE MATHEMATICS—comprising Arithmetic, Algebra, Geometry, Mensuration, Trigonometry, Conic Sections, Properties of Curves. Part II. MIXED MATHEMATICS—comprising Mechanics in general, Statics, Dynamics, Hydrostatics, Hydrodynamics, Pneumatics, Mechanical Agents, Strength of Materials. With an Appendix of copious Logarithmic and other Tables. By OLINTHUS GREGORY, LL.D., F.R.A.S. Enlarged by HENRY LAW, C.E. 4th Edition, carefully revised and corrected by J. R. YOUNG, formerly Professor of Mathematics, Belfast College; Author of "A Course of Mathematics," &c. With 13 Plates. Medium 8vo, 1l. 1s. cloth.

"As a standard work on mathematics it has not been excelled."—*Artizan.*

"The engineer or architect will here find ready to his hand, rules for solving nearly every mathematical difficulty that may arise in his practice. The rules are in all cases explained by means of examples, in which every step of the process is clearly worked out."—*Builder.*

"One of the most serviceable books to the practical mechanics of the country. . . . . In the edition just brought out, the work has again been revised by Professor Young. He has modernised the notation throughout, introduced a few paragraphs here and there, and corrected the numerous typographical errors which have escaped the eyes of the former Editor. The book is now as complete as it is possible to make it. It is an instructive book for the student, and a Text-book for him who having once mastered the subjects it treats of, needs occasionally to refresh his memory upon them."—*Building News.*

The Metric System.

A SERIES OF METRIC TABLES, in which the British Standard Measures and Weights are compared with those of the Metric System at present in use on the Continent. By C. H. DOWLING, C. E. Second Edition, revised and enlarged. 8vo, 10s. 6d. strongly bound.

"Mr. Dowling's Tables, which are well put together, come just in time as a ready reckoner for the conversion of one system into the other."—*Athenæum.*

"Their accuracy has been certified by Prof. Airy, Astronomer-Royal."—*Builder.*

"Resolution 8.—That advantage will be derived from the recent publication of Metric Tables, by C. H. Dowling, C.E."—*Report of Section F, Brit. Assoc. Bath.*

Comprehensive Weight Calculator.

THE WEIGHT CALCULATOR; being a Series of Tables upon a New and Comprehensive Plan, exhibiting at one Reference the exact Value of any Weight from 1lb. to 15 tons, at 300 Progressive Rates, from 1 Penny to 168 Shillings per cwt., and containing 186,000 Direct Answers, which with their Combinations, consisting of a single addition (mostly to be performed at sight), will afford an aggregate of 10,266,000 Answers; the whole being calculated and designed to ensure Correctness and promote Despatch. By HENRY HARBEN, Accountant, Sheffield, Author of 'The Discount Guide.' An entirely New Edition, carefully revised. Royal 8vo, strongly half-bound, 30s. [*Just Published.*

Comprehensive Discount Guide.

THE DISCOUNT GUIDE; comprising several Series of Tables for the use of Merchants, Manufacturers, Ironmongers, and others, by which may be ascertained the exact profit arising from any mode of using Discounts, either in the Purchase or Sale of Goods, and the method of either Altering a Rate of Discount, or Advancing a Price, so as to produce, by one operation, a sum that will realise any required profit after allowing one or more Discounts: to which are added Tables of Profit or Advance from 1¼ to 90 per cent., Tables of Discount from 1½ to 98¼ per cent., and Tables of Commission, &c., from ⅛ to 10 per cent. By HENRY HARBEN, Accountant, Author of "The Weight Calculator." New Edition, carefully Revised and Corrected. In a handsome demy 8vo. volume (544 pp.), strongly and elegantly half-bound, price £1 5s. [*Just published*.

Inwood's Tables, greatly enlarged and improved.

TABLES FOR THE PURCHASING of ESTATES, Freehold, Copyhold, or Leasehold; Annuities, Advowsons, &c., and for the Renewing of Leases held under Cathedral Churches, Colleges, or other corporate bodies; for Terms of Years certain, and for Lives; also for Valuing Reversionary Estates, Deferred Annuities, Next Presentations, &c., together with Smart's Five Tables of Compound Interest, and an Extension of the same to Lower and Intermediate Rates. By WILLIAM INWOOD, Architect. The 20th edition, with considerable additions, and new and valuable Tables of Logarithms for the more Difficult Computations of the Interest of Money, Discount, Annuities, &c., by M. FÉDOR THOMAN, of the Société Crédit Mobilier of Paris. 12mo, 8s. cloth.

"Those interested in the purchase and sale of estates, and in the adjustment of compensation cases, as well as in transactions in annuities, life insurances, &c., will find the present edition of eminent service."—*Engineering*.

"Inwood's Tables still maintain a most enviable reputation. The new issue has been enriched by large additional contributions by M. Fédor Thoman, whose carefully arranged Tables of Logarithms for the more Difficult Computations of the Interest of Money, Discount, Annuities, &c., cannot fail to be of the utmost utility."—*Mining Journal*.

Geometry for the Architect, Engineer, &c.

PRACTICAL GEOMETRY, for the Architect, Engineer, and Mechanic; giving Rules for the Delineation and Application of various Geometrical Lines, Figures and Curves. By E. W. TARN, M.A., Architect, Author of "The Science of Building," &c. With 164 Illustrations. Demy 8vo. 12s. 6d.

"No book with the same objects in view has ever been published in which the clearness of the rules laid down and the illustrative diagrams have been so satisfactory."—*Scotsman*.

Compound Interest and Annuities.

THEORY of COMPOUND INTEREST and ANNUITIES; with Tables of Logarithms for the more Difficult Computations of Interest, Discount, Annuities, &c., in all their Applications and Uses for Mercantile and State Purposes. With an elaborate Introduction. By FÉDOR THOMAN, of the Société Crédit Mobilier, Paris. 12mo, cloth, 5s.

"A very powerful work, and the Author has a very remarkable command of his subject."—*Professor A. de Morgan*.

"We recommend it to the notice of actuaries and accountants."—*Athenæum*.

PUBLISHED BY CROSBY LOCKWOOD & CO.

SCIENCE AND ART.

The Military Sciences.

AIDE-MÉMOIRE to the MILITARY SCIENCES. Framed from Contributions of Officers and others connected with the different Services. Originally edited by a Committee of the Corps of Royal Engineers. Second Edition, most carefully revised by an Officer of the Corps, with many additions; containing nearly 350 Engravings and many hundred Woodcuts. 3 vols. royal 8vo, extra cloth boards, and lettered, price 4*l*. 10*s*.

"A compendious encyclopædia of military knowledge."—*Edinburgh Review*.
"The most comprehensive work of reference to the military and collateral sciences."—*Volunteer Service Gazette*.

Field Fortification.

A TREATISE on FIELD FORTIFICATION, the ATTACK of FORTRESSES, MILITARY MINING, and RECONNOITRING. By Colonel I. S. MACAULAY, late Professor of Fortification in the R. M. A., Woolwich. Sixth Edition, crown 8vo, cloth, with separate Atlas of 12 Plates, price 12*s*. complete.

Field Fortification.

HANDBOOK OF FIELD FORTIFICATION, intended for the Guidance of Officers preparing for Promotion, and especially adapted to the requirements of Beginners. By Major W. W. KNOLLYS, F.R.G.S., 93rd Sutherland Highlanders, &c. With 163 Woodcuts. Crown 8vo, 3*s*. 6*d*. cloth.

Storms.

STORMS: their Nature, Classification, and Laws, with the Means of Predicting them by their Embodiments, the Clouds. By WILLIAM BLASIUS. With Coloured Plates and numerous Wood Engravings. Crown 8vo, 10*s*. 6*d*. cloth boards.

Light-Houses.

EUROPEAN LIGHT-HOUSE SYSTEMS; being a Report of a Tour of Inspection made in 1873. By Major GEORGE H. ELLIOT, Corps of Engineers, U.S.A. Illustrated by 51 Engravings and 31 Woodcuts in the Text. 8vo, 21*s*. cloth.

Dye-Wares and Colours.

THE MANUAL of COLOURS and DYE-WARES; their Properties, Applications, Valuation, Impurities, and Sophistications. For the Use of Dyers, Printers, Dry Salters, Brokers, &c. By J. W. SLATER. Post 8vo, cloth, price 7*s*. 6*d*.

"A complete encyclopædia of the *materia tinctoria*. The information given respecting each article is full and precise, and the methods of determining the value of articles such as these, so liable to sophistication, are given with clearness, and are practical as well as valuable."—*Chemical Druggist*.

Electricity.

A MANUAL of ELECTRICITY; including Galvanism, Magnetism, Diamagnetism, Electro-Dynamics, Magneto-Electricity, and the Electric Telegraph. By HENRY M. NOAD, Ph.D., F.C.S., Lecturer on Chemistry at St. George's Hospital. Fourth Edition, entirely rewritten. Illustrated by 500 Woodcuts. 8vo, 1l. 4s. cloth.

"The commendations already bestowed in the pages of the *Lancet* on the former editions of this work are more than ever merited by the present. The accounts given of electricity and galvanism are not only complete in a scientific sense, but, which is a rarer thing, are popular and interesting."—*Lancet*.

Text-Book of Electricity.

THE STUDENT'S TEXT-BOOK OF ELECTRICITY. By HENRY M. NOAD, Ph.D., Lecturer on Chemistry at St. George's Hospital. New Edition, revised and enlarged, with additions on Telegraphy, by G. E. PREECE, Esq. Upwards of 400 Illustrations.
[*In Preparation.*

Rudimentary Magnetism.

RUDIMENTARY MAGNETISM: being a concise exposition of the general principles of Magnetical Science, and the purposes to which it has been applied. By Sir W. SNOW HARRIS, F.R.S. New and enlarged Edition, with considerable additions by Dr. NOAD, Ph.D. With 165 Woodcuts. 12mo, cloth, 4s. 6d.

"As concise and lucid an exposition of the phenomena of magnetism as we believe it is possible to write."—*English Mechanic*.

"Not only will the scientific student find this volume an invaluable book of reference, but the general reader will find in it as much to interest as to inform his mind. Though a strictly scientific work, its subject is handled in a simple and readable style."—*Illustrated Review*.

"There is a good index, and this volume of 419 pages may be considered the best possible manual on the subject of magnetism."—*Mechanics' Magazine*.

Chemical Analysis.

THE COMMERCIAL HANDBOOK of CHEMICAL ANALYSIS; or Practical Instructions for the determination of the Intrinsic or Commercial Value of Substances used in Manufactures, in Trades, and in the Arts. By A. NORMANDY, Author of "Practical Introduction to Rose's Chemistry," and Editor of Rose's "Treatise on Chemical Analysis." *New Edition.* Enlarged, and to a great extent re-written, by HENRY M. NOAD, Ph.D., F.R.S. With numerous Illustrations. Cr. 8vo, 12s. 6d. cloth.

"We recommend this book to the careful perusal of every one; it may be truly affirmed to be of universal interest, and we strongly recommend it to our readers as a guide, alike indispensable to the housewife as to the pharmaceutical practitioner."—*Medical Times*.

"Will be found to be essential to the analysts appointed under the new Act.... In all cases the most recent results are given, and the work is well edited and carefully written."—*Nature*.

Mollusca.

A MANUAL OF THE MOLLUSCA; being a Treatise on Recent and Fossil Shells. By Dr. S. P. WOODWARD, A.L.S. With Appendix by RALPH TATE, A.L.S. F.G.S. With numerous Plates and 300 Woodcuts. Third Edition. Crown 8vo, 7s. 6d. cloth gilt.

PUBLISHED BY CROSBY LOCKWOOD & CO.   25

Clocks, Watches, and Bells.

RUDIMENTARY TREATISE on CLOCKS, and WATCHES, and BELLS. By Sir EDMUND BECKETT, Bart. (late E. B. Denison), LL.D., Q.C., F.R.A.S., Author of "Astronomy without Mathematics," &c. Sixth edition, thoroughly revised and enlarged, with numerous Illustrations. Limp cloth (No. 67, Weale's Series), 4s. 6d.; cloth boards, 5s. 6d.

"As a popular and practical treatise it is unapproached." — *English Mechanic.*

"The best work on the subject probably extant. So far as we know it has no competitor worthy of the name. The treatise on bells is undoubtedly the best in the language. It shows that the author has contributed very much to their modern improvement, if indeed he has not revived this art, which was decaying here. To call it a rudimentary treatise is a misnomer, at least as respects clocks and bells. It is something more. It is the most important work of its kind in English." — *Engineering.*

"The only modern treatise on clock-making." — *Horological Journal.*

"We do not know whether to wonder most at the extraordinary cheapness of this admirable treatise on clocks, by the most able authority on such a subject, or the thorough completeness of his work. The chapter on bells is singular and amusing, and will be a real treat even to the uninitiated general reader. The illustrations, notes, and indices, make the work completely perfect of its kind." — *Standard.*

"There is probably no book in the English language on a technical subject so easy to read, and to read through, as the treatise on clocks, watches, and bells, written by the eminent Parliamentary Counsel, Mr. E. B. Denison—now Sir Edmund Beckett, Bart." — *Architect.*

Gold and Gold-Working.

THE PRACTICAL GOLD-WORKER; or, The Goldsmith's and Jeweller's Instructor. The Art of Alloying, Melting, Reducing, Colouring, Collecting and Refining. The processes of Manipulation, Recovery of Waste, Chemical and Physical Properties of Gold, with a new System of Mixing its Alloys; Solders, Enamels, and other useful Rules and Recipes, &c. By GEORGE E. GEE. Crown 8vo, cloth, 7s. 6d. [*Now Ready.*

"A good, sound, technical educator, and will be generally accepted as an authority. It gives full particulars for mixing alloys and enamels, is essentially a book for the workshop, and exactly fulfils the purpose intended." — *Horological Journal.*

"The best work yet printed on its subject for a reasonable price. We have no doubt that it will speedily become a standard book which few will care to be without." — *Jeweller and Metalworker.*

Science and Scripture.

SCIENCE ELUCIDATIVE OF SCRIPTURE, AND NOT ANTAGONISTIC TO IT; being a Series of Essays on—1. Alleged Discrepancies; 2. The Theory of the Geologists and Figure of the Earth; 3. The Mosaic Cosmogony; 4. Miracles in general—Views of Hume and Powell; 5. The Miracle of Joshua— Views of Dr. Colenso: The Supernaturally Impossible; 6. The Age of the Fixed Stars—their Distances and Masses. By Professor J. R. YOUNG, Author of "A Course of Elementary Mathematics," &c. &c. Fcap. 8vo, price 5s. cloth lettered.

"Distinguished by the true spirit of scientific inquiry, by great knowledge, by keen logical ability, and by a style peculiarly clear, easy, and energetic." — *Nonconformist.*

"No one can rise from its perusal without being improved with a sense of the singular weakness of modern scepticism." — *Baptist Magazine.*

"A valuable contribution to controversial theological literature." — *City Press.*

Practical Philosophy.

A SYNOPSIS of PRACTICAL PHILOSOPHY. By the Rev. JOHN CARR, M.A., late Fellow of Trin. Coll., Cambridge. Second Edition. 18mo, 5s. cloth.

DR. LARDNER'S POPULAR WORKS.

Dr. Lardner's Museum of Science and Art.

THE MUSEUM OF SCIENCE AND ART. Edited by DIONYSIUS LARDNER, D.C.L., formerly Professor of Natural Philosophy and Astronomy in University College, London. With upwards of 1200 Engravings on Wood. In 6 Double Volumes. Price £1 1s., in a new and elegant cloth binding; or handsomely bound in half morocco, 31s. 6d.

"The 'Museum of Science and Art' is the most valuable contribution that has ever been made to the Scientific Instruction of every class of society."—*Sir David Brewster in the North British Review.*

"Whether we consider the liberality and beauty of the illustrations, the charm of the writing, or the durable interest of the matter, we must express our belief that there is hardly to be found among the new books, one that would be welcomed by people of so many ages and classes as a valuable present."—*Examiner.*

** *Separate books formed from the above, suitable for Workmen's Libraries, Science Classes, &c.*

COMMON THINGS EXPLAINED. Containing Air, Earth, Fire, Water, Time, Man, the Eye, Locomotion, Colour, Clocks and Watches, &c. 233 Illustrations, cloth gilt, 5s.

THE MICROSCOPE. Containing Optical Images, Magnifying Glasses, Origin and Description of the Microscope, Microscopic Objects, the Solar Microscope, Microscopic Drawing and Engraving, &c. 147 Illustrations, cloth gilt, 2s.

POPULAR GEOLOGY. Containing Earthquakes and Volcanoes, the Crust of the Earth, etc. 201 Illustrations, cloth gilt, 2s. 6d.

POPULAR PHYSICS. Containing Magnitude and Minuteness, the Atmosphere, Meteoric Stones, Popular Fallacies, Weather Prognostics, the Thermometer, the Barometer, Sound, &c. 85 Illustrations, cloth gilt, 2s. 6d.

STEAM AND ITS USES. Including the Steam Engine, the Locomotive, and Steam Navigation. 89 Illustrations, cloth gilt, 2s.

POPULAR ASTRONOMY. Containing How to Observe the Heavens. The Earth, Sun, Moon, Planets. Light, Comets, Eclipses, Astronomical Influences, &c. 182 Illustrations, 4s. 6d.

THE BEE AND WHITE ANTS: Their Manners and Habits. With Illustrations of Animal Instinct and Intelligence. 135 Illustrations, cloth gilt, 2s.

THE ELECTRIC TELEGRAPH POPULARISED. To render intelligible to all who can Read, irrespective of any previous Scientific Acquirements, the various forms of Telegraphy in Actual Operation. 100 Illustrations, cloth gilt, 1s. 6d.

Scientific Class-Books, by Dr. Lardner.

NATURAL PHILOSOPHY FOR SCHOOLS. By DR. LARDNER. 328 Illustrations. Fifth Edition. 1 vol. 3s. 6d. cloth.

"Conveys, in clear and precise terms, general notions of all the principal divisions of Physical Science."—*British Quarterly Review.*

ANIMAL PHYSIOLOGY FOR SCHOOLS. By DR. LARDNER. With 190 Illustrations. Second Edition. 1 vol. 3s. 6d. cloth.

"Clearly written, well arranged, and excellently illustrated."—*Gardeners' Chronicle.*

DR. LARDNER'S SCIENTIFIC WORKS.

Astronomy.

Animal Physics.

Electric Telegraph.

LARDNER'S COURSE
Mechanics.

THE HANDBOOK OF MECHANICS. Enlarged and almost rewritten by BENJAMIN LOEWY, F.R.A.S. With 378 Illustrations. Post 8vo, 6s. cloth.

"The perspicuity of the original has been retained,' and chapters which had become obsolete, have been replaced by others of more modern character. The explanations throughout are studiously popular, and care has been taken to show the application of the various branches of physics to the industrial arts, and to the practical business of life."—*Mining Journal.*

Heat.

Hydrostatics and Pneumatics.

Electricity, Magnetism, and Acoustics.

Optics.

Geology and Genesis Harmonised.

THE TWIN RECORDS of CREATION; or, Geology and Genesis, their Perfect Harmony and Wonderful Concord. By GEORGE W. VICTOR LE VAUX. With numerous Illustrations. Fcap. 8vo, price 5s. cloth.

"We can recommend Mr. Le Vaux as an able and interesting guide to a popular appreciation of geological science."—*Spectator*.

"The author combines an unbounded admiration of science with an unbounded admiration of the Written Record."—*London Review*.

Geology, Physical.

PHYSICAL GEOLOGY. (Partly based on Major-General Portlock's Rudiments of Geology.) By RALPH TATE, A.L.S., F.G.S. Numerous Woodcuts. 12mo, 2s.

Geology, Historical.

HISTORICAL GEOLOGY. (Partly based on Major-General Portlock's Rudiments of Geology.) By RALPH TATE, A.L.S., F.G.S. Numerous Woodcuts. 12mo, 2s. 6d.

*** Or PHYSICAL and HISTORICAL GEOLOGY, bound in One Volume, price 5s.

Wood-Carving.

INSTRUCTIONS in WOOD-CARVING, for Amateurs; with Hints on Design. By A LADY. In emblematic wrapper, handsomely printed, with Ten large Plates, price 2s. 6d.

"The handicraft of the wood-carver, so well as a book can impart it, may be learnt from 'A Lady's' publication."—*Athenæum*.

"A real *practical guide*. It is very complete."—*Literary Churchman*.

"The directions given are plain and easily understood, and it forms a very good introduction to the practical part of the carver's art."—*English Mechanic*.

Popular Work on Painting.

PAINTING POPULARLY EXPLAINED; with Historical Sketches of the Progress of the Art. By THOMAS JOHN GULLICK, Painter, and JOHN TIMBS, F.S.A. Second Edition, revised and enlarged. With Frontispiece and Vignette. In small 8vo, 6s. cloth.

*** *This Work has been adopted as a Prize-book in the Schools of Art at South Kensington.*

"A work that may be advantageously consulted. Much may be learned, even by those who fancy they do not require to be taught, from the careful perusal of this unpretending but comprehensive treatise."—*Art Journal*.

"A valuable book, which supplies a want. It contains a large amount of original matter, agreeably conveyed, and will be found of value, as well by the young artist seeking information as by the general reader. We give a cordial welcome to the book, and augur for it an increasing reputation."—*Builder*.

Grammar of Colouring.

A GRAMMAR OF COLOURING, applied to Decorative Painting and the Arts. By GEORGE FIELD. New edition, enlarged and adapted to the use of the Ornamental Painter and Designer, by ELLIS A. DAVIDSON. With new Coloured Diagrams and numerous Engravings on Wood. 12mo, 3s. cloth boards.

"One of the most useful of student's books, and probably the best known of the few we have on the subject."—*Architect*.

"The book is a most useful *résumé* of the properties of pigments."—*Builder*.

"This treatise forms a most valuable *vade mecum* for the ornamental painter and designer."—*Scotsman*.

Delamotte's Works on Illumination & Alphabets.

A PRIMER OF THE ART OF ILLUMINATION; for the use of Beginners: with a Rudimentary Treatise on the Art, Practical Directions for its Exercise, and numerous Examples taken from Illuminated MSS., printed in Gold and Colours. By F. DELAMOTTE. Small 4to, price 9s. Elegantly bound, cloth antique.

"A handy book, beautifully illustrated; the text of which is well written, and calculated to be useful.... The examples of ancient MSS recommended to the student, which, with much good sense, the author chooses from collections accessible to all, are selected with judgment and knowledge, as well as taste."—*Athenæum.*

ORNAMENTAL ALPHABETS, ANCIENT and MEDIÆVAL; from the Eighth Century, with Numerals; including Gothic, Church-Text, large and small, German, Italian, Arabesque, Initials for Illumination, Monograms, Crosses, &c. &c., for the use of Architectural and Engineering Draughtsmen, Missal Painters, Masons, Decorative Painters, Lithographers, Engravers, Carvers, &c. &c. &c. Collected and engraved by F. DELAMOTTE, and printed in Colours. Royal 8vo, oblong, price 4s. cloth.

"A well-known engraver and draughtsman has enrolled in this useful book the result of many years' study and research. For those who insert enamelled sentences round gilded chalices, who blazon shop legends over shop-doors, who letter church walls with pithy sentences from the Decalogue, this book will be useful."—*Athenæum.*

EXAMPLES OF MODERN ALPHABETS, PLAIN and ORNAMENTAL; including German, Old English, Saxon, Italic, Perspective, Greek, Hebrew, Court Hand, Engrossing, Tuscan, Riband, Gothic, Rustic, and Arabesque; with several Original Designs, and an Analysis of the Roman and Old English Alphabets, large and small, and Numerals, for the use of Draughtsmen, Surveyors, Masons, Decorative Painters, Lithographers, Engravers, Carvers, &c. Collected and engraved by F. DELAMOTTE, and printed in Colours. Royal 8vo, oblong, price 4s. cloth.

"To artists of all classes, but more especially to architects and engravers, this very handsome book will be invaluable. There is comprised in it every possible shape into which the letters of the alphabet and numerals can be formed, and the talent which has been expended in the conception of the various plain and ornamental letters is wonderful."—*Standard.*

MEDIÆVAL ALPHABETS AND INITIALS FOR ILLUMINATORS. By F. DELAMOTTE, Illuminator, Designer, and Engraver on Wood. Containing 21 Plates, and Illuminated Title, printed in Gold and Colours. With an Introduction by J. WILLIS BROOKS. Small 4to, 6s. cloth gilt.

"A volume in which the letters of the alphabet come forth glorified in gilding and all the colours of the prism interwoven and intertwined and intermingled, sometimes with a sort of rainbow arabesque. A poem emblazoned in these characters would be only comparable to one of those delicious love letters symbolized in a bunch of flowers well selected and cleverly arranged."—*Sun.*

THE EMBROIDERER'S BOOK OF DESIGN; containing Initials, Emblems, Cyphers, Monograms, Ornamental Borders, Ecclesiastical Devices, Mediæval and Modern Alphabets, and National Emblems. Collected and engraved by F. DELAMOTTE, and printed in Colours. Oblong royal 8vo, 2s. 6d. in ornamental boards.

AGRICULTURE, &c.

Youatt and Burn's Complete Grazier.
THE COMPLETE GRAZIER, and FARMER'S and CATTLE-BREEDER'S ASSISTANT. A Compendium of Husbandry. By WILLIAM YOUATT, ESQ., V.S. 11th Edition, enlarged by ROBERT SCOTT BURN, Author of "The Lessons of My Farm," &c. One large 8vo volume, 784 pp, with 215 Illustrations, 1*l*. 1*s*. half-bd.

"The standard and text-book, with the farmer and grazier."—*Farmer's Magazine.*
"A treatise which will remain a standard work on the subject as long as British agriculture endures."—*Mark Lane Express.*

Spooner on Sheep.
SHEEP; THE HISTORY, STRUCTURE, ECONOMY, AND DISEASES OF. By W. C. SPOONER, M.R.V.C., &c. Third Edition, considerably enlarged; with numerous fine engravings, including some specimens of New and Improved Breeds. Fcp. 8vo, 366 pp., price 6*s*. cloth.

"The book is decidedly the best of the kind in our language."—*Scotsman.*
"Mr. Spooner has conferred upon the agricultural class a lasting benefit by embodying in this work the improvements made in sheep stock by such men as Humphreys, Rawlence, Howard, and others."—*Hampshire Advertiser.*
"The work should be in possession of every flock-master."—*Banbury Guardian.*

Scott Burn's System of Modern Farming.
OUTLINES OF MODERN FARMING. By R. SCOTT BURN. Soils, Manures, and Crops—Farming and Farming Economy, Historical and Practical—Cattle, Sheep, and Horses—Management of the Dairy, Pigs, and Poultry, with Notes on the Diseases of Stock—Utilisation of Town-Sewage, Irrigation, and Reclamation of Waste Land. New Edition. In 1 vol. 1250 pp., half-bound, profusely illustrated, price 12*s*.

"There is sufficient stated within the limits of this treatise to prevent a farmer from going far wrong in any of his operations."—*Observer.*

Horton's Underwood and Woodland Tables.
TABLES FOR PLANTING AND VALUING UNDERWOOD AND WOODLAND; also Lineal, Superficial, Cubical, Wages, Marketing, and Decimal Tables. Together with Tables for Converting Land-measure from one denomination to another, and instructions for Measuring Round Timber. By RICHARD HORTON. 12mo. 2*s*. strongly bound in leather.

Good Gardening.
A PLAIN GUIDE TO GOOD GARDENING; or, How to Grow Vegetables, Fruits, and Flowers. With Practical Notes on Soils, Manures, Seeds, Planting, Laying-out of Gardens and Grounds, and on the various kinds of Garden Structures. By SAMUEL WOOD (late gardener to Sir L. P. Wrey, Bart.), Author of 'Gardening for the Cottage.' Second Edition, with very considerable Additions, &c., and numerous Illustrations. Crown 8vo, pp. 416, cloth elegant, price 5*s*.

"A very good book, and one to be highly recommended as a practical guide. The practical directions are excellent."—*Athenaeum.*
"A thoroughly useful guidebook for the amateur gardener who may want to make his plot of land not merely pretty, but useful and profitable."—*Daily Telegraph.*

Ewart's Land Improver's Pocket-Book.

THE LAND IMPROVER'S POCKET-BOOK OF FORMULÆ, TABLES, and MEMORANDA, required in any Computation relating to the Permanent Improvement of Landed Property. By JOHN EWART, Land Surveyor and Agricultural Engineer. Royal 32mo, oblong, leather, gilt edges, with elastic band, 4s.

"Admirably calculated to serve its purpose."—*Scotsman.*
"A compendious and handy little volume."—*Spectator.*

Hudson's Tables for Land Valuers.

THE LAND VALUER'S BEST ASSISTANT; being Tables, on a very much improved Plan, for Calculating the Value of Estates. With Tables for reducing Scotch, Irish, and Provincial Customary Acres to Statute Measure; also, Tables of Square Measure, and of the Dimensions of an Acre by which the Contents of any Plot of Ground may be ascertained without the expense of a regular Survey; &c. By R. HUDSON, C.E. New Edition, royal 32mo, oblong, leather, gilt edges, with elastic band, 4s.

"Of incalculable value to the country gentleman and professional man."—*Farmer's Journal.*

Complete Agricultural Surveyor's Pocket-Book.

THE LAND VALUER'S AND LAND IMPROVER'S COMPLETE POCKET-BOOK; consisting of the above two works bound together, leather, gilt edges, with strap, 7s. 6d.

☞ *The above forms an unequalled and most compendious Pocket Vade-mecum for the Land Agent and Agricultural Engineer.*

"We consider Hudson's book to be the best ready-reckoner on matters relating to the valuation of land and crops we have ever seen, and its combination with Mr. Ewart's work greatly enhances the value and usefulness of the latter-mentioned. It is most useful as a manual for reference to those for whom it is intended."—*North of England Farmer.*

The Management of Estates.

LANDED ESTATES MANAGEMENT: Treating of the Varieties of Lands, Peculiarities of its Farms, Methods of Farming, the Setting-out of Farms and their Fields, Construction of Roads, Fences, Gates, and Farm Buildings, of Waste or Unproductive Lands, Irrigation, Drainage, Plantation, &c. By R. SCOTT BURN, Fcp. 8vo, numerous Illustrations, 3s. 6d.   [*Now Ready.*

Scott Burn's Introduction to Farming.

THE LESSONS of MY FARM: a Book for Amateur Agriculturists, being an Introduction to Farm Practice, in the Culture of Crops, the Feeding of Cattle, Management of the Dairy, Poultry, and Pigs, and in the Keeping of Farm-work Records. By ROBERT SCOTT BURN. With numerous Illustrations. Fcp. 6s. cloth.

"A most complete introduction to the whole round of farming practice."—*John Bull.*

The Laws of Mines and Mining Companies.

A PRACTICAL TREATISE on the LAW RELATING to MINES and MINING COMPANIES. By WHITTON ARUNDELL, Attorney-at-Law. Crown 8vo, 4s. cloth.

"A Complete Epitome of the Laws of this Country."

EVERY MAN'S OWN LAWYER; a Handy-Book of the Principles of Law and Equity. By A BARRISTER. 14th Edition, Revised to the end of last Session. Including a Summary of the Judicature Acts, and the principal Acts of the past Session, viz.—The Act for Amending the Law Relating to Crossed Cheques, The Merchant Shipping Act, The Vivisection or Cruelty to Animals Amendment Act, The Rivers' Pollution Prevention Act, The Wild-Fowl Preservation Act, &c., &c. With Notes and References to the Authorities. Crown 8vo, price 6s. 8d. (saved at every consultation), strongly bound.

COMPRISING THE LAWS OF

BANKRUPTCY—BILLS OF EXCHANGE—CONTRACTS AND AGREEMENTS—COPYRIGHT—DOWER AND DIVORCE—ELECTIONS AND REGISTRATION INSURANCE—LIBEL AND SLANDER—MORTGAGES—SETTLEMENTS—STOCK EXCHANGE PRACTICE—TRADE MARKS AND PATENTS—TRESPASS, NUISANCES, ETC.—TRANSFER OF LAND, ETC.—WARRANTY—WILLS AND AGREEMENTS, ETC. Also Law for Landlord and Tenant—Master and Servant—Workmen and Apprentices—Heirs, Devisees, and Legatees—Husband and Wife—Executors and Trustees—Guardian and Ward—Married Women and Infants—Partners and Agents—Lender and Borrower—Debtor and Creditor—Purchaser and Vendor—Companies and Associations—Friendly Societies—Clergymen, Churchwardens—Medical Practitioners, &c.—Bankers—Farmers—Contractors—Stock and Share Brokers—Sportsmen and Gamekeepers—Farriers and Horse-Dealers—Auctioneers, House-Agents—Innkeepers, &c.—Pawnbrokers—Surveyors—Railways and Carriers, &c. &c.

"No Englishman ought to be without this book."—*Engineer.*

"What it professes to be—a complete epitome of the laws of this country, thoroughly intelligible to non-professional readers."—*Bell's Life.*

Auctioneer's Assistant.

THE APPRAISER, AUCTIONEER, BROKER, HOUSE AND ESTATE AGENT, AND VALUER'S POCKET ASSISTANT, for the Valuation for Purchase, Sale, or Renewal of Leases, Annuities, and Reversions, and of property generally; with Prices for Inventories, &c. By JOHN WHEELER, Valuer, &c. Third Edition, enlarged, by C. NORRIS. Royal 32mo, cloth, 5s.

"A neat and concise book of reference, containing an admirable and clearly-arranged list of prices for inventories, and a very practical guide to determine the value of furniture, &c."—*Standard.*

Pawnbroker's Legal Guide.

THE PAWNBROKER'S, FACTOR'S, and MERCHANT'S GUIDE to the LAW of LOANS and PLEDGES. By H. C. FOLKARD, Esq., Barrister-at-Law, Author of the "Law of Slander and Libel," &c. With Additions and Corrections to 1876. 12mo, cloth boards, price 3s. 6d.

House Property.

HANDBOOK OF HOUSE PROPERTY: a Popular and Practical Guide to the Purchase, Mortgage, Tenancy, and Compulsory Sale of Houses and Land; including the Law of Dilapidations and Fixtures; with Explanations and Examples of all kinds of Valuations, and useful Information and Advice on Building. By EDWARD LANCE TARBUCK, Architect and Surveyor. 12mo, 5s. cloth boards.

"We are glad to be able to recommend it."—*Builder.*

"The advice is thoroughly practical."—*Law Journal.*

Bradbury, Agnew, & Co., Printers, Whitefriars, London.

Weale's Rudimentary Series

PHILADELPHIA, 1876.
THE PRIZE MEDAL
Was awarded to the Publishers for
Books: Rudimentary Scientific,
"WEALE'S SERIES," ETC.

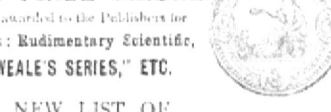

A NEW LIST OF
WEALE'S SERIES
RUDIMENTARY SCIENTIFIC, EDUCATIONAL,
AND CLASSICAL.

LONDON, 1862.
THE PRIZE MEDAL
Was awarded to the Publishers of
"WEALE'S SERIES."

These popular and cheap Series of Books, now comprising nearly Three Hundred distinct works in almost every department of Science, Art, and Education, are recommended to the notice of Engineers, Architects, Builders, Artisans, and Students generally, as well as to those interested in Workmen's Libraries, Free Libraries, Literary and Scientific Institutions, Colleges, Schools, Science Classes, &c., &c.

N.B.—In ordering from this List it is recommended, as a means of facilitating business and obviating error, to quote the numbers affixed to the volumes, as well as the titles and prices.

*** The books are bound in limp cloth, unless otherwise stated.

RUDIMENTARY SCIENTIFIC SERIES.

ARCHITECTURE, BUILDING, ETC.

No.
16. *ARCHITECTURE—ORDERS*—The Orders and their Æsthetic Principles. By W. H. LEEDS. Illustrated. 1s. 6d.
17. *ARCHITECTURE—STYLES*—The History and Description of the Styles of Architecture of Various Countries, from the Earliest to the Present Period. By T. TALBOT BURY, F.R.I.B.A., &c. Illustrated. 2s.
*** ORDERS AND STYLES OF ARCHITECTURE, *in One Vol.*, 3s. 6d.
18. *ARCHITECTURE—DESIGN*—The Principles of Design in Architecture, as deducible from Nature and exemplified in the Works of the Greek and Gothic Architects. By E. L. GARBETT, Architect. Illustrated. 2s.
*** The three preceding Works, in One handsome Vol., half bound, entitled "MODERN ARCHITECTURE," Price 6s.
22. *THE ART OF BUILDING*, Rudiments of. General Principles of Construction, Materials used in Building, Strength and Use of Materials, Working Drawings, Specifications, and Estimates. By EDWARD DOBSON, M.R.I.B.A., &c., Illustrated. 2s.
23. *BRICKS AND TILES*, Rudimentary Treatise on the Manufacture of; containing an Outline of the Principles of Brickmaking. By EDW. DOBSON, M.R.I.B.A. With Additions by C. TOMLINSON, F.R.S. Illustrated. 3s.

CROSBY LOCKWOOD AND CO., 7, STATIONERS' HALL COURT, E.C.

Architecture, Building, etc., *continued*.

25. *MASONRY AND STONECUTTING*, Rudimentary Treatise on; in which the Principles of Masonic Projection and their application to the Construction of Curved Wing-Walls, Domes, Oblique Bridges, and Roman and Gothic Vaulting, are concisely explained. By EDWARD DOBSON, M.R.I.B.A., &c. Illustrated with Plates and Diagrams. 2s. 6d.

44. *FOUNDATIONS AND CONCRETE WORKS*, a Rudimentary Treatise on; containing a Synopsis of the principal cases of Foundation Works, with the usual Modes of Treatment, and Practical Remarks on Footings, Planking, Sand, Concrete, Béton, Pile-driving, Caissons, and Cofferdams. By E. DOBSON, M.R.I.B.A., &c. Fourth Edition, revised by GEORGE DODD, C.E. Illustrated. 1s. 6d.

42. *COTTAGE BUILDING.* By C. BRUCE ALLEN, Architect. Eleventh Edition, revised and enlarged. Numerous Illustrations. 1s. 6d.

45. *LIMES, CEMENTS, MORTARS, CONCRETES, MASTICS,* PLASTERING, &c. By G. R. BURNELL, C.E. Ninth Edition. 1s. 6d.

57. *WARMING AND VENTILATION*, a Rudimentary Treatise on; being a concise Exposition of the General Principles of the Art of Warming and Ventilating Domestic and Public Buildings, Mines, Lighthouses, Ships, &c. By CHARLES TOMLINSON, F.R.S., &c. Illustrated. 3s.

83**. *CONSTRUCTION OF DOOR LOCKS.* Compiled from the Papers of A. C. HOBBS, Esq., of New York, and Edited by CHARLES TOMLINSON, F.R.S. To which is added, a Description of Fenby's Patent Locks, and a Note upon IRON SAFES by ROBERT MALLET, M.I.C.E. Illus. 2s. 6d.

111. *ARCHES, PIERS, BUTTRESSES, &c.:* Experimental Essays on the Principles of Construction in; made with a view to their being useful to the Practical Builder. By WILLIAM BLAND. Illustrated. 1s. 6d.

116. *THE ACOUSTICS OF PUBLIC BUILDINGS;* or, The Principles of the Science of Sound applied to the purposes of the Architect and Builder. By T. ROGER SMITH, M.R.I.B.A., Architect. Illustrated. 1s. 6d.

124. *CONSTRUCTION OF ROOFS,* Treatise on the, as regards Carpentry and Joinery. Deduced from the Works of ROBISON, PRICE, and TREDGOLD. Illustrated. 1s. 6d.

127. *ARCHITECTURAL MODELLING IN PAPER,* the Art of. By T. A. RICHARDSON, Architect. Illustrated. 1s. 6d.

128. *VITRUVIUS—THE ARCHITECTURE OF MARCUS VITRUVIUS POLLIO.* In Ten Books. Translated from the Latin by JOSEPH GWILT, F.S.A., F.R.A.S. With 23 Plates. 5s.

130. *GRECIAN ARCHITECTURE,* An Inquiry into the Principles of Beauty in; with a Historical View of the Rise and Progress of the Art in Greece. By the EARL OF ABERDEEN. 1s.

*** *The two Preceding Works in One handsome Vol., half bound, entitled "*ANCIENT ARCHITECTURE.*" Price 6s.*

132. *DWELLING-HOUSES,* a Rudimentary Treatise on the Erection of. By S. H. BROOKS, Architect. New Edition, with Plates. 2s. 6d.

156. *QUANTITIES AND MEASUREMENTS,* How to Calculate and Take them in Bricklayers', Masons', Plasterers', Plumbers', Painters', Paperhangers', Gilders', Smiths', Carpenters', and Joiners' Work. By A. C. BEATON, Architect and Surveyor. New and Enlarged Edition. Illus. 1s. 6d.

175. *LOCKWOOD & CO.'S BUILDER'S AND CONTRACTOR'S* PRICE BOOK, for 1877, containing the latest Prices of all kinds of Builders' Materials and Labour, and of all Trades connected with Building: Lists of the Members of the Metropolitan Board of Works, of Districts, District Offices, and District Surveyors, and the Metropolitan Bye-laws. Edited by FRANCIS T. W. MILLER, Architect and Surveyor. 3s. 6d.

182. *CARPENTRY AND JOINERY*—THE ELEMENTARY PRINCIPLES OF CARPENTRY. Chiefly composed from the Standard Work of THOMAS TREDGOLD, C.E. With Additions from the Works of the most Recent Authorities, and a TREATISE ON JOINERY by E. WYNDHAM TARN, M.A. Numerous Illustrations. 3s. 6d.

LONDON: CROSBY LOCKWOOD AND CO.,

WEALE'S RUDIMENTARY SERIES. 3

Architecture, Building, etc., *continued.*

182*. *CARPENTRY AND JOINERY. ATLAS* of 35 Plates to accompany the foregoing book. With Descriptive Letterpress. 4to. 6s.

187. *HINTS TO YOUNG ARCHITECTS.* By GEORGE WIGHTWICK. New, Revised, and enlarged Edition. By G. HUSKISSON GUILLAUME, Architect. With numerous Woodcuts. 3s. 6d.

188. *HOUSE PAINTING, GRAINING, MARBLING, AND SIGN WRITING:* A Practical Manual of. With 9 Coloured Plates of Woods and Marbles, and nearly 150 Wood Engravings. By ELLIS A. DAVIDSON. Second Edition, carefully revised, 5s. [*Just published.*

189. *THE RUDIMENTS OF PRACTICAL BRICKLAYING.* In Six Sections: General Principles; Arch Drawing, Cutting, and Setting; Pointing; Paving, Tiling, Materials; Slating and Plastering; Practical Geometry, Mensuration, &c. By ADAM HAMMOND. Illustrated. 1s. 6d.

191. *PLUMBING.* A Text-Book to the Practice of the Art or Craft of the Plumber. With Chapters upon House Drainage, embodying the latest Improvements. Containing about 300 Illustrations. By W. P. BUCHAN, Sanitary Engineer. 3s. [*Just published.*

192. *THE TIMBER IMPORTER'S, TIMBER MERCHANT'S,* and BUILDER'S STANDARD GUIDE; comprising copious and valuable Memoranda for the Retailer and Builder. By RICHARD E. GRANDY. Second Edition, Revised. 3s.

CIVIL ENGINEERING, ETC.

13. *CIVIL ENGINEERING,* the Rudiments of; for the Use of Beginners, for Practical Engineers, and for the Army and Navy. By HENRY LAW, C.E. Including a Section on Hydraulic Engineering, by GEORGE R. BURNELL, C.E. 5th Edition, with Notes and Illustrations by ROBERT MALLET, A.M., F.R.S. Illustrated with Plates and Diagrams. 7s.

29. *THE DRAINAGE OF DISTRICTS AND LANDS.* By G. DRYSDALE DEMPSEY, C.E. New Edition, enlarged. Illustrated. 1s. 6d.

30. *THE DRAINAGE OF TOWNS AND BUILDINGS.* By G. DRYSDALE DEMPSEY, C.E. New Edition. Illustrated. 2s. 6d.
*** With "*Drainage of Districts and Lands,*" in One Vol., 3s. 6d.

31. *WELL-DIGGING, BORING, AND PUMP-WORK.* By JOHN GEORGE SWINDELL, Assoc. R.I.B.A. New Edition, revised by G. R. BURNELL, C.E. Illustrated. 1s. 6d.

35. *THE BLASTING AND QUARRYING OF STONE,* for Building and other Purposes. With Remarks on the Blowing up of Bridges. By Gen. Sir JOHN BURGOYNE, Bart., K.C.B. Illustrated. 1s. 6d.

43. *TUBULAR AND OTHER IRON GIRDER BRIDGES.* Particularly describing the BRITANNIA and CONWAY TUBULAR BRIDGES. With a Sketch of Iron Bridges, and Illustrations of the Application of Malleable Iron to the Art of Bridge Building. By G. D. DEMPSEY, C.E. New Edition, with Illustrations. 1s. 6d.

62. *RAILWAY CONSTRUCTION,* Elementary and Practical Instruction on. By Sir MACDONALD STEPHENSON, C.E. New Edition, enlarged by EDWARD NUGENT, C.E. Plates and numerous Woodcuts. 3s.

80*. *EMBANKING LANDS FROM THE SEA,* the Practice of. Treated as a Means of Profitable Employment for Capital. With Examples and Particulars of actual Embankments, and also Practical Remarks on the Repair of old Sea Walls. By JOHN WIGGINS, F.G.S. New Edition, with Notes by ROBERT MALLET, F.R.S. 2s.

81. *WATER WORKS,* for the Supply of Cities and Towns. With a Description of the Principal Geological Formations of England as influencing Supplies of Water; and Details of Engines and Pumping Machinery for raising Water. By SAMUEL HUGHES, F.G.S., C.E. New Edition, revised and enlarged, with numerous Illustrations. 4s.

82**. *GAS WORKS,* and the Practice of Manufacturing and Distributing Coal Gas. By SAMUEL HUGHES, C.E. New Edition, revised by W. RICHARDS, C.E. Illustrated. 3s. 6d.

7, STATIONERS' HALL COURT, LUDGATE HILL, E.C.

Civil Engineering, etc., *continued*.

117. *SUBTERRANEOUS SURVEYING*; an Elementary and Practical Treatise on. By THOMAS FENWICK. Also the Method of Conducting Subterraneous Surveys without the Use of the Magnetic Needle, and other modern Improvements. By THOMAS BAKER, C.E. Illustrated. 2s. 6d.
118. *CIVIL ENGINEERING IN NORTH AMERICA*, a Sketch of. By DAVID STEVENSON, F.R.S.E., &c. Plates and Diagrams. 3s.
121. *RIVERS AND TORRENTS*. With the Method of Regulating their Courses and Channels. By Professor PAUL FRISI, F.R.S., of Milan. To which is added, AN ESSAY ON NAVIGABLE CANALS. Translated by Major-General JOHN GARSTIN, of the Bengal Engineers. Plates. 2s. 6d.
197. *ROADS AND STREETS (THE CONSTRUCTION OF)* in two Parts: I. THE ART OF CONSTRUCTING COMMON ROADS, by HENRY LAW, C.E., revised and condensed by D. KINNEAR CLARK, C.E.; II. RECENT PRACTICE IN THE CONSTRUCTION OF ROADS AND STREETS, including pavements of Stone, Wood, and Asphalte, by D. K. CLARK, M.I.C.E., with numerous Illustrations. 4s. 6d. [*Just published.*

MECHANICAL ENGINEERING, ETC.

33. *CRANES*, the Construction of, and other Machinery for Raising Heavy Bodies for the Erection of Buildings, and for Hoisting Goods. By JOSEPH GLYNN, F.R.S., &c. Illustrated. 1s. 6d.
34. *THE STEAM ENGINE*, a Rudimentary Treatise on. By Dr. LARDNER. Illustrated. 1s. 6d.
59. *STEAM BOILERS:* their Construction and Management. By R. ARMSTRONG, C.E. Illustrated. 1s. 6d.
63. *AGRICULTURAL ENGINEERING:* Farm Buildings, Motive Power, Field Machines, Machinery, and Implements. By G. H. ANDREWS, C.E. Illustrated. 3s.
67. *CLOCKS, WATCHES, AND BELLS*, a Rudimentary Treatise on. By Sir EDMUND BECKETT (late EDMUND BECKETT DENISON, LL.D., Q.C.) A new, Revised, and considerably Enlarged Edition (the 6th), with very numerous Illustrations. 4s. 6d. [*Just published.*
77*. *THE ECONOMY OF FUEL*, particularly with Reference to Reverbatory Furnaces for the Manufacture of Iron, and to Steam Boilers. By T. SYMES PRIDEAUX. 1s. 6d.
82. *THE POWER OF WATER*, as applied to drive Flour Mills, and to give motion to Turbines and other Hydrostatic Engines. By JOSEPH GLYNN, F.R.S., &c. New Edition, Illustrated. 2s.
98. *PRACTICAL MECHANISM*, the Elements of; and Machine Tools. By T. BAKER, C.E. With Remarks on Tools and Machinery, by J. NASMYTH, C.E. Plates. 2s. 6d.
114. *MACHINERY*, Elementary Principles of, in its Construction and Working. Illustrated by numerous Examples of Modern Machinery for different Branches of Manufacture. By C. D. ABEL, C.E. 1s. 6d.
15. *ATLAS OF PLATES*. Illustrating the above Treatise. By C. D. ABEL, C.E. 7s. 6d.
125. *THE COMBUSTION OF COAL AND THE PREVENTION OF SMOKE*, Chemically and Practically Considered. With an Appendix. By C. WYE WILLIAMS, A.I.C.E. Plates. 3s.
139. *THE STEAM ENGINE*, a Treatise on the Mathematical Theory of, with Rules at length, and Examples for the Use of Practical Men. By T. BAKER, C.E. Illustrated. 1s. 6d.
162. *THE BRASS FOUNDER'S MANUAL;* Instructions for Modelling, Pattern-Making, Moulding, Turning, Filing, Burnishing, Bronzing, &c. With copious Receipts, numerous Tables, and Notes on Prime Costs and Estimates. By WALTER GRAHAM. Illustrated. 2s. 6d.
164. *MODERN WORKSHOP PRACTICE*, as applied to Marine, Land, and Locomotive Engines, Floating Docks, Dredging Machines, Bridges, Cranes, Ship-building, &c., &c. By J. G. WINTON. Illustrated. 3s.

LONDON: CROSBY LOCKWOOD AND CO.,

Mechanical Engineering, etc., *continued.*

165. *IRON AND HEAT,* exhibiting the Principles concerned in the Construction of Iron Beams, Pillars, and Bridge Girders, and the Action of Heat in the Smelting Furnace. By J. Armour, C.E. 2s. 6d.
166. *POWER IN MOTION:* Horse-Power, Motion, Toothed-Wheel Gearing, Long and Short Driving Bands, Angular Forces. By James Armour, C.E. With 73 Diagrams. 2s. 6d.
167. *THE APPLICATION OF IRON TO THE CONSTRUCTION OF BRIDGES, GIRDERS, ROOFS, AND OTHER WORKS.* By Francis Campin, C.E. Second Edition, revised and corrected. Numerous Woodcuts. 2s. 6d.
171. *THE WORKMAN'S MANUAL OF ENGINEERING DRAWING.* By John Maxton, Engineer, Instructor in Engineering Drawing, Royal Naval College, Greenwich. Third Edition. Illustrated with 7 Plates and nearly 350 Woodcuts. 3s. 6d.
190. *STEAM AND THE STEAM ENGINE,* Stationary and Portable. Being an extension of Mr. John Sewell's "Treatise on Steam." By D. Kinnear Clark, M.I.C.E., Author of "Railway Machinery," &c., &c. With numerous Illustrations. 3s. 6d.

SHIPBUILDING, NAVIGATION, MARINE ENGINEERING, ETC.

51. *NAVAL ARCHITECTURE,* the Rudiments of; or, an Exposition of the Elementary Principles of the Science, and their Practical Application to Naval Construction. Compiled for the Use of Beginners. By James Peake, School of Naval Architecture, H.M. Dockyard, Portsmouth. Fourth Edition, corrected, with Plates and Diagrams. 3s. 6d.
53*. *SHIPS FOR OCEAN AND RIVER SERVICE,* Elementary and Practical Principles of the Construction of. By Hakon A. Sommerfeldt, Surveyor of the Royal Norwegian Navy. With an Appendix. 1s.
53**. *AN ATLAS OF ENGRAVINGS* to Illustrate the above. Twelve large folding plates. Royal 4to, cloth. 7s. 6d.
54. *MASTING, MAST-MAKING, AND RIGGING OF SHIPS,* Rudimentary Treatise on. Also Tables of Spars, Rigging, Blocks; Chain, Wire, and Hemp Ropes, &c., relative to every class of vessels. Together with an Appendix of Dimensions of Masts and Yards of the Royal Navy of Great Britain and Ireland. By Robert Kipping, N.A. Fourteenth Edition. Illustrated. 2s.
54*. *IRON SHIP-BUILDING.* With Practical Examples and Details for the Use of Ship Owners and Ship Builders. By John Grantham, Consulting Engineer and Naval Architect. 5th Edition, with Additions. 4s.
54**. *AN ATLAS OF FORTY PLATES* to Illustrate the above. Fifth Edition, Including the latest Examples, such as H.M. Steam Frigates "Warrior," "Hercules," "Bellerophon;" H.M. Troop Ship "Serapis," Iron Floating Dock, &c., &c. 4to, boards. 38s.
55. *THE SAILOR'S SEA BOOK;* a Rudimentary Treatise on Navigation. I. How to Keep the Log and Work it off. II. On Finding the Latitude and Longitude. By James Greenwood, B.A., of Jesus College, Cambridge. To which are added, Directions for Great Circle Sailing; an Essay on the Law of Storms and Variable Winds; and Explanations of Terms used in Ship-building. Ninth Edition, with several Engravings and Coloured Illustrations of the Flags of Maritime Nations. 2s.
80. *MARINE ENGINES, AND STEAM VESSELS,* a Treatise on. Together with Practical Remarks on the Screw and Propelling Power, as used in the Royal and Merchant Navy. By Robert Murray, C.E., Engineer-Surveyor to the Board of Trade. With a Glossary of Technical Terms, and their Equivalents in French, German, and Spanish. Fifth Edition, revised and enlarged. Illustrated. 3s.

7, STATIONERS' HALL COURT, LUDGATE HILL, E.C.

Shipbuilding, Navigation, etc., *continued.*

83*bis*. *THE FORMS OF SHIPS AND BOATS:* Hints, Experimentally Derived, on some of the Principles regulating Ship-building. By W. BLAND. Sixth Edition, revised, with numerous Illustrations and Models. 1s. 6d.

99. *NAVIGATION AND NAUTICAL ASTRONOMY*, in Theory and Practice. With Attempts to facilitate the Finding of the Time and the Longitude at Sea. By J. R. YOUNG, formerly Professor of Mathematics in Belfast College. Illustrated. 2s. 6d.

100*. *TABLES* intended to facilitate the Operations of Navigation and Nautical Astronomy, as an Accompaniment to the above Book. By J. R. YOUNG. 1s. 6d.

106. *SHIPS' ANCHORS*, a Treatise on. By GEORGE COTSELL, N.A. Illustrated. 1s. 6d.

149. *SAILS AND SAIL-MAKING*, an Elementary Treatise on. With Draughting, and the Centre of Effort of the Sails. Also, Weights and Sizes of Ropes; Masting, Rigging, and Sails of Steam Vessels, &c., &c. Tenth Edition, enlarged, with an Appendix. By ROBERT KIPPING, N.A., Sailmaker, Quayside, Newcastle. Illustrated. 2s. 6d.

155. *THE ENGINEER'S GUIDE TO THE ROYAL AND MERCANTILE NAVIES.* By a PRACTICAL ENGINEER. Revised by D. F. M'CARTHY, late of the Ordnance Survey Office, Southampton. 3s.

PHYSICAL SCIENCE, NATURAL PHILOSOPHY, ETC.

1. *CHEMISTRY*, for the Use of Beginners. By Professor GEORGE FOWNES, F.R.S. With an Appendix, on the Application of Chemistry to Agriculture. 1s.

2. *NATURAL PHILOSOPHY*, Introduction to the Study of; for the Use of Beginners. By C. TOMLINSON, Lecturer on Natural Science in King's College School, London. Woodcuts. 1s. 6d.

4. *MINERALOGY*, Rudiments of; a concise View of the Properties of Minerals. By A. RAMSAY, Jun. Woodcuts and Steel Plates. 3s.

6. *MECHANICS*, Rudimentary Treatise on; being a concise Exposition of the General Principles of Mechanical Science, and their Applications. By CHARLES TOMLINSON, Lecturer on Natural Science in King's College School, London. Illustrated. 1s. 6d.

7. *ELECTRICITY*; showing the General Principles of Electrical Science, and the purposes to which it has been applied. By Sir W. SNOW HARRIS, F.R.S., &c. With considerable Additions by R. SABINE, C.E., F.S.A. Woodcuts. 1s. 6d.

7*. *GALVANISM*, Rudimentary Treatise on, and the General Principles of Animal and Voltaic Electricity. By Sir W. SNOW HARRIS. New Edition, revised, with considerable Additions, by ROBERT SABINE, C.E., F.S.A. Woodcuts. 1s. 6d.

8. *MAGNETISM*; being a concise Exposition of the General Principles of Magnetical Science, and the Purposes to which it has been applied. By Sir W. SNOW HARRIS. New Edition, revised and enlarged by H. M. NOAD, Ph.D., Vice-President of the Chemical Society, Author of "A Manual of Electricity," &c., &c. With 165 Woodcuts. 3s. 6d.

1. *THE ELECTRIC TELEGRAPH*; its History and Progress; with Descriptions of some of the Apparatus. By R. SABINE, C.E., F.S.A., &c. Woodcuts. 3s.

12. *PNEUMATICS*, for the Use of Beginners. By CHARLES TOMLINSON. Illustrated. 1s. 6d.

72. *MANUAL OF THE MOLLUSCA*; a Treatise on Recent and Fossil Shells. By Dr. S. P. WOODWARD, A.L.S. With Appendix by RALPH TATE, A.L.S., F.G.S. With numerous Plates and 300 Woodcuts, 6s. 6d. Cloth boards, 7s. 6d.

LONDON : CROSBY LOCKWOOD AND CO.,

Physical Science, Natural Philosophy, etc., *continued.*

79**. *PHOTOGRAPHY*, Popular Treatise on; with a Description of the Stereoscope, &c. Translated from the French of D. Van Monckhoven, by W. H. Thornthwaite, Ph.D. Woodcuts. 1s. 6d.

96. *ASTRONOMY.* By the Rev. R. Main, M.A., F.R.S., &c. New and enlarged Edition, with an Appendix on "Spectrum Analysis." Woodcuts. 1s. 6d.

97. *STATICS AND DYNAMICS*, the Principles and Practice of; embracing also a clear development of Hydrostatics, Hydrodynamics, and Central Forces. By T. Baker, C.E. 1s. 6d.

138. *TELEGRAPH*, Handbook of the; a Manual of Telegraphy, Telegraph Clerks' Remembrancer, and Guide to Candidates for Employment in the Telegraph Service. By R. Bond. Fourth Edition, revised and enlarged; to which is appended, QUESTIONS on MAGNETISM, ELECTRICITY, and PRACTICAL TELEGRAPHY, for the Use of Students, by W. McGregor, First Assistant Superintendent, Indian Gov. Telegraphs. Woodcuts. 3s.

143. *EXPERIMENTAL ESSAYS.* By Charles Tomlinson. I. On the Motions of Camphor on Water. II. On the Motion of Camphor towards the light. III. History of the Modern Theory of Dew. Woodcuts. 1s.

173. *PHYSICAL GEOLOGY*, partly based on Major-General Portlock's "Rudiments of Geology." By Ralph Tate, A.L.S., &c. Numerous Woodcuts. 2s.

174. *HISTORICAL GEOLOGY*, partly based on Major-General Portlock's "Rudiments." By Ralph Tate, A.L.S., &c. Woodcuts. 2s. 6d.

173 & 174. *RUDIMENTARY TREATISE ON GEOLOGY*, Physical and Historical. Partly based on Major-General Portlock's "Rudiments of Geology." By Ralph Tate, A.L.S., F.G.S., &c., &c. Numerous Illustrations. In One Volume, 4s. 6d.

183 & 184. *ANIMAL PHYSICS*, Handbook of. By Dionysius Lardner, D.C.L., formerly Professor of Natural Philosophy and Astronomy in University College, London. With 520 Illustrations. In One Volume, cloth boards. 7s. 6d.

*** *Sold also in Two Parts, as follows :—*

183. Animal Physics. By Dr. Lardner. Part I., Chapter I—VII. 4s.
184. Animal Physics. By Dr. Lardner. Part II. Chapter VIII—XVIII. 3s.

MINING, METALLURGY, ETC.

117. *SUBTERRANEOUS SURVEYING*, Elementary and Practical Treatise on, with and without the Magnetic Needle. By Thomas Fenwick, Surveyor of Mines, and Thomas Baker, C.E. Illustrated. 2s. 6d.

133. *METALLURGY OF COPPER*; an Introduction to the Methods of Seeking, Mining, and Assaying Copper, and Manufacturing its Alloys. By Robert H. Lamborn, Ph.D. Woodcuts. 2s. 6d.

134. *METALLURGY OF SILVER AND LEAD.* A Description of the Ores; their Assay and Treatment, and valuable Constituents. By Dr. R. H. Lamborn. Woodcuts. 2s.

135. *ELECTRO-METALLURGY*; Practically Treated. By Alexander Watt, F.R.S.S.A. New Edition, enlarged. Woodcuts. 2s. 6d.

172. *MINING TOOLS*, Manual of. For the Use of Mine Managers, Agents, Students, &c. Comprising Observations on the Materials from, and Processes by, which they are manufactured; their Special Uses, Applications, Qualities, and Efficiency. By William Morgans, Lecturer on Mining at the Bristol School of Mines. 2s. 6d.

172*. *MINING TOOLS*, ATLAS of Engravings to Illustrate the above, containing 235 Illustrations of Mining Tools, drawn to Scale. 4to. 4s. 6d.

7, STATIONERS' HALL COURT, LUDGATE HILL, E.C.

Mining, Metallurgy, etc., *continued.*

176. *METALLURGY OF IRON*, a Treatise on the. Containing History of Iron Manufacture, Methods of Assay, and Analyses of Iron Ores, Processes of Manufacture of Iron and Steel, &c. By H. BAUERMAN, F.G.S. Fourth Edition, enlarged, with numerous Illustrations. 4s. 6d.
180. *COAL AND COAL MINING*: A Rudimentary Treatise on. By WARINGTON W. SMYTH, M.A., F.R.S., &c., Chief Inspector of the Mines of the Crown and of the Duchy of Cornwall. New Edition, revised and corrected. With numerous Illustrations. 3s. 6d.
195. *THE MINERAL SURVEYOR AND VALUER'S COMPLETE GUIDE*, with new Traverse Tables; and Descriptions of Improved Instruments; also the Correct Principles of Laying out and Valuing Mineral Properties. By WILLIAM LINTERN, Mining and Civil Engineer. With four Plates of Diagrams, Plans, &c. 3s. 6d. [*Now Ready.*

EMIGRATION.

154. *GENERAL HINTS TO EMIGRANTS.* Containing Notices of the various Fields for Emigration. With Hints on Preparation for Emigrating, Outfits, &c., &c. With Directions and Recipes useful to the Emigrant. With a Map of the World. 2s.
157. *THE EMIGRANT'S GUIDE TO NATAL.* By ROBERT JAMES MANN, F.R.A.S., F.M.S. Second Edition, carefully corrected to the present Date. Map. 2s.
159. *THE EMIGRANT'S GUIDE TO AUSTRALIA*, New South Wales, Western Australia, South Australia, Victoria, and Queensland. By the Rev. JAMES BAIRD, B.A. Map. 2s. 6d.
160. *THE EMIGRANT'S GUIDE TO TASMANIA and NEW ZEALAND.* By the Rev. JAMES BAIRD, B.A. With a Map. 2s.
159 & *THE EMIGRANT'S GUIDE TO AUSTRALASIA.* By the
160. Rev. J. BAIRD, B.A. Comprising the above two volumes, cloth boards. 5s.

AGRICULTURE.

29. *THE DRAINAGE OF DISTRICTS AND LANDS.* By G. DRYSDALE DEMPSEY, C.E. Illustrated. 1s. 6d.
    _{*} With "*Drainage of Towns and Buildings*," in One Vol., 3s. 6d.
63. *AGRICULTURAL ENGINEERING*: Farm Buildings, Motive Powers and Machinery of the Steading, Field Machines, and Implements. By G. H. ANDREWS, C.E. Illustrated. 3s.
66. *CLAY LANDS AND LOAMY SOILS.* By Professor DONALDSON. 1s.
131. *MILLER'S, MERCHANT'S, AND FARMER'S READY RECKONER*, for ascertaining at sight the value of any quantity of Corn, from One Bushel to One Hundred Quarters, at any given price, from £1 to £5 per Qr. With approximate values of Millstones, Millwork, &c. 1s.
140. *SOILS, MANURES, AND CROPS.* (Vol. 1. OUTLINES OF MODERN FARMING.) By R. SCOTT BURN. Woodcuts. 2s.
141. *FARMING AND FARMING ECONOMY*, Notes, Historical and Practical, on. (Vol. 2. OUTLINES OF MODERN FARMING.) By R. SCOTT BURN. Woodcuts. 3s.
142. *STOCK; CATTLE, SHEEP, AND HORSES.* (Vol. 3. OUTLINES OF MODERN FARMING.) By R. SCOTT BURN. Woodcuts. 2s. 6d.
145. *DAIRY, PIGS, AND POULTRY*, Management of the. By R. SCOTT BURN. With Notes on the Diseases of Stock. (Vol. 4. OUTLINES OF MODERN FARMING.) Woodcuts. 2s.
146. *UTILIZATION OF SEWAGE, IRRIGATION, AND RECLAMATION OF WASTE LAND.* (Vol. 5. OUTLINES OF MODERN FARMING.) By R. SCOTT BURN. Woodcuts. 2s. 6d.
    _{*} Nos. 140-1-2-5-6, in One Vol., handsomely half-bound, entitled "OUTLINES OF MODERN FARMING." By ROBERT SCOTT BURN. Price 12s.
177. *FRUIT TREES*, The Scientific and Profitable Culture of. From the French of DU BREUIL. Revised by GEO. GLENNY. 187 Woodcuts. 3s. 6d.

LONDON : CROSBY LOCKWOOD AND CO.,

FINE ARTS.

20. *PERSPECTIVE FOR BEGINNERS.* Adapted to Young Students and Amateurs in Architecture, Painting, &c. By GEORGE PYNE, Artist. Woodcuts. 2s.
40 & 41. *GLASS STAINING;* or, Painting on Glass, The Art of. Comprising Directions for Preparing the Pigments and Fluxes, laying them upon the Glass, and Firing or Burning in the Colours. From the German of Dr. GESSERT. To which is added, an Appendix on THE ART OF ENAMELLING, &c., with THE ART OF PAINTING ON GLASS, from the German of EMANUEL OTTO FROMBERG. In One Volume, 2s. 6d.
69. *MUSIC,* A Rudimentary and Practical Treatise on. With numerous Examples. By CHARLES CHILD SPENCER. 2s. 6d.
71. *PIANOFORTE,* The Art of Playing the. With numerous Exercises and Lessons. Written and Selected from the Best Masters, by CHARLES CHILD SPENCER. 1s. 6d.
181. *PAINTING POPULARLY EXPLAINED,* including Fresco, Oil, Mosaic, Water Colour, Water-Glass, Tempera, Encaustic, Miniature, Painting on Ivory, Vellum, Pottery, Enamel, Glass, &c. With Historical Sketches of the Progress of the Art by THOMAS JOHN GULLICK, assisted by JOHN TIMBS, F.S.A. Third Edition, revised and enlarged, with Frontispiece and Vignette, 5s.
186. *A GRAMMAR OF COLOURING,* applied to Decorative Painting and the Arts. By GEORGE FIELD. New Edition, enlarged and adapted to the Use of the Ornamental Painter and Designer. By ELLIS A. DAVIDSON, Author of "Drawing for Carpenters," &c. With two new Coloured Diagrams and numerous Engravings on Wood. 2s. 6d.

ARITHMETIC, GEOMETRY, MATHEMATICS, ETC.

32. *MATHEMATICAL INSTRUMENTS,* a Treatise on; in which their Construction and the Methods of Testing, Adjusting, and Using them are concisely Explained. By J. F. HEATHER, M.A., of the Royal Military Academy, Woolwich. Original Edition, in 1 vol., Illustrated. 1s. 6d.
*** In ordering the above, be careful to say, "*Original Edition,*" or give the number in the Series (32) to distinguish it from the *Enlarged Edition* in 3 vols. (Nos. 168-9-70.)
60. *LAND AND ENGINEERING SURVEYING,* a Treatise on; with all the Modern Improvements. Arranged for the Use of Schools and Private Students; also for Practical Land Surveyors and Engineers. By T. BAKER, C.E. New Edition, revised by EDWARD NUGENT, C.E. Illustrated with Plates and Diagrams. 2s.
61*. *READY RECKONER FOR THE ADMEASUREMENT OF LAND.* By ABRAHAM ARMAN, Schoolmaster, Thurleigh, Beds. To which is added a Table, showing the Price of Work, from 2s. 6d. to £1 per acre, and Tables for the Valuation of Land, from 1s. to £1,000 per acre, and from one pole to two thousand acres in extent, &c., &c. 1s. 6d.
76. *DESCRIPTIVE GEOMETRY,* an Elementary Treatise on; with a Theory of Shadows and of Perspective, extracted from the French of G. MONGE. To which is added, a description of the Principles and Practice of Isometrical Projection; the whole being intended as an introduction to the Application of Descriptive Geometry to various branches of the Arts. By J. F. HEATHER, M.A. Illustrated with 14 Plates. 2s.
178. *PRACTICAL PLANE GEOMETRY:* giving the Simplest Modes of Constructing Figures contained in one Plane and Geometrical Construction of the Ground. By J. F. HEATHER, M.A. With 215 Woodcuts. 2s.
179. *PROJECTION:* Orthographic, Topographic, and Perspective: giving the various Modes of Delineating Solid Forms by Constructions on a Single Plane Surface. By J. F. HEATHER, M.A. [*In preparation.*
*** The above three volumes will form a COMPLETE ELEMENTARY COURSE OF MATHEMATICAL DRAWING.

7, STATIONERS' HALL COURT, LUDGATE HILL, E.C.

Arithmetic, Geometry, Mathematics, etc., *continued*.

83. *COMMERCIAL BOOK-KEEPING*. With Commercial Phrases and Forms in English, French, Italian, and German. By JAMES HADDON, M.A., Arithmetical Master of King's College School, London. 1s.

84. *ARITHMETIC*, a Rudimentary Treatise on: with full Explanations of its Theoretical Principles, and numerous Examples for Practice. For the Use of Schools and for Self-Instruction. By J. R. YOUNG, late Professor of Mathematics in Belfast College. New Edition, with Index. 1s. 6d.

85.*. A KEY to the above, containing Solutions in full to the Exercises, together with Comments, Explanations, and Improved Processes, for the Use of Teachers and Unassisted Learners. By J. R. YOUNG. 1s. 6d.

85. *EQUATIONAL ARITHMETIC*, applied to Questions of Interest.

85.*. Annuities, Life Assurance, and General Commerce; with various Tables by which all Calculations may be greatly facilitated. By W. HIPSLEY. 2s.

86. *ALGEBRA*, the Elements of. By JAMES HADDON, M.A., Second Mathematical Master of King's College School. With Appendix, containing miscellaneous Investigations, and a Collection of Problems in various parts of Algebra. 2s.

86.*. A KEY AND COMPANION to the above Book, forming an extensive repository of Solved Examples and Problems in Illustration of the various Expedients necessary in Algebraical Operations. Especially adapted for Self-Instruction. By J. R. YOUNG. 1s. 6d.

88. *EUCLID*, THE ELEMENTS OF: with many additional Propositions
89. and Explanatory Notes; to which is prefixed, an Introductory Essay on Logic. By HENRY LAW, C.E. 2s. 6d.

*** *Sold also separately, viz.:—*

88. EUCLID, The First Three Books. By HENRY LAW, C.E. 1s.
89. EUCLID, Books 4, 5, 6, 11, 12. By HENRY LAW, C.E. 1s. 6d.

90. *ANALYTICAL GEOMETRY AND CONIC SECTIONS*, a Rudimentary Treatise on. By JAMES HANN, late Mathematical Master of King's College School, London. A New Edition, re-written and enlarged by J. R. YOUNG, formerly Professor of Mathematics at Belfast College. 2s.

91. *PLANE TRIGONOMETRY*, the Elements of. By JAMES HANN, formerly Mathematical Master of King's College, London. 1s.

92. *SPHERICAL TRIGONOMETRY*, the Elements of. By JAMES HANN. Revised by CHARLES H. DOWLING, C.E. 1s.

*** *Or with "The Elements of Plane Trigonometry," in One Volume,* 2s.

93. *MENSURATION AND MEASURING*, for Students and Practical Use. With the Mensuration and Levelling of Land for the Purposes of Modern Engineering. By T. BAKER, C.E. New Edition, with Corrections and Additions by E. NUGENT, C.E. Illustrated. 1s. 6d.

94. *LOGARITHMS*, a Treatise on; with Mathematical Tables for facilitating Astronomical, Nautical, Trigonometrical, and Logarithmic Calculations; Tables of Natural Sines and Tangents and Natural Cosines. By HENRY LAW, C.E. Illustrated. 2s. 6d.

101.*. *MEASURES, WEIGHTS, AND MONEYS OF ALL NATIONS*, and an Analysis of the Christian, Hebrew, and Mahometan Calendars. By W. S. B. WOOLHOUSE, F.R.A.S., &c. 1s. 6d.

102. *INTEGRAL CALCULUS*, Rudimentary Treatise on the. By HOMERSHAM COX, B.A. Illustrated. 1s.

103. *INTEGRAL CALCULUS*, Examples on the. By JAMES HANN, late of King's College, London. Illustrated. 1s.

101. *DIFFERENTIAL CALCULUS*, Examples of the. By W. S. B. WOOLHOUSE, F.R.A.S., &c. 1s. 6d.

104. *DIFFERENTIAL CALCULUS*, Examples and Solutions of the. By JAMES HADDON, M.A. 1s.

Arithmetic, Geometry, Mathematics, etc., *continued*.

105. *MNEMONICAL LESSONS.*—GEOMETRY, ALGEBRA, AND TRIGONOMETRY, in Easy Mnemonical Lessons. By the Rev. THOMAS PENYNGTON KIRKMAN, M.A. 1s. 6d.
136. *ARITHMETIC,* Rudimentary, for the Use of Schools and Self-Instruction. By JAMES HADDON, M.A. Revised by ABRAHAM ARMAN. 1s. 6d.
137. A KEY TO HADDON'S RUDIMENTARY ARITHMETIC. By A. ARMAN. 1s. 6d.
147. *ARITHMETIC,* STEPPING-STONE TO; being a Complete Course of Exercises in the First Four Rules (Simple and Compound), on an entirely new principle. For the Use of Elementary Schools of every Grade. Intended as an Introduction to the more extended works on Arithmetic. By ABRAHAM ARMAN. 1s.
148. A KEY TO STEPPING-STONE TO ARITHMETIC. By A. ARMAN. 1s.
158. *THE SLIDE RULE, AND HOW TO USE IT;* containing full, easy, and simple Instructions to perform all Business Calculations with unexampled rapidity and accuracy. By CHARLES HOARE, C.E. With a Slide Rule in tuck of cover. 3s.
168. *DRAWING AND MEASURING INSTRUMENTS.* Including I. Instruments employed in Geometrical and Mechanical Drawing, and in the Construction, Copying, and Measurement of Maps and Plans. II. Instruments used for the purposes of Accurate Measurement, and for Arithmetical Computations. By J. F. HEATHER, M.A., late of the Royal Military Academy, Woolwich, Author of "Descriptive Geometry," &c. &c. Illustrated. 1s. 6d.
169. *OPTICAL INSTRUMENTS.* Including (more especially) Telescopes, Microscopes, and Apparatus for producing copies of Maps and Plans by Photography. By J. F. HEATHER, M.A. Illustrated. 1s. 6d.
170. *SURVEYING AND ASTRONOMICAL INSTRUMENTS.* Including—I. Instruments Used for Determining the Geometrical Features of a portion of Ground. II. Instruments Employed in Astronomical Observations. By J. F. HEATHER, M.A. Illustrated. 1s. 6d.

_{*} *The above three volumes form an enlargement of the Author's original work, "Mathematical Instruments: their Construction, Adjustment, Testing, and Use," the Eleventh Edition of which is on sale, price 1s. 6d. (See No. 32 in the Series.)*

168.} *MATHEMATICAL INSTRUMENTS.* By J. F. HEATHER,
169.} M.A. Enlarged Edition, for the most part entirely re-written. The 3 Parts as
170.} above, in One thick Volume. With numerous Illustrations. 4s. 6d.

185. *THE COMPLETE MEASURER;* setting forth the Measurement of Boards, Glass, &c., &c.; Unequal-sided, Square-sided, Octagonal-sided, Round Timber and Stone, and Standing Timber. With a Table showing the solidity of hewn or eight-sided timber, or of any octagonal-sided column. Compiled for the accommodation of Timber-growers, Merchants, and Surveyors, Stonemasons, Architects, and others. By RICHARD HORTON. Third Edition, with valuable additions. 5s.
196. *THEORY OF COMPOUND INTEREST AND ANNUITIES;* with Tables of Logarithms for the more Difficult Computations of Interest, Discount, Annuities, &c. By FÉDOR THOMAN, of the Société Crédit Mobilier, Paris. 4s. [*Now ready.*

LEGAL TREATISES.

50. *THE LAW OF CONTRACTS FOR WORKS AND SERVICES.* By DAVID GIBBONS. Third Edition, revised and considerably enlarged. 3s. [*Just published.*
151. *A HANDY BOOK ON THE LAW OF FRIENDLY, INDUSTRIAL & PROVIDENT BUILDING & LOAN SOCIETIES.* With copious Notes. By NATHANIEL WHITE, of H.M. Civil Service. 1s.
163. *THE LAW OF PATENTS FOR INVENTIONS;* and on the Protection of Designs and Trade Marks. By F. W. CAMPIN, Barrister-at-Law. 2s.

7, STATIONERS' HALL COURT, LUDGATE HILL, E.C.

MISCELLANEOUS VOLUMES.

36. *A DICTIONARY OF TERMS used in ARCHITECTURE, BUILDING, ENGINEERING, MINING, METALLURGY, ARCHÆOLOGY, the FINE ARTS, &c.* By JOHN WEALE. Fifth Edition. Revised by ROBERT HUNT, F.R.S., Keeper of Mining Records. Numerous Illustrations. 5s.
112. *MANUAL OF DOMESTIC MEDICINE.* By R. GOODING, B.A., M.B. Intended as a Family Guide in all Cases of Accident and Emergency. 2s.
112*. *MANAGEMENT OF HEALTH.* A Manual of Home and Personal Hygiene. By the Rev. JAMES BAIRD, B.A. 1s.
113. *FIELD ARTILLERY ON SERVICE.* By TAUBERT, Captain Prussian Artillery. Translated by Lieut.-Col. H. H. MAXWELL. 1s. 6d.
113*. *SWORDS, AND OTHER ARMS.* By Col. MAREY. Translated by Col. H. H. MAXWELL. With Plates. 1s.
150. *LOGIC*, Pure and Applied. By S. H. EMMENS. Third Edition. 1s. 6d.
152. *PRACTICAL HINTS FOR INVESTING MONEY.* With an Explanation of the Mode of Transacting Business on the Stock Exchange. By FRANCIS PLAYFORD, Sworn Broker. 1s. 6d.
153. *SELECTIONS FROM LOCKE'S ESSAYS ON THE HUMAN UNDERSTANDING.* With Notes by S. H. EMMENS. 2s.
193. *HANDBOOK OF FIELD FORTIFICATION*, intended for the Guidance of Officers Preparing for Promotion, and especially adapted to the requirements of Beginners. By Major W. W. KNOLLYS, F.R.G.S., 93rd Sutherland Highlanders, &c. With 163 Woodcuts. 3s.
194. *THE HOUSE MANAGER;* Being a Guide to Housekeeping, Practical Cookery, Pickling and Preserving, Household Work, Dairy Management, the Table and Dessert, Cellarage of Wines, Home-brewing and Wine-making, the Boudoir and Dressing-room, Travelling, Stable Economy, Gardening Operations, &c. By AN OLD HOUSEKEEPER. 3s. 6d.

EDUCATIONAL AND CLASSICAL SERIES.

HISTORY.

1. **England, Outlines of the History of**; more especially with reference to the Origin and Progress of the English Constitution. A Text Book for Schools and Colleges. By WILLIAM DOUGLAS HAMILTON, F.S.A., of Her Majesty's Public Record Office. Fourth Edition, revised. Maps and Woodcuts. 5s.; cloth boards, 6s.
5. **Greece, Outlines of the History of**; in connection with the Rise of the Arts and Civilization in Europe. By W. DOUGLAS HAMILTON, of University College, London, and EDWARD LEVIEN, M.A., of Balliol College, Oxford. 2s. 6d.; cloth boards, 3s. 6d.
7. **Rome, Outlines of the History of**: from the Earliest Period to the Christian Era and the Commencement of the Decline of the Empire. By EDWARD LEVIEN, of Balliol College, Oxford. Map, 2s. 6d.; cl. bds. 3s. 6d.
9. **Chronology of History, Art, Literature, and Progress**, from the Creation of the World to the Conclusion of the Franco-German War. The Continuation by W. D. HAMILTON, F.S.A., of Her Majesty's Record Office. 3s.; cloth boards, 3s. 6d.
50. **Dates and Events in English History**, for the use of Candidates in Public and Private Examinations. By the Rev. E. RAND. 1s.

LONDON: CROSBY LOCKWOOD AND CO.,

ENGLISH LANGUAGE AND MISCELLANEOUS.

11. **Grammar of the English Tongue**, Spoken and Written. With an Introduction to the Study of Comparative Philology. By HYDE CLARKE, D.C.L. Third Edition. 1s.
11*. **Philology**: Handbook of the Comparative Philology of English, Anglo-Saxon, Frisian, Flemish or Dutch, Low or Platt Dutch, High Dutch or German, Danish, Swedish, Icelandic, Latin, Italian, French, Spanish, and Portuguese Tongues. By HYDE CLARKE, D.C.L. 1s.
12. **Dictionary of the English Language**, as Spoken and Written. Containing above 100,000 Words. By HYDE CLARKE, D.C.L. 3s. 6d.; cloth boards, 4s. 6d.; complete with the GRAMMAR, cloth bds., 5s. 6d.
48. **Composition and Punctuation**, familiarly Explained for those who have neglected the Study of Grammar. By JUSTIN BRENAN. 16th Edition. 1s.
49. **Derivative Spelling-Book**: Giving the Origin of Every Word from the Greek, Latin, Saxon, German, Teutonic, Dutch, French, Spanish, and other Languages; with their present Acceptation and Pronunciation. By J. ROWBOTHAM, F.R.A.S. Improved Edition. 1s. 6d.
51. **The Art of Extempore Speaking**: Hints for the Pulpit, the Senate, and the Bar. By M. BAUTAIN, Vicar-General and Professor at the Sorbonne. Translated from the French. Sixth Edition, carefully corrected. 2s. 6d.
52. **Mining and Quarrying**, with the Sciences connected therewith. First Book of, for Schools. By J. H. COLLINS, F.G.S., Lecturer to the Miners' Association of Cornwall and Devon. 1s.
53. **Places and Facts in Political and Physical Geography**, for Candidates in Public and Private Examinations. By the Rev. EDGAR RAND, B.A. 1s.
54. **Analytical Chemistry**, Qualitative and Quantitative, a Course of. To which is prefixed, a Brief Treatise upon Modern Chemical Nomenclature and Notation. By WM. W. PINK, Practical Chemist, &c., and GEORGE E. WEBSTER, Lecturer on Metallurgy and the Applied Sciences, Nottingham. 2s.

THE SCHOOL MANAGERS' SERIES OF READING BOOKS,

Adapted to the Requirements of the New Code. Edited by the Rev. A. R. GRANT, Rector of Hitcham, and Honorary Canon of Ely; formerly H.M. Inspector of Schools.

INTRODUCTORY PRIMER, 3d.

	s. d.		s. d.
FIRST STANDARD	0 6	FOURTH STANDARD	1 2
SECOND ,,	0 10	FIFTH ,,	1 4
THIRD ,,	1 0	SIXTH ,,	1 6

LESSONS FROM THE BIBLE, Part I. Old Testament. 1s.
LESSONS FROM THE BIBLE, Part II. New Testament, to which is added THE GEOGRAPHY OF THE BIBLE, for very young Children. By Rev. C. THORNTON FORSTER. 1s. 2d. *₀* Or the Two Parts in One Volume. 2s.

FRENCH.

24. **French Grammar.** With Complete and Concise Rules on the Genders of French Nouns. By G. L. STRAUSS, Ph.D. 1s.
25. **French-English Dictionary.** Comprising a large number of New Terms used in Engineering, Mining, on Railways, &c. By ALFRED ELWES. 1s. 6d.
26. **English-French Dictionary.** By ALFRED ELWES. 2s.
25,26. **French Dictionary** (as above). Complete, in One Vol., 3s.; cloth boards, 3s. 6d. *₀* Or with the GRAMMAR, cloth boards, 4s. 6d.

7, STATIONERS' HALL COURT, LUDGATE HILL, E.C.

French, *continued.*

47. **French and English Phrase Book**; containing Introductory Lessons, with Translations, for the convenience of Students; several Vocabularies of Words, a Collection of suitable Phrases, and Easy Familiar Dialogues. 1s.

GERMAN.

39. **German Grammar.** Adapted for English Students, from Heyse's Theoretical and Practical Grammar, by Dr. G. L. STRAUSS. 1s.
40. **German Reader:** A Series of Extracts, carefully culled from the most approved Authors of Germany; with Notes, Philological and Explanatory. By G. L. STRAUSS, Ph.D. 1s.
41. **German Triglot Dictionary.** By NICHOLAS ESTERHAZY S. A. HAMILTON. Part I. English-German-French. 1s.
42. **German Triglot Dictionary.** Part II. German-French-English. 1s.
43. **German Triglot Dictionary.** Part III. French-German-English. 1s.
41-43. **German Triglot Dictionary** (as above), in One Vol., 3s.; cloth boards, 4s. *⁎* Or with the GERMAN GRAMMAR, cloth boards, 5s.

ITALIAN.

27. **Italian Grammar**, arranged in Twenty Lessons, with a Course of Exercises. By ALFRED ELWES. 1s.
28. **Italian Triglot Dictionary**, wherein the Genders of all the Italian and French Nouns are carefully noted down. By ALFRED ELWES. Vol. 1. Italian-English-French. 2s.
30. **Italian Triglot Dictionary.** By A. ELWES. Vol. 2. English-French-Italian. 2s.
32. **Italian Triglot Dictionary.** By ALFRED ELWES. Vol. 3. French-Italian-English. 2s.
28,30,32. **Italian Triglot Dictionary** (as above). In One Vol., 6s.; cloth boards, 7s. 6d. *⁎* Or with the ITALIAN GRAMMAR, cloth bds., 8s. 6d.

SPANISH AND PORTUGUESE.

34. **Spanish Grammar,** in a Simple and Practical Form. With a Course of Exercises. By ALFRED ELWES. 1s. 6d.
35. **Spanish-English and English-Spanish Dictionary.** Including a large number of Technical Terms used in Mining, Engineering, &c., with the proper Accents and the Gender of every Noun. By ALFRED ELWES. 4s.; cloth boards, 5s. *⁎* Or with the GRAMMAR, cloth boards, 6s.
55. **Portuguese Grammar,** in a Simple and Practical Form. With a Course of Exercises. By ALFRED ELWES, Author of "A Spanish Grammar," &c. 1s. 6d. [*Just published.*

HEBREW.

46*. **Hebrew Grammar.** By Dr. BRESSLAU. 1s. 6d.
44. **Hebrew and English Dictionary,** Biblical and Rabbinical; containing the Hebrew and Chaldee Roots of the Old Testament Post-Rabbinical Writings. By Dr. BRESSLAU. 6s. *⁎* Or with the GRAMMAR, 7s.
46. **English and Hebrew Dictionary.** By Dr. BRESSLAU. 3s.
44,46. **Hebrew Dictionary** (as above), in Two Vols., complete, with 46*. the GRAMMAR, cloth boards, 12s.

LONDON: CROSBY LOCKWOOD AND CO.,

LATIN.

19. **Latin Grammar.** Containing the Inflections and Elementary Principles of Translation and Construction. By the Rev. Thomas Goodwin, M.A., Head Master of the Greenwich Proprietary School. 1s.
20. **Latin-English Dictionary.** Compiled from the best Authorities. By the Rev. Thomas Goodwin, M.A. 2s.
22. **English-Latin Dictionary;** together with an Appendix of French and Italian Words which have their origin from the Latin. By the Rev. Thomas Goodwin, M.A. 1s. 6d.
20,22. **Latin Dictionary** (as above). Complete in One Vol., 3s. 6d.; cloth boards, 4s. 6d. *⁎* Or with the Grammar, cloth boards, 5s. 6d.

LATIN CLASSICS. With Explanatory Notes in English.

1. **Latin Delectus.** Containing Extracts from Classical Authors, with Genealogical Vocabularies and Explanatory Notes, by Henry Young, lately Second Master of the Royal Grammar School, Guildford. 1s.
2. **Cæsaris Commentarii de Bello Gallico.** Notes, and a Geographical Register for the Use of Schools, by H. Young. 2s.
12. **Ciceronis Oratio pro Sexto Roscio Amerino.** Edited, with an Introduction, Analysis, and Notes Explanatory and Critical, by the Rev. James Davies, M.A. 1s.
14. **Ciceronis Cato Major, Lælius, Brutus,** sive de Senectute, de Amicitia, de Claris Oratoribus Dialogi. With Notes by W. Brownrigg Smith, M.A., F.R.G.S. 2s.
3. **Cornelius Nepos.** With Notes. Intended for the Use of Schools. By H. Young. 1s.
6. **Horace;** Odes, Epode, and Carmen Sæculare. Notes by H. Young. 1s. 6d.
7. **Horace;** Satires, Epistles, and Ars Poetica. Notes by W. Brownrigg Smith, M.A., F.R.G.S. 1s. 6d.
21. **Juvenalis Satiræ.** With Prolegomena and Notes by T. H. S. Escott, B.A., Lecturer on Logic at King's College, London. 1s. 6d.
16. **Livy; History of Rome.** Notes by H. Young and W. B. Smith, M.A. Part 1. Books i., ii., 1s. 6d.
16*. ——— Part 2. Books iii., iv., v., 1s. 6d.
17. ——— Part 3. Books xxi., xxii., 1s. 6d.
8. **Sallustii Crispi Catalina et Bellum Jugurthinum.** Notes Critical and Explanatory, by W. M. Donne, B.A., Trinity College, Cambridge. 1s. 6d.
10. **Terentii Adelphi, Hecyra, Phormio.** Edited, with Notes, Critical and Explanatory, by the Rev. James Davies, M.A. 2s.
9. **Terentii Andria et Heautontimorumenos.** With Notes, Critical and Explanatory, by the Rev. James Davies, M.A. 1s. 6d.
11. **Terentii Eunuchus, Comœdia.** Edited, with Notes, by the Rev. James Davies, M.A. 1s. 6d. Or the Adelphi, Andria, and Eunuchus, 3 vols. in 1, cloth boards, 6s.
4. **Virgilii Maronis Bucolica et Georgica.** With Notes on the Bucolics by W. Rushton, M.A., and on the Georgics by H. Young. 1s. 6d.
5. **Virgilii Maronis Æneis.** Notes, Critical and Explanatory, by H. Young. 2s.
19. **Latin Verse Selections,** from Catullus, Tibullus, Propertius, and Ovid. Notes by W. B. Donne, M.A., Trinity College, Cambridge. 2s.
20. **Latin Prose Selections,** from Varro, Columella, Vitruvius, Seneca, Quintilian, Florus, Velleius Paterculus, Valerius Maximus Suetonius, Apuleius, &c. Notes by W. B. Donne, M.A. 2s.

Other Volumes are in Preparation.

7, STATIONERS' HALL COURT, LUDGATE HILL., E.C.

GREEK.

14. **Greek Grammar**, in accordance with the Principles and Philological Researches of the most eminent Scholars of our own day. By HANS CLAUDE HAMILTON. 1s. 6d.
15,17. **Greek Lexicon.** Containing all the Words in General Use, with their Significations, Inflections, and Doubtful Quantities. By HENRY R. HAMILTON. Vol. 1. Greek-English, 2s.; Vol. 2. English-Greek, 2s. Or the Two Vols. in One, 4s.; cloth boards, 5s.
14,15. **Greek Lexicon** (as above). Complete, with the GRAMMAR, in 17. One Vol., cloth boards, 6s.

GREEK CLASSICS. With Explanatory Notes in English.

1. **Greek Delectus.** Containing Extracts from Classical Authors, with Genealogical Vocabularies and Explanatory Notes, by H. YOUNG. New Edition, with an improved and enlarged Supplementary Vocabulary, by JOHN HUTCHISON, M.A., of the High School, Glasgow. 1s.
30. **Æschylus:** Prometheus Vinctus: The Prometheus Bound. From the Text of DINDORF. Edited, with English Notes, Critical and Explanatory, by the Rev. JAMES DAVIES, M.A. 1s.
32. **Æschylus:** Septem Contra Thebes: The Seven against Thebes. From the Text of DINDORF. Edited, with English Notes, Critical and Explanatory, by the Rev. JAMES DAVIES, M.A. 1s.
40. **Aristophanes:** Acharnians. Chiefly from the Text of C. H. WEISE. With Notes, by C. S. T. TOWNSHEND, M.A. 1s. 6d.
26. **Euripides:** Alcestis. Chiefly from the Text of DINDORF. With Notes, Critical and Explanatory, by JOHN MILNER, B.A. 1s.
23. **Euripides:** Hecuba and Medea. Chiefly from the Text of DINDORF. With Notes, Critical and Explanatory, by W. BROWNRIGG SMITH, M.A., F.R.G.S. 1s. 6d.
14-17. **Herodotus,** The History of, chiefly after the Text of GAISFORD. With Preliminary Observations and Appendices, and Notes, Critical and Explanatory, by T. H. L. LEARY, M.A., D.C.L.
   Part 1. Books i., ii. (The Clio and Euterpe), 2s.
   Part 2. Books iii., iv. (The Thalia and Melpomene), 2s.
   Part 3. Books v.-vii. (The Terpsichore, Erato, and Polymnia), 2s.
   Part 4. Books viii., ix. (The Urania and Calliope) and Index, 1s. 6d.
5-12. **Homer,** The Works of. According to the Text of BAEUMLEIN. With Notes, Critical and Explanatory, drawn from the best and latest Authorities, with Preliminary Observations and Appendices, by T. H. L. LEARY, M.A., D.C.L.

THE ILIAD: Part 1. Books i. to vi., 1s. 6d. | Part 3. Books xiii. to xviii., 1s. 6d.
         Part 2. Books vii. to xii., 1s. 6d. | Part 4. Books xix. to xxiv., 1s. 6d.
THE ODYSSEY: Part 1. Books i. to vi., 1s. 6d. | Part 3. Books xiii. to xviii., 1s. 6d.
         Part 2. Books vii. to xii., 1s. 6d. | Part 4. Books xix. to xxiv., and Hymns, 2s.

4. **Lucian's Select Dialogues.** The Text carefully revised, with Grammatical and Explanatory Notes, by H. YOUNG. 1s.
13. **Plato's Dialogues:** The Apology of Socrates, the Crito, and the Phaedo. From the Text of C. F. HERMANN. Edited with Notes, Critical and Explanatory, by the Rev. JAMES DAVIES, M.A. 2s.
18. **Sophocles:** Œdipus Tyrannus. Notes by H. YOUNG. 1s.
20. **Sophocles:** Antigone. From the Text of DINDORF. Notes, Critical and Explanatory, by the Rev. JOHN MILNER, B.A. 2s.
41. **Thucydides:** History of the Peloponnesian War. Notes by H. YOUNG. Book 1. 1s.
2, 3. **Xenophon's Anabasis;** or, The Retreat of the Ten Thousand. Notes and a Geographical Register, by H. YOUNG. Part 1. Books i. to iii., 1s. Part 2. Books iv. to vii., 1s.
42. **Xenophon's Panegyric on Agesilaus.** Notes and Introduction by Ll. F. W. JEWITT. 1s. 6d.

☞ *Other Volumes are in Preparation.*

www.ingramcontent.com/pod-product-compliance
Lightning Source LLC
Chambersburg PA
CBHW031333230426
43670CB00006B/329